the BREATH of ISIS

Naomi 1985 © Rick Spink

the BREATH of ISIS

Autobiography of a Priestess
A Tale of Being and Becoming
NAOMI OZANIEC

Thoth Publications

Copyright © Naomi Ozaniec 2013.
This edition published by Thoth Publications 2025.
First published as *The Breath of Isis*
by House of Life E-books.

Naomi Ozaniec asserts the moral right to be identified as the author of this work.

A CIP catalogue record for this book is available from the British Library

All rights reserved. No part of this publication may be reproduced, stored in a retrieval system, or transmitted, in any form or by any means, electronic, mechanical, photocopying, recording or otherwise, without the prior permission of the publishers.

Cover design and text design by Helen Surman

Published by Thoth Publications
Markfield,
Leicestershire LE67 9QB

ISBN 978-1-913660-44-4
Web address: www.thothpublications.com
Email: enquiries@thoth.co.uk

I have had the blessed opportunity to read this book in manuscript. At every page, I felt inspired and marvelled at the way in which Isis called Naomi and indeed, calls all of her priestesses. The magic in this book is familiar and palpable. The characters she has met over the years, and yes, some of them are indeed, characters, are quite amazing. I loved Daughters of the Goddess *and bought several copies of it for friends. I thrilled and jealously guard her books on the Qabalah! With this new book, I cannot sing its praises enough. Everybody out there – Go out and get your own. You won't regret it.*

Normandi Ellis, November 2013

These words are dedicated to Isis of Ten Thousand Names

WORDS 2009

Soul, ba-bird where do you dwell?
In some far away heaven,
Or do you whisper in my ear at night and show me where to look by day
So that I pick up your clues like morsels left for a hungry dog,
Or the white pebbles cast for Hansel and Gretel so that they could find
the way home.
Why then am I lost?

Travel no further, look neither up nor down but straight into the heart.
Give up the face of pain,
Put down the fear that writhes like a snake.
Tear down the veil behind your eyes.
Undress yourself.

Smile as the child you were,
Breathe like the babe newborn.
See as the mind on Christmas morn'
Stand.
This moment is your life, a patchwork quilt of your own making,
Good let the tears flow – dissolution then, not regret.
Resolve, take down the drawbridge, put down the shield.
Step forward.
Where have you been hiding pretty one

With your sistrum and your drum,
Magnificent and exalted are your secret words.
Lay them down on the altar of the ordinary and the everyday.
Write them large and let them burn inside
All that separates stands in your way.
Dressed in the finery of the past, you cannot reach today
In case you should trip on the hem or forget the words of power.
Weighed down by words, now you must travel with none prepared.
Words will come from the endless source, the star inside.
Speech will never fail for the spirit speaks without ceasing
Even in silence.
Reach out,
Ways new to you open like the lotus flower.
Each day will hold a surprise and a promise.
Magnetise not with the mind – a parlour trick so easy to perform,
But with the heart – slumbering still, across the abyss of becoming.
Set your sight on the jewelled isle.
Reach out for a gem and send it on its way.
This is your new altar.

CONTENTS

Preface   11

Introduction   13

Chapter One
AWAKENING   15

Chapter Two
THE CALL OF ISIS   36

Chapter Three
THE MANTLE OF ISIS   52

Chapter Four
THE RITES OF ISIS   76

Chapter Five
THE GARMENTS OF ISIS   97

Chapter Six
THE BREATH OF ISIS   112

Chapter Seven
THE LIGHT OF ISIS   129

Chapter Eight
THE MYSTERIES OF ISIS   152

Chapter Nine
THE SORROWS OF ISIS   164

Words form the Archive	183
I: THE ASCENSION OF OSIRIS	192
II: THE ADORATION OF SEKHMET	211
III: THE BLESSINGS OF HATHOR	238
IV: THE ROSES OF ISIS	259
V: THE RE-MEMBERING OF OSIRIS	272
VI: THE MARRIAGE OF HEAVEN AND EARTH	286
Addendum I	304
Addendum II	308
Addendum III	312
Postscript	313
Contact Details	314

Preface

WHEN someone asked me why I was writing this book, I replied quite simply that Isis had asked me to do so. I could see at once that my answer was unacceptable, I had strayed into territories of bad taste. But that remains my answer. Moreover, it was pointed out, that writing a magical autobiography was a task reserved for those distinguished by a life of magic, an accolade I had clearly not earned, and I was not at the end of an illustrious magical career. Finally, it was pointed out, again in no uncertain terms that anyone of any real magical stature knew that Isis just did not speak in this way! I can only apologise in advanced for my folly, but my answer remains the same. I wrote the book because Isis instructed me to. I received the inspiration on a long train journey when Isis gave me the task of telling this tale. She dropped her chosen words into my mind like bright jewels and by the time I arrived at my destination, I had received the title and an outline. Fulfilling my obligation to complete the task has taken a little longer than expected !

I too have wondered about the purpose of writing such a personal book but my own questions have been unexpectedly answered. The second part of the book arose in my mind without any pre-planning and suddenly the book has become something more than an autobiography. Writing from the Archive has given me a curious perspective on the events of my life, which up to this point had seemed to be purely idiosyncratic. But the overview gifted by the long view, has revealed patterns that I had simply missed at close quarters. Additionally, I have been provided with an opportunity to add more recent insights and understandings to works originally written many years ago. The material from the Archive is presented as a resource for anyone sufficiently interested in this tradition. The shaping of my life is probably less important than the work that has flowed from it and it is I think merely the container in which the resource may rest. And so, I cautiously open the book of my life so that you might peer in and observe how Isis is still willing and able to share in the human condition, if like my well-meaning friend, you are offended, I sincerely apologise in advance.

March 6, 2013

Introduction

THIS book has been written in stages. It was begun in 2009 and left to gestate. I returned to it in 2013 and then left it again for another ten years without even trying to find a publisher. Now in 2024, the work calls me to attend to its birth as a midwife at the bedside. The publishing world, as in so many other areas of life has shifted considerably in recent decades, now anyone and everyone may have a voice in the new realm of social media. Here is a manifestation of the Aquarian impetus appearing on the horizon as a new dawn. Astrology describes the Aquarian characteristic as those of communication combined with technology, the results of this intermarriage are revolutionary. This new drive for individual presence in the world chimes with my intention to create a Mystery School readied for the initiating waters of Aquarius inspired by the words and ideas of Dion Fortune, an Inner Plane mentor.

The book takes the form of an autobiography as a record of a particular journey, it is an unveiling of a relationship between the divine and the mortal realms central to Kemetic metaphysical theology, and it is in this possibility that the purpose of the book is to be found.

In reviewing my own life with the eye of objectivity, I have been struck by the long and arduous processes of my own unmaking required to strip away a persona suited for our time, even while small seeds, often invisible were placed waiting to be unfolded.

At a social and cultural level, this process is being repeated in so many different ways, beneath the familiarity of greed, profit and falsehood, new voices call to be heard; the many headed monster of our time shows itself to be ugly and deformed; change is inevitable.

It is my hope that these few pages will speak to wise knowing: the intelligence of the heart as the place of spiritual union between the divine and the mortal. My journey still has far to go, a new phase opens full of greened promise just as the green faced Osiris was ever the beloved of the lady of wisdom and magic.

July 2024

CHAPTER ONE
AWAKENING

The journey from the inner to the outer world is like no other, from consciousness to un-consciousness, a falling into a sleep-like state before finally awakening to life. Is this really the fabled Fall? This journey into flesh and forgetting. Journeying towards the birth canal and breath, nine months of becoming passes in a state of active passivity, all unfolds of itself, quietly and in accordance with an invisible cellular clock, until with assured inevitability, we are each disgorged from the place of heaven and cut loose from our peaceful unity; the prime separation is completed. What is it that we bring with us as we pass into form by taking on limbs and function? Is it possible that the gifts of the stars are secretly encoded along with our becoming, hidden in prepared time capsules like jewelled gifts to be presented to the sleeping beauty. I wonder about such things, but now I realise that I have wondered about many strange and eccentric things. I look back over my shoulder to the life that has already passed from possibility to actuality. I recall the things that took place and wonder what happened to other expectations, dreams and intentions, all stillborn in the face of circumstance. Memories lay like pieces of a jigsaw puzzle. Hindsight alone permits me to make sense of the pattern. Events and landmarks serve as chronological markers but the journey is not linear and sequential but disorderly, confused and

THE BREATH OF ISIS

meandering in the manner of its living. Connections seem evident, but only afterwards; at the time the way ahead is always unclear. Words are now my salvation, a way of remembering all that has been and also a way of recording such a strange passage through life. I am a priestess because I was born a priestess. Through every personal and experience, I have been a priestess even when my feet wandered far from the path. My entire life has revolved around this single theme, it has haunted me with half remembered knowing, driven me to seek understanding and forced me to accept my place, chasing me relentlessly through every hiding place that life can offer.

I entered into the world on 19th January 1951 at 4.10am. It was a difficult and horrible entry. A flu epidemic raged and nursing staff were in short supply. My mother aged just 18 was unattended throughout her labour. Left alone in a darkened room, she struggled against nature; no-one knew that the umbilical cord was laced around my stomach. Every attempt to push me into life was thwarted until after bearing down for too many hours, I was finally expelled with such force that I landed upon her feet; mother and baby were not doing well. Had the cord been wrapped around my neck, I would have been suffocated by my own birth, as it was, unseen damage had been done, the wall of my stomach had been ruptured, I had created an umbilical hernia. My early life was spent in and out of hospital until my hernia was finally stitched with an operation and of course I still have the scar. In a story told to me many times in my childhood, my mother marvelled at the mature composure of so young a child. Apparently, I made no fuss, I did not cry even as she left me in the hands of the hospital staff. When I came round from the anaesthetic, my mother of course was sitting waiting and I am told that I simply said, "I knew you would come." Now with the hindsight of a mother, I too wonder at this extraordinary acceptance and trust. But my adult magical mind recognises other circumstances when it is timely to lie in the dark between the worlds waiting to be resuscitated by attendants

AWAKENING

at the appointed moment, neither sooner nor later but at the exact moment. Somewhere deep in my child's mind the template of complete trust had already been formed.

I was by all accounts a precocious child. I cut my teeth early, I spoke early, and at once asked my parents, *"Why does the moon stop when we stop?"* My question was based on observation, when travelling by a car on a dark clear night, the moon seemed to keep pace with us as we moved along, when we stopped, the moon appeared to halt too. So, it seemed that the moon had occupied my mind even as a young child. I was ill more often than most children of my age. My poor start in life seemed to have left me vulnerable to all sorts of infections. Despite many absences, I did well at school learning easily and with the confidence that comes from a genuine curiosity about the world. Though I could not have known it, I had been born into an unusual home. My father was exiled from a wealthy colonial background in Hong-Kong, my mother was the daughter of a Russian émigré who moved for love just ahead of the revolutionary wave. Escaping unwittingly from political turmoil to a new life, my grandmother was eventually abandoned with her five children by the man for whom she had left everything. My mother was raised in deprivation, my father was raised in excess, such extremes rarely meet and even less often make successful partnerships, but my parents were married long and made a happiness of it. I grew up in the space created between forgotten privilege and stunted hope, where the aspiration of intelligence through education proved to be our escape route.

As a child I was deeply affected by myth, magic and flights of the imagination. I hoped it was possible to find the glass mountain or like the children on the way to Narnia, to walk through the wardrobe and find another world. I loved the idea of the Wood between the Worlds and was dumbstruck by my first encounter with Queen Jadis in the Hall of Images in the city of Charn. These imaginary encounters served to stir my deepest remembering and longings.

THE BREATH OF ISIS

We grew amidst financial hardship and remembrances of especially awful incidents were handed down liked cautionary tales. Once my father lost his wages, the pay-packet that slipped so easily from his pocket was doubtless a miraculous find for someone else, but for our family it was disaster. On another occasion, my father bumped into a lost relation who promptly offered him a job in the bosom of the family once more. My father declined with breezy indifference and, unemployed but with personal pride high, he returned home to a pregnant wife and no prospects. My mother was resourceful and hardworking. I had no sense that we were in any way different from our neighbours but in fact we were. Lacking any cultural roots, our little family just bobbed along without any of the usual reference points. My father was misplaced in the economic wasteland frequented in those days mainly by the uneducated. His education in Hong-Kong was interrupted by the outbreak of war and he missed the professional career that should have come his way. Instead, five years in a Japanese prisoner of war camp left him indelibly marked. My mother was likewise misplaced in undemanding jobs peopled by the unskilled. Her education was foreshortened by circumstance, not ability and she found the path to a profession late in life; she became a teacher and a good one. We were a family of cultural refugees, excluded from the support of an extended family and ill at ease with the normal activities of the economically disadvantaged. My father wrote poetry and pined for classical music, my mother wrote stories for me, thought deeply and philosophised about life. By the time I became an adult our family had finally camouflaged itself into a suburban mould; we were pretty indistinguishable from everyone else, on the outside at least. This untypical background gifted me with mental freedom. I carried no imposed baggage being neither middle class nor working class. A lifelong friend from my school days was the daughter of a refugee Polish family. I think we instinctively knew that we were outsiders, and this sense has never faded from my mind. From

AWAKENING

my earliest days, I was expected only to, 'do my best,' this charge never failed to lure; more demanding than any other expectation, it freed me from failure while exhorting me to succeed. My parents imposed no religious yoke, my father, estranged by choice from his orthodox Jewish background had no desire to impose what he had already rejected and my mother though nominally a member of the Church of England expressed no interest in turning the family into church-goers. My father was a sceptic, my mother was a natural psychic, an interesting combination!

Reaching deeply into my child-mind, it seems to me now that I had a deep and abiding curiosity in all things religious. I think that I wondered about God from the moment I heard his name, where was he? How might I get to know him? But the more I heard the less I wanted to know. When I was eight years old, I was sent to a convent school. We had moved to a new area and every other school was full. I was, I believe, an adaptable child, full of life and curiosity, but my brief time in the hands of nuns was utterly dispiriting. Looking back, I can recall my uniform, the slightly scratchy blue gingham frock, the cream straw hat and the stiff grey blazer. The convent was a long walk from home. Sitting proudly at the crest of a hill occupying the highest ground, it did not look like a school at all, wrought iron gates opened onto gardens and the main building was of grey stone with high windows. Above the central doorway a statue of the Madonna and Child looked out impassively. My memories are fragmented, silent classrooms, enforced silence in all corridors at all times, an oppressive atmosphere, black robed nuns, unsmiling and unforgiving, prayers and more prayers. I remember almost no education, other than daily English and incomprehensible maths, no history or geography, no art, no science and certainly nothing approaching fun. I recall being cold during games lessons in the playground and being called out from my class to sit written examinations. Confession of personal misdemeanours was regular and effective. It was a miserable, friendless place obsessed with just one thing: God.

THE BREATH OF ISIS

"Stand up anyone who did not go to church on Sunday."
"Stand up anyone who spoke on the way back from assembly."
"Stand up anyone who................."

Well, I always stood up for failure to go to church and the best reason I could think of was, "I'm Jewish miss." Actually, even as I spoke the words, I knew it was not fully true, but it turned my very Jewish surname: Goldenberg, to good use. Soon my reflex to stand up and confess was just dismissed. *"Oh, do sit down, we don't mean you."* The day was punctuated by moments of prayer, a shared grace before meals but also a private moment before leaving the dining hall, a prayer at the end of the school morning and of course another at the end of the day and so it went on. I sat bewildered through lessons on catechism and mumbled my way through prayers. I sat attentive but confused when a Father came in to speak with us. What did I learn in my brief stay here educationally? – absolutely nothing. But I learned other things instead, that these nuns were neither kind nor loving, that these strange words were meaningless and that I did not belong. When a place in a local school became available, I was able to escape and only then did I cry. With the best will in the world, my parents had inadvertently exposed me to the very pressures and influences which together they found to be repugnant in orthodox religion.

Recently a forgotten memory has surfaced, the school had a substantial garden complete with winding paths and one of these paths lead directly to a life-size statue of the Madonna carrying the infant Jesus. For some reason I liked to stand and look at her, I thought she had a beautiful face. She was dressed in pale blue robe, wore a gold crown and carried her infant son in her arms; she was of course Regina Coeli. Although my father had no time for religion, it was however never a forgotten subject in our household, instead it was a matter of great debate. My father displayed the intellectual detachment much vaunted in the Bohemian set in which he once moved when he first came to London; quite simply God was Dead,

AWAKENING

alive only in the minds of simpletons, the needy and the foolish. Actually, his beliefs probably had a good deal more to do with his prison camp experiences than with any philosophy and this had indeed given him reason to despair of human folly. Through the years and as I grew, I became accustomed to his humanistic rational philosophy of life. For him faith of any kind was an obstacle to clear thinking, blind faith produced the kind of obedience which delighted dictators, tyrants and all opponents of personal liberty. He saw religion as a kind of personal brain-washing which anaesthetized a nation and created wars. He ridiculed the tenets of the Church and knew that its doctrine had justified appalling behaviour. He placed his faith in science, education and rationalism. His arguments were compelling and well thought out. I was inclined to agree with him. These conversations had perhaps whetted my appetite for philosophical thinking and religious enquiry. I cannot really explain better except to say that his wide-ranging references to comparative religion, human superstition, history, mythology and the like had raised more questions than he could answer, and I just wanted to answer my own questions. I was I think already developing an untypical view of the world.

Before I was ten, I heard a story from my mother, made all the more real and powerful simply because I knew it was true. I do not know how the conversation arose, I cannot imagine that she suddenly decided to tell me a ghost story, but tell me she did. Early in my parent's married life, they looked for rented accommodation and found a spacious flat in London at a very reasonable rent. It seemed to be heaven-sent although apparently my mother did not in truth, like the feel of the place even at the outset. But as the saying goes, 'beggars can't be choosers' and the opportunity was just too good to pass up. They unpacked and as the day drew to its close prepared for bed, and now comes the bit where the story became very spooky. I can imagine my eyes widening and my heart fluttering as she told me that as she climbed into bed on one side

THE BREATH OF ISIS

and my father climbed in from the other, a third figure unseen and unknown except by an unsavoury and unwholesome sense of presence intervened between them. My mother even said the place in the bed between them visibly sunk as if a large and heavy body lay there! Apparently, my father dropped to his knees and slipped straight back into Jewish prayers invoking the protection of blessed sanctity on them. My mother just ran out of the room. They packed their bags instantly and by first light, with their sheets strapped to the outside of the suitcase with a belt, so unclean and contaminated did they feel, that they took themselves off to the nearest priest for a blessing – so much for sceptics. If I had read this in a book, it might have left some mark but being told this tale first hand by my mother it was planted indelibly into my memory bank simply because I knew it to be true.

I was an avid and precocious reader. When I discovered the inner world of mythology, I devoured it like food. Given an adult ticket to the library ages 11, I wasted no time in exploring its shelves. I had already gutted the junior library and was quite satiated by its undemanding repertoire. I happily read about all sorts of things, from history to architecture from gardening to nutrition. But once I had discovered the so called, 'occult' shelf of the library, I read along its entire length without pause. I read everything in the library on witchcraft which I found to be boring. I discovered psychology and comparative religion, world mythology and much more. When my parents voiced disapproval at my reading An Encyclopaedia of Occultism, I simply stopped taking books home and instead sat for hours transfixed at a small reading desk in the library. Novels were a little less contentious being only, 'stories' so quite soon, I had navigated my way around the world through the great stories of heroes and heroines, gods and goddesses, shamans, witches, sorcerers, magicians and demons. I discovered the world of historical novels set in ancient places. Such stories drew me like a magnet, and it was here that I first encountered the Goddess. One

AWAKENING

particular incident described in a book left an indelible imprint in my mind.

In a Cretan setting a young priestess crossed a courtyard filled with rough soldiers. One blocked her way and with malicious intent slowly began to lift her skirt before his friends thinking to shame her prove himself masterful. *"Do you dare to lift the veil of the Goddess?"* demanded the young priestess. Her words reduced him to a shamefaced silence. And in that single moment I seemed to know that he who defiles a priestess, robs from the lap of the Goddess and is himself diminished. Even at the time this purely imaginary incident touched me very deeply. I was no more than 12 when I read these words, yet this tale had a searing impact on me. It remained with me for many years as a symbol of the mysterious power that a woman possesses when she walks in the light of the Goddess. Though I had entirely forgotten the title of the book, my sister easily remembered it on reading my manuscript, it was *The Crown of Violets* by Geoffrey Trease. The book must have left an impression on her too.

I discovered Robert Graves aged 11 and chose to present an essay on the book *King Jesus* when asked to write a book review at school. Here were not simple answers but complex questions of culture, belief and real personal experience. I was a precocious reader finding Frazer's *Golden Bough*, *The White Goddess* and a whole host of historical novels by Henry Treece and Geoffrey Trease. I discovered the works of Alice Bailey and also read *The Cosmic Doctrine* by Dion Fortune in the same year. The book filled my mind, and I ordered it over and over again from the library, but it was not until many decades later that I discovered it to be a key teaching text of a particular esoteric school. At that time, I could not know that Dion Fortune would become a big influence in my life and that I would in the fullness of time found a conference to honour her work, but that is to jump far ahead. During this period, I came across a copy of Charles Leadbeater's work on the chakras.

THE BREATH OF ISIS

Published in 1927 it was one of the earliest books on the subject. I can still remember the beautiful colour plates especially the pink and gold shimmering crown chakra. Little did I know then, that I would also write a book on the same subject, but that all lay waiting in the future. I once read a paragraph aloud from Alice Bailey to my father so that we might discuss it. He told me in no uncertain terms that it was all unintelligible gobbledygook. To my unformed adolescent curious mind this new genre all made perfect sense, I could not understand why other people did not want to lap it up too.

I remember it was about this time that I taught myself to dowse. I was in the first year of my secondary school, so I would have been about 12. It began with a simple throw-away remark of my mother's. She mentioned that some people believed it was possible to tell the sex of an unborn child by holding a threaded needle or ring suspended over the pregnant mother's stomach, if it turned one way the child was a boy, if it turned the other was the baby was a girl. The idea seemed utterly preposterous but somehow interesting to my mind. I cannot now imagine what promoted me, there were no pregnant women around, but I threaded up a long needle all the same. Having threaded a needle, I imagine that my natural curiosity took over and I probably experimented by holding it over myself. I think I discarded the needle pretty quickly, it is light in comparison to a ring and I know that I had soon persuaded my mum to take off my grandmother's ring and let me thread it onto a length of cotton. I soon discovered that when held over one side of the body, knees and hands being easy to use, the ring moved in clockwise motion, while when held over the other side, the ring travelled in the exactly the opposite way. Now I considered this to be perfectly normal and just a bit of harmless fun. With the naivety of a child with nothing to hide, testing everything became my new game. My father was not impressed, sitting me down he explained that really, 'I' was doing it all, it was all a just childish deception. He had placed himself quite

AWAKENING

deliberately in the position of the Doubting Thomas. He did not believe that I could dowse because dowsing had no intrinsic reality. Instinctively I felt he was wrong and perhaps it was here that the clash between our two views began to crystallise. Our difference of opinion continued throughout the decades and did not cease until a few years before his death when we both called a truce. But at that time as the parent, he held the upper hand, he told me that I until I could show him some positive proof, he would simply put it all down to the tricks of the mind. I took his challenge in good humour and curiously it prepared me for the future. I learned very early that contentious statements required good intellectual backup, so I set about acquiring it. It seems ironic that my father who genuinely set out to show me the error of my ways, was in actuality preparing me to defend my cause more effectively. He showed me the face of society, disbelieving, disapproving and at heart, disinterested. My instinctive belief in things that could not be seen, heard, measured or otherwise proved, was I think an affront to his rational and logical mind. So, I learned to offer explanation, argument, justification and rationale.

The dowsing challenge continued until we both gave up trying to convince the other. What I took to be evidential, he regarded as coincidental. He created test conditions: dowsing while observed with eyes closed or letting someone else hold the actual thread while my hand just rested on theirs. Once he asked me to see if a pendulum could still move while it was suspended from a wooden rod without any physical contact to me whatsoever! My failure to move it was taken as proof that it was, 'all in my mind.' Actually, he was right but not in the way that he meant it and we finally agreed to disagree. I of course carried on dowsing, much later I even wrote the book, *Dowsing for Beginners*. However, he taught me another valuable lesson; the Doubting Thomas Syndrome is not open to being convinced, it is a preconceived view masquerading as an open mind. Having failed to convince me that I couldn't dowse he did

THE BREATH OF ISIS

come to express a mild interest in what he observed. He finally recognized that he just did not understand it and he put it all down to some peculiarity of mine – just like my mother!

My early teenage years passed uneventfully enough. I went to school and at weekends I often spent Saturday afternoons in the library. I was an able student but beneath my academic ease, an abiding fascination with all things spiritual/occult, never vanished. It was a ceaseless inner voice, unheard to all but me. I learned, much to my own surprise that such interests seemed to make people uncomfortable, I never understood why. I had an intense brooding about death, much more focussed and consuming I think than is common or even normal. I simply wanted to know what happened after death. It struck me as a perfectly reasonable question, one for the specialists I thought, and I was liable to plague anyone and everyone I came across who showed any religious leanings with my questions. I was perplexed that even avowedly religious people had no particular knowledge on the matter but were prepared to take things on trust. The question bothered me and most of all it bothered me that no-one else seemed to be bothered! So, I continued to read and think, and time passed.

One day in school some time in between our A Level exams and the results, I sat around idly with my friends. We were expected to attend school but there were no classes on the timetable. Someone suggested, "Let's have a séance." I know that it was not me, I would never have paraded my interests so publicly. And it was suggested in the spirit of idle curiosity, not my style at all. But in a whirl of activity, preparations were suddenly under way, tables were pushed together, and dissenting minds moved out of the way or left the room. In answer to the question, *"But what do we do?"* Someone shouted, *"We need a glass and some paper,"* and before I knew it a dozen adolescent girls were squashed around a couple of tables hastily pushed together. An upturned tumbler sat ominously in the middle of a circle formed by the alphabet and the words, '*Yes*'

AWAKENING

and, 'No' 'written on scraps of paper. The giggling stopped and an expectant but nervous hush descended.

I had never done anything like this before but in the dubious spirit of a party game, several girls were familiar with the procedure. Those who could reach the glass with ease placed a finger tentatively on its upturned surface, *"Now what?"* Someone said, *"You just ask, is there anybody there?"* Being bossy by nature I took charge of the opening question and spoke out in the silence, feeling just a bit silly, *"Is anybody there?"* I had my finger on the glass, and I experienced a strange sensation, as if it was already trying to move, jiggling slightly under our fingers. Of course, the theory is that since the glass is in fact moved by the subconscious minds of those present, the sense of tension at the glass is more about the competing muscular impulses generated by different minds than anything else. However, the glass moved or more correctly was moved by our minds towards the word YES. There was a long pause, now I did not know how to respond, I had not really expected anything to happen. I was not afraid but genuinely curious so I asked, *"Do you know anybody here?"* The glass still resting beside the *'Yes'* nudged it once more. Well, this at least seemed easy enough to deal with, I simply started with the person on my left and asked, *"Do you have a message for...?"* The glass moved firmly to the, 'No' position where it stayed as I passed around the circle repeating the same question until at last there remained just one person left, me. I had to ask once more *"Do you have a message for me?"* When the glass moved or was moved to the, 'Yes' position, I felt a sense of astonishment more than anything else. I was curious and naturally asked the next logical question, *"Who are you?"* The glass began to move under, what volition who can say, and in sequence it stopped seemingly with deliberation at the following letters O.L.E.G. I had already sat back, prepared to write things down from a detached executive role. Now I was doubly dumbstruck. Oleg was my father's cousin who I had always called Uncle Olly. He had died of a brain tumour

THE BREATH OF ISIS

suddenly aged 29. I had gone to visit him in hospital with my father and he had died just before we arrived. In my early childhood, he was my favourite person, taking me to the ballet when I was only three. As another representative of our somewhat eccentric family, he too was exiled in London, quite impoverished but still deeply wedded to culture, classical music, the arts, ballet, music and as I learned much later, he had more than a passing interest in, 'the occult.' But at that precise moment, my mind went into a bit of a spin. I neither believed nor disbelieved what was taking place in front of my eyes. I didn't really know how to react or what to say, so I simply asked the next obvious question. *"What is the message that you have for me?"* *"Good news mum."* Then I asked, *"Is there any other message?"* *"Tell Alan,"* was the answer. I think I had run out of things to say or even think. The dialogue seemed to have run its natural course. There was nothing left to do but finish. Now I had a real problem. Should I, 'Tell Alan' (my father) as directed or just pretend that the event never happened. Deliberate fraud seemed ridiculous, so I went home and did as I had been asked, though it seems I told my mother and allowed her to tell my father. I did not get to hear his reaction straightaway. My strange bombshell was followed by one of those incomprehensible synchronicities that appear from nowhere and pack a mighty punch. Within a very short time of my revelation, my father saw a medium on the television, usually he would just be scornful and mocking but her face seemed familiar, and he was pretty sure she lived on his delivery round. Recent research has shown me that Jessie Nason caused such a stir when she appeared on the David Frost Show in 1963 that the phone lines were blocked for days. My father must have seen this too. I now wonder how many lives were also redirected by her appearance. He said nothing to me but on his next delivery to the address, he simply knocked at her door and she invited him in. This informality may seem a little strange, but Jessie Nason was known to be informal and very down to earth, and of course a medium will

AWAKENING

always follow the voice of spirit. In conversation many years later, my father told me that while standing at a bus-stop he had been approached by a woman who had tried to give him a message from Sprit. He clearly thought her quite mad, and his blanked response proved to be the end of that conversation. But now he was ready to initiate his own conversation. After some 35 years my memory is a little hazy as to the exact sequence of events. But when turning out an attic in 2006, I came across a box of records relating to this period. I opened the box on September 17th and found my father's own typed manuscript on the subject. His words, written so much nearer the time offer a more accurate account. Moreover, it seems fitting that his words should be included.

> *The date now at the time of starting to write this down is August 1970 and I can see already that notes we have made in the intervening period are becoming so jumbled as to become almost unintelligible for reasons which will become clearer as I progress. I have to attempt get this piece of writing done before memory becomes unreliable.*

Writing in detail of his encounter with Mrs Jessie Nason, my father wrote.

> *Before I even got round to asking her sitting fees she said,*
> *"I can tell you this, right now I am getting someone with you. He is very happy at this event." Oleg, I thought. "He is limping, dragging his leg, but he is smiling." Her words cut right across my train of thought, this was not correct. This is not what I had expected. There had been nothing wrong with Oleg's leg. Here was no confirmation. I could think of no-one I knew who limped. "He is telling, me is glad to be with you. He is bouncing with vitality – this person, trying to convey his personality. He tries to give me a name. That is it. He says Jo. The name is Jo."*

THE BREATH OF ISIS

I was nonplussed. I could think of no one called Jo, no-one who limped, that is. I had been expecting if anything were to come from this interview, if there were any truth in these ideas, the name she would have given me would have been Oleg, but it was not. Her next words began to make some slight sense. "He looks a bit oriental. He is young."

Years before I had spent five years of my young life as a prisoner of war, first in Hong-Kong and then in Japan. There had been nine of us who managed to stick together throughout the period of captivity four of us had remained in close touch in London for a time after the war. Jo was one of these. Jo was one of these gregarious, exuberant types one sometimes meets. He was only half Chinese. If there was a Camp Concert Party to be organised, he was in the middle of it. When he died, after the war in London, the circumstances had been somewhat sad to state. He had been madly in love with a young woman whose mother would not have accepted him as a son-in-law at any price, due to his part Chinese Ancestry which showed in his appearance. He had become deranged and had to be committed to a mental home and it was there that he had been allowed to contract pneumonia, from which he had died. But he had not limped the last time I had known him. It was not until afterwards that we found the answer. His leg had been damaged after I saw him last; that is, his last days in the institution.

"There is another gentleman man now. He gives the name Ebrahim or something like that. He is an older man. He is related to you. He wants you to know he is here." She was now describing someone whom she could not possibly have known about, guessed at or lifted in any way from my mind. He was not in my mind. When she was speaking about Jo, I had been thinking about Oleg. My godfather's name was Ezra Abraham it was about 28 years since I had seen him. The rest

AWAKENING

of my consultation with Mrs Nason was in like vein just more and more personal detail…………….By the time I had left Mrs Nason's and resumed my day's work I had no doubt left in my mind that survival was indeed a fact.

So, made ready by his timely visit to Mrs Nason, we sat together, my mother, my father and myself, a glass tumbler and the alphabet laid out in a circle. What an unlikely beginning for an adventure that was to last for five years. I am unable to convey the impact of that first encounter. It was as if years of resistance to the very ideas of survival just tumbled in the face of experience. He was utterly convinced of the authenticity of the communication and my father was no fool. Writing briefly of that evening he simply recorded:

I am not such a skilled practitioner with words as to try and convey the wealth of emotions experienced in that short reunion which lasted about two hours, but it was of an intensity which I still remember very clearly two years later. I am not adept at describing my own emotions but they were of the variety where one discovers one has a lump in the throat, so hard that it hurts, when one's breath comes sometimes in short gulps, when moisture is discovered in the corner of ones yes, where it has no business to be. This was to be the most completely personal seance we were to conduct for a very long time in which we became reunited with a whole phalanx of relatives and ancestors.

As I review these experiences so many decades later, I am struck by extraordinary nature of what took place: incredulity turned into firm belief, dialogue turned into teaching, wondering turned into solid experience. Always following the same procedure, Oleg remained our first point of contact, and others, initially family members but later teaching figures, were brought by him to join our conversation. I have no way of measuring quite how unusual this

THE BREATH OF ISIS

level of experience might be even among Spiritualist groups, but I have a feeling that by most standards this regular and committed conversation across the planes remains most unusual. In time even my school friends came as guests and as ever the procedure remained the same and always the level of proof remained high. My father's scepticism was put on one side, his curiosity was aroused, his experimental approach remained. Quite early on in these experiences, I remember that he decided to replace the regular glass tumbler with a huge glass carboy, a container normally used for wine, now it was filled with freon gas, to this day I don't know what he was trying to do! The large heavy container filled with smoky freon, not surprisingly did not move but sat immobilised and cold in the centre of the table. Needless to say, we did not try this particular experiment again. However undaunted, my father clearly wondered about the effect of different physical substances and on another occasion, he placed a large circle made of copper beneath the feet of the sitters. If I remember rightly, it had immediate and disastrous effect upon the communication, words made no sense and the glass lurched wildly across the table. I have no sensible explanation for this but many years later I had my own problems with a spiral of copper. The introduction of the copper had been quite spectacular, and I have a feeling that my father planned to experiment with copper headbands, until my mother drew the line and we just held, 'ordinary' séances as if this was quite the norm! Even in this wild departure from normal family life, we did not do the obvious thing and join others of a like mindedness. My father retained his natural suspicion of all groups, organisations and dogmas. We did not seek out the nearest Spiritualist Church and declare our new-found interest but just carried on in our own private way, wondering and questioning all the while. In such strange territory, fraud and delusion are great dangers, but in our unusual situation, neither really applied; we all muddled through together without preconceptions. On reflection our lack of appropriate training was

AWAKENING

probably a bonus, having no preconceptions, we were not bound by a set of expectations. My mother gradually developed into a natural medium including becoming a trance medium on occasion. My father developed no psychic sensitivity whatsoever. As for me, when I had my finger to the glass, as soon as the contact was made, I experienced a strong sensation rising through my arm, akin to an electrical current and sometimes almost painful. This soon settled down and seemed to occur only during the opening moments. It is impossible to say what curious twists of fate and circumstance made all this possible - a bored afternoon, a chance recognition of a medium, an insatiable curiosity, a restless spirit, who can say! And yes, my mother did receive some good news - she had passed a necessary exam.

This period eventually wore itself out for a number of reasons; the group had consumed its momentum. My school friends each went away to university. I moved away too. However, the group had served a purpose: a bridge had been built in understanding; individually and together we had been gifted with the first-hand practical experience of survival, a wonderful blessing indeed. I really do not remember quite how things ended. I think meetings became fewer until they just did not happen anymore. We simply had no need to continue meeting. We required no further proof; evidence of survival had been supplied continuously. A seed had been deeply planted. Throughout the whole period, I had taken to reading widely, often bringing my questions to the table for comment and consideration. When the group ceased, I continued to read even more widely and branched out into metaphysical philosophy, comparative religion, psychology, anthropology, mythology, in fact anything and everything that might shed light on the essential nature of being. My mother closed down her mediumship as easily as she had opened herself up. She continued to be intuitive and highly sensitive. My father seemed completed by the experience itself. In his first flush of enthusiasm, he became quite passionate

THE BREATH OF ISIS

about Spiritualism as a means of proving survival and he expended much time and energy in compiling his thoughts and recording our experiences. He remained unorthodox in his views, seeking neither a personal god nor a religious creed. He needed only proof of survival and that he was given in full measure. At the time, I thought that my encounter with spirit was over, it fact it had just begun, with hindsight this period proved to be a firm foundation.

NOTES

1. Robert Graves : poet, novelist and scholar specialising in the ideas, history and philosophy of the classical world. His lifelong fascination with pre-Christian existence led to works of translation, biography and history and to a uniquely unorthodox perspective. He envisaged poetry as divine inspiration vision through a living relationship with a muse described as *The White Goddess*. His engagement with the classical past created a rich literary legacy in which ancient history was illuminated by a profound understanding of myth. He was cousin to Lady Oliver Robertson whose life was also rooted in the goddess mysteries of the ancient past.

2. Alice Bailey: telepathic communicator, mediator author. Alice Bailey was born to a wealthy, aristocratic and conventional Christian family. But on June 30, 1895, when she was only fifteen, a stranger wearing a turban walked into the living-room and told her that she needed to develop self-control to prepare for certain work planned for her. At the age of twenty two, she went to India where she became deeply involved in the Theosophical Society. Here she recognized a portrait of the Master Koot Hoomi as the oriental visitor from her youth. This set her upon a unique path as an extraordinary telepathic writer. She wrote daily for 30 years resulting in 24 books. She founded the Lucis Trust with her husband Foster Bailey and wrote *The Great Invocation*, a meditation which continues to be used globally.

3. Dion Fortune: British occultist and writer. Dion Fortune was born Violet Mary Firth. Her chosen name is derived from the Latin motto, Deo Non-Fortuna meaning, 'God, not Luck.' She was a key figure in the occult revival of the early twentieth century and her work remains significant today. She founded The Society of the Inner Light which is still in existence.

AWAKENING

4. Charles Webster Leadbeater: spiritual pilgrim, author, priest, theosophist. Leadbeater became a leading figure in late Victorian esotericism. In 1879 he was ordained as Anglican priest. He travelled to Ceylon with Henry Olcott, the first president of the Theosophy Society and together they founded the English Buddhist Academy. Leadbeater became its headmaster and the school expanded to become the Ananda College which exists to this day. In 1909 he discovered the fourteen year old Jiddu Krishnamurti, once proclaimed as a new world teacher. He remains an important but controversial figure due to his sexual proclivities.

5. Jessie Nason was an internationally known medium. She worked from a hall in Peckham in South London and then moved to Dulwich Library where she led regular meetings for 28 years. When she appeared on *The David Frost Show* in 1963 the switchboard was blocked with calls for days. In recognition of her extraordinary success *Psychic News* awarded her The Spiritualist of the Year. Jessie became well known in the USA and Canada where she gave many demonstrations and often appeared on TV. Despite her international recognition, she remained down to earth and accessible. Her work was carried on by her son David. TV mediumship in the twenty-first century has become normal and popular, Jessie Nason was a forerunner. Her life story is told in the book, *The Medium: Biography of Jessie Nason* by Maurice Leonard.

CHAPTER TWO

THE CALL OF ISIS

A fter this extended episode, my life subsided back into the trappings of normality. I married and trained to be a teacher. I found no like-minds at college. Time passed uneventfully. It was 1977, I was in every respect quite like others of my generation. Married, my thoughts centred on the kind of thing that young married people thought about. My husband, despite his presence during the many years of our home circle proved to be remarkably indifferent to any ideas of further psychic or spiritual exploration. I felt cheated. He continuously intimated that when he had, 'more time,' he would happily accompany me to whatever I wanted to do but of course he never found that elusive quality. Instead, all his energies were expended into his career. His spiritual interests evaporated while mine just coalesced, it was a hidden current silent and deep always seeking its way back to the things of the spirit. So inside my outwardly normal life, other thoughts also moved. My childhood knowing covered itself by a respectable intellectual curiosity, I continued to read and to think.

My awakening to things Egyptian was in the way of these things, seemingly a quirk of fate, yet some thirty years later, I can concede that some greater intention had worked its way to the forefront of my life weaving threads ancient and modern into a new tapestry of being. Yet this awakening, so central to the direction of my adult life, did not come with ease, as a new ship might pass into view on the horizon but instead as a lightning bolt which strikes and

THE CALL OF ISIS

then is gone leaving destruction as its indelible fingerprint. So it was that I entered The Mysteries in this life neither by study and meditation, nor by dream and devotion, but suddenly and without prior warning; some piece of ancient circuitry watchfully asleep, heard its secret name called and was honour bound to answer and awake. Aged 26, I was widely read, satiated with comparative religion, immersed in psychology, touched by psychic realities and still asking questions. Consciously seeking the company and conversation of the like-minded, and disappointed by the total lack of spiritual interest in my own home, I answered an advert placed by a local discussion group. Nowadays an invitation to an Aquarian Discussion Group would be just so much small beer, but at that time answering such an advert called for a little personal courage and an independence of spirit. It was a clarion call for the spiritually disenfranchised, the rebellious, perhaps even the mildly eccentric, on a Sunday afternoon, I set out and walked to an address just a few streets away and turned into a broad tree lined avenue in a pleasant suburb. When I arrived at the house, I saw that it was a huge Victorian property clearly divided into flats and set into a large and manicured garden. I opened the gate and walked along the path with nervous anticipation in my heart. I pushed open the dark heavy external doors to find myself in a cool lobby. A staircase led upstairs, and I walked to the door of the flat on the left and knocked.

As the door was opened, without knowing it, I stepped into a new world that in time I would come to inhabit like a second skin. I was made welcome and shown into a large Victorian parlour. Almost instantly, even as he introduced himself, I was aware of a quality I had not met in life before and could not quite fathom. Our host superbly conveyed an aura of mystery, which begged the question, was this real authority or a studied mystique designed to impress. Such conscious thoughts were far from my mind, I was a little unnerved and more than a little impressed. My eyes wandered

THE BREATH OF ISIS

around the room, it was like no other I had seen up to that moment. The scent of incense filled the air, it was new to me, but I liked it. The room, Victorian in every way, was disguised by dark green drapery which hung from ceiling to floor hiding the wallpaper. A piano was set against one wall, a green sofa was set against another, a number of chairs were arranged in the window bay and occasional tables were set with unusual ornaments. A single chair with wooden arms and faded cushions was placed adjacent to the fireplace facing the window bay. A standard lamp stood beside it. One alcove was filled with books. The mantelpiece was set with matched candlesticks and an assortment of placed items. The room carried its own atmosphere which I could not place, it had the flavour of a spiritualist's parlour, table turning would have been quite in keeping here yet somehow such antics would have seemed inadequate, there was another quality which eluded me. I was in unfamiliar territory.

Others knocked at the front door and soon the room was filled by the psychic and the curious. I sat on a chair in the window bay, watching our host who smoked cigarettes from a long holder and languorously chaired the proceedings from the seat beside the fireplace. I listened as others spoke and when my time came, I just burbled and babbled, there was so much to say, and I said it all badly. Here in this new company, sitting between a middle aged medium and a male witch, my psychic experiences just melted into the background; everyone had their own story to tell. Our host whom I shall refer to by his initial D, commented knowingly after each person's contribution. He appeared to be most knowledgeable. My attention vacillated between the speakers and our host as the dialogue moved clockwise around the room. I have never been able to explain quite how my mind became focused on a single image. I do not know where it came from, or how I came to watch it moving into my mind, but as our host spoke, I received the impression that he wore something large and golden at his chest. Despite my psychic

THE CALL OF ISIS

interests, I was not used to this kind of thing. The idea would not leave me but kept tugging at my sleeve. So at coffee break, more to empty myself of the vision than anything else, I plucked up the courage to mention it. He listened with interest but made no comment. Coffee-break over, we all gathered again and waited for him to join us. He was as they say, fashionably late. Finally, the door opened, and he walked in now wearing a long black robe with an embroidered golden circular motif which filled his chest. I was needless to say, speechless, my mind was in a whirl. In retrospect his response was theatrical, deliberately intended to form a private dialogue between the two of us. He might have responded by simply telling me that my vision was accurate enough to make sense. But such a sufficient and measured response lacked impact and drama. Sweeping into a darkened room made a statement, all eyes were upon him, mine especially, he was in his element.

I do not remember what he talked about in detail, my mind was still reeling. I expect to balance the disclosures from the participants he was obliged to talk about his own journey. As my mind settled, I heard new terms for the first time – The Tree of Life, esoteric, Qabalah. I did not know what he was talking about but of course it did not matter, I was already hooked. This was occultism on show, it was the theatrical presentation of a lifestyle orchestrated for effect but as I was to discover eventually, quite lacking in real content. Much later in my life, I came to meet real magical practitioners and found them to be both ordinary and extraordinary in blended measure but since our host was not extraordinary, he could not bear to be thought ordinary. Instead, he had cultivated a studied air of unusualness with great success. It was an effective act, still undoubtedly repeated by pseudo-occultists who create an air of being powerful in compensation for lack of personal power, choosing rather to seek power over others in the place of empowering others. Such realisations do not belong in the moment but only to reflection. In the moment, the illusion was perfectly substantial.

THE BREATH OF ISIS

I do not remember the order in which the events of that summer took place but in those few brief months, the course of my life completely changed, the expectations and assumptions which glued my daily existence together just vanished, almost overnight. My other silent secret-self had found an opportunity in which to awaken and speak. Such peak moments can appear suddenly in life, conjured as if from nowhere, but they are not in truth without foundation, rather their roots are deeply hidden in the fertile soil of the psyche. These seeds sleep, waiting for the circumstances in which they will waken, where such seeds originate is quite another question. That summer, I spent a great deal of time in the atmosphere of that room walking from my house and my ordinary life just a few streets away. Every visit took me into new realms, taking me further away from the constraints of home, marriage and career. At first, I held onto a degree of caution, still keeping up my guard despite the first flurry of psychic excitement but as the saying goes, 'curiosity killed the cat' and I was very curious. All the while he maintained an air of mystery suggesting though never quite saying, that he, 'knew things.' When he told me that he used hypnosis to take people back to past lives, I of course volunteered to be a subject. It was quite true that I had an interest in the idea of reincarnation. In fact, I had built up quite a belief that I might have had a life in Georgian London. Ironically, some several decades later, I realized that I was of Georgian descent but at the time I had quite a fixation on the trappings of the period, so if my conscious expectations were focused anywhere, it was on the architectural lines of Georgian culture. I arrived excited but nervous and still with some reserve but reserve and deep trance are mutually exclusive!

He wore dark trousers and a dark blue turtle-neck jumper, a massage table had been set up in the centre of the room with as folded blanket on it. He put me at my ease, and I lay down comforted by the softness of the blanket. I did not know what to expect. He simply spoke to me using deep beguiling honeyed tones that were

THE CALL OF ISIS

his speciality. To my surprise, I found my mind moving elsewhere, away from an awareness of the room and even his presence. There was nothing to see in my mind but a darkness then without warning I suddenly felt that I could indeed, 'see' inside my own head, it was a very curious sensation which I have become used to over the years, but at that moment it was quite new and disconcerting. When he asked me to describe what I could see, I answered in some strange far-away voice that I hardly recognized. I found myself standing beside a wall and I was experiencing the fierce heat of a different environment, this was not Georgian London that much I knew straightaway. He asked me to look around and describe what was in my mind's eye. I mentally surveyed the wall. "*What do you see?*" he asked. I replied with spine tingling clarity, "*I see men-animals.*" "*What do you mean?*"- "*I see men with animal heads.*" A thought appeared from the other side of my brain, 'oops this is definitely not Georgian England.' I knew I was in Egypt. The knowing shocked me utterly. As the session unfolded. I could see my sandaled feet and feel the linen of my dress, and later as the session progressed, I provided an acceptable Egyptian name which I slowly and painstakingly sounded out syllable by syllable. When asked to write it in hieroglyphs, my fingers traced invisible shapes in the air and my mind outlined pictograms. It was such a strange process, questions were answered only slowly as if a part of my mind was literally looking into an old file. Answers formed as pictures or through feelings. There was curious suspension of thought quite unlike everyday thinking. No thoughts other than those presented to me through question arose spontaneously. Normally the mind wanders happily from past to present, from present to future but here in this state there was nowhere to wander. My mind waited in suspended animation for the next request and as words shaped themselves and ideas followed, I was surprised at myself. I know now that I have a capacity to move easily into a trance state but then, I knew only what was happening moment by moment. He

THE BREATH OF ISIS

asked the kind of questions that common sense dictates in the circumstances but then he changed the line of enquiry and asked a question that changed everything. *"Is there anyone in your present life with connections to this far memory experience?"* The answer came back with utter clarity and speed in a single word. *"You."* The response ricocheted through me, even now I regard it as genuine answer, quite unpremeditated and as much of a surprise to me as it must have been to him. But there it was, out in the open hanging between us like a thunderclap, a word that could not be denied or sidestepped. Revealing no trace of emotional interest in my answer, he carried on with further questions to ascertain the nature of the relationship. My answers were clear and unequivocal, 'he' had been a father to me. I provided a name, it was hardly a historical reference, but it certainly was an Egyptian name, once again it was slowly sounded out syllable by syllable not consciously knowing how the word might end once it was begun.

When the session was completed and I was returned to waking consciousness, I was faintly embarrassed and somewhat bemused. He retained a level of interest but complete detachment in the unanswered question, was this claim true? Was this an emotional projection? Was this possibly telepathy? Was it a crafty piece of wish fulfilment? Was it an over-active imagination? Was it a desire to impress? I did not know. However, there were many things I did not know. My soon-to-be teacher was already deeply immersed in things spiritual, occult and psychic, especially things Egyptian. Though I did not know it, two rooms in the flat were painted with full size Egyptian murals and much of his conscious life energy had already been taken up with delving into a presumed Egyptian past. He was looking for his own answer to a single question. In this lifetime, he had neither psychic ability nor any inner sensitivity, all such avenues were dead. In fact, according to his own understanding, all these avenues had been completely and deliberately blocked. Apparently, the mediums and psychics he had visited over the years told pretty

THE CALL OF ISIS

much the same story, yes, he had been a person of some authority in an Egyptian setting but through some misuse of personal power, a decision had been made and acted upon to, 'close him down.' None of this was known to me. Moreover, due to his total psychic blindness, he was constantly searching for a woman with gifted sight to both diagnose and even remedy this situation. This was the loaded trap I had inadvertently sprung. It was quite impossible for either of us to walk away from the evening as if nothing had happened, the moment was just too charged with possibilities. For him, fate had delivered, psychic giftedness compounded by naivety and inexperience. For me, fate had also delivered, a new world was inviting me in and conveniently just on my doorstep! We arranged to meet on another evening but this time in contrast to the first session which never moved from an intellectual exchange, despite my apparent revelation, the following session overspilled with emotion as we sought to explore the possible nature of a past relationship. Outside the confines of therapy, it is impossible to convey the painful way in which the mind moves towards its goal of knowing what it does not wish to remember, incrementally edging its way beyond the safety of a comfort zone where all is well. This is how it was for me, first the appearance of a memory almost out of reach, next, its apprehension as the mind grapples with the enormity and suddenness of realisation. As memory rises taking shape and form, breaking through barriers of self-protection, dragging repressed emotion in its wake and overwhelming the cocoon of forgetting, so the mind faces what it has been asked to find. For me, it was an apparent memory of patricide, of taking a life to spare the suffering of a man deformed by a condition of mind and body so devastating that quiet mercy was preferable to unending madness. Was this behind the misuse of power which he suspected of himself? Lunacy is terrible enough but when compounded by the right to exercise authority, the results are no longer personal; history books are littered with the power mad and the insane living in the same mind.

THE BREATH OF ISIS

This is essence is the nature of what erupted into my twentieth century life; needless to say, it did not fit easily. This realisation whether true or false, the distinction was irrelevant, this calling into mind carried with it all the emotional response that might be expected from a loving daughter reunited with a father. None of this made any rational sense, either then or now, but it made perfect irrational sense. Integrating these sudden and unexpected feelings into my life proved quite impossible, it was as if I had quietly offered someone a poisoned draught only last week. Chronological time was irrelevant. I believed I was responsible for a death. I believed I had taken a life. Moreover, the Egyptian imagery in my mind now became so powerful and overwhelming that I felt I was living in two worlds, the present and the past.

My aspirations and interest changed almost overnight, I wanted to read about Egypt and to consume its imagery, to become immersed in what I understood only dimly. In truth what I needed most was probably a period of quiet adjustment and integration. However my, 'teacher' spurred on by the pace at which things had already moved, was hungry for more and he had a range of waiting activities up his sleeve. I do not think he ever developed any real caring for me as a person, I was a fascinating experimental subject with a natural facility for trance and an inborn aptitude for things magical which he must have been able to recognize almost at once, although I did not understand it myself until much later. I simply became a pet project, responsive, highly suggestible and eager to learn. Time with the group was clearly inadequate so in the way of these things I was included in a sub-group and we also spent much time by ourselves. Once again, I did not know that I was a new part of a long-established pattern, promising candidates, selected and primed for magical partnership passed through his hands with regularity, though such a coarse and common description would not have been to his liking. He had a way with words which turned all things to his advantage. His partner took an instant and irrevocable

THE CALL OF ISIS

dislike to me, hardly surprising but quite unnecessary. We never became friends because he had a way of setting people against each other if it suited his purposes. He expended much time telling just how psychic and gifted she was, no matter what I did I could never match her. For me there was no competition involved, so I found such comments out of place, but it was the time-honoured practice of divide and rule.

The hypnosis sessions had put me on an emotional roller coaster, magical talk fired my mind and when he began to work with my subtle energies a whole new explosion took place. In those days interest in the chakras was minimal, books were absent, information was sparse. But since knowledge is always power, he had enough knowledge to appear powerful. As I already knew, the body is surrounded and interpenetrated by more subtle vehicles of consciousness marked by the nodal chakra points. What I did not appreciate is just how sensitised the energy field can become. At first these energy exchanges were more like games done almost in a spirit of fun and exploration quite openly in the group, normally quite harmless. For instance, one person might lie down with eyes closed while a partner placed a hand over a part of the body and the first person might be asked to sense a location. Or again working with a partner, energy could be passed from person through the hands. These were and are innocent enough exercises. Once again, I responded with unexpected ease, playing with these living energies was fun. However, my natural aptitude coupled with the magnetic chemistry which had opened up between us produced dramatic and unexpected results. He always loved the grand gesture and like Mesmer loved to experiment using magnetic passes. I experienced huge shifts in prana; creeping sensations over my body, fiery flushes, flowing energies strange inexplicable sensations. My mind was reeling, now I could not sleep, could not eat. I was hyped, running too fast on an overload of energy. Any sensible teacher would have known it was time to slow down but the process had escaped his

THE BREATH OF ISIS

control. I felt as if a protective skin has been ripped away, colours were unbearably bright, sounds horribly accentuated, feelings greatly intensified. My family thought I had gone mad, what could I say? For me, contact with esoteric teaching was like exposing potassium to air, the effect was instant, explosive and devastating. I do not remember how long this state initial of intensity lasted, probably a matter of weeks, but it changed me completely. Slowly I regained my own self-control and composure but I had radically altered in outlook, intention and aspiration. I began to meditate in my own faltering way and started to read Dion Fortune's *The Mystical Qabalah*, which remained utterly unintelligible for a long time. I began to learn about Tarot and astrology both in the group and on my own. He lent me books. I was a good and able student in the thrall of a charismatic and persuasive teacher. He never appeared troubled by the upheaval which had been precipitated, rather he behaved like the proverbial cat who had swallowed the cream. Jealousies were considered unbecoming, he was always right and his actions were apparently beyond reproach. He had an answer, an occult platitude for everything, his favourite and most often used was, 'some things are necessary,' always said with a far-away meaningful look as if he were at that very moment reading the Akashic Record. It was used a great deal and covered every possible situation.

My life took on the hue of a bad occult novel where a young woman meets a charismatic occult teacher, a well-worn cliché but nonetheless true. How can I convey the reality of this time! I had gone through a dramatic process of spiritual awakening, an initiation of sorts. But this sort of manufactured experience brings many problems in its wake. Disturbing kundalini in this way, by etheric magnetism alone, is in truth an invasive abuse of another person's sacred space, releasing tumultuous and unpredictable personal energy which will run its course as best it can. Moreover, by its very nature, this kind of polarised practice will always

THE CALL OF ISIS

produce a sexualised manifestation whether it is intended or not. As the energy moves from the base chakra upwards into the sacral chakra it will pick up a sexual charge carrying it upwards towards the higher centres. Since the same chakra houses subconscious energies, including memories and feelings, an unprepared release is nothing but troublesome. Arousing a sexually charged energy outside a personal relationship with the intention of stoking passion to fuel kundalini's rising might also be thought morally dubious. Nevertheless, this was my path into the spiritual life. Eventually it produced all sorts of problems, quite apart from the emotional turmoil and psychic upheaval. The drain on my sacral chakra was very great using this centre to pump prana upwards actually left a deficit. One day my sacral chakra just stopped functioning. Subsequently and I had trouble with my periods which became completely irregular and hormone treatment produced only the appearance of normality. It was while hearing a lecture on acupuncture some two years later that the penny dropped and I suddenly realised that this excessive energy work on the etheric had transferred itself into my physical body. In hindsight I wonder why it took me so long to make the connection. I booked an appointment with an acupuncturist and my period returned with 24 hours of treatment and thankfully resumed a normal cycle. My book on the chakras, *The Elements of The Chakras* was written as a direct response to my personal circumstances. It took two years to fully recover physically and mentally from my baptism of fire. In a short space of time, I was skyrocketed into a magical maelstrom. The intensity of the first few weeks abated but explosive possibilities were never far from the surface. I was invited into a newly convened sub-group, the agenda was never quite clear, though we met regularly enough. I am not sure what I learned here, it was a very fraught emotional environment. The group included the male witch who sat beside me on the first meeting - I was never convinced of his competence and a self-professed medium who did not stay with the group for more

THE BREATH OF ISIS

than a few meetings, D. and his partner and myself, an interesting combination! There was much talk of ritual and magic, though I am not sure we ever produced either. One memory does stand out. It took place no more than a few weeks after everything had erupted. I was in one room with D. hearing about the Mysteries of Osiris and the door opened rather hesitantly. It was our wiccan friend. He seemed a bit abashed. *"Sorry to interrupt, err, have you got a minute, seem to be having a bit of problem."* We both stood up and followed him into the front room where we saw that the lady of the house was laid out in the floor. "What happened?" *"Errr, well, we were doing some chakra work and she just passed out. I can't wake her."* This seemed absurd, we all gathered around, and she seemed quite oblivious to our presence. When asked to be more precise about what exactly had happened, it became clear that he had been intoning sounds into each of the chakras and she had simply passed out. D. knelt down, called her name, tapped her hands but with no effect. He made magnetic passes over in sweeping movements over her body but with no effect either. Some time had passed by now and I think we all began to feel concerned. She seemed completely unconscious. Whether a cold flannel might have revived her, I cannot say. But instead, and much to my surprise, I was asked, *"Can you go out and find her?'* I somehow felt obliged to at least try to comply with the request. I was asked to lay down beside her and take her hand to make contact, a light trance was induced. I hadn't got a clue as to how to proceed but I tried to focus my thoughts on her, and to my surprise in my mind's eye an image of her arose floating in the darkness of space like a magician's assistant suspended on the air. I found myself by her side and began to call her name. It seemed to me that as she heard her name, a convulsive wave rolled through her, but she did not wake here. Then quite suddenly the scene changed, and we both seemed to me outside a temple of some kind. I seemed to be running after her and she continued to run away from me. I felt that she did not want to be found, I did

THE CALL OF ISIS

not feel I would succeed in bringing her back. I returned myself to ordinary consciousness a little dazed. She was still lying on the floor partly covered by a blanket. She was still unconscious, though there seemed to have been a small change, now as her name was called a shiver ran visibly through her body. She seemed to be in a more natural and deep sleep, her body showed signs of involuntary movement. At last, she opened her eyes and slowly sat up. What did she remember, not much, but she spoke about being locked out of a temple. All this took hours, I crept home in the small hours of the morning hoping my husband would not wake – what could I say?

The main group continued to hold Sunday meetings which began in the afternoon and often sprawled into the late evening. We studied the Tree of Life which I found fascinating but incomprehensible and for the first time I encountered Tarot. Nowadays I think it would be quite difficult to reach the mid-twenties without any awareness of Tarot cards. Tarot still carried a certain mystique; it was not quite respectable. Curiously, I brought no pre-existing prejudices or fears to the subject, I had never even seen a Tarot card, the whole subject was a complete blank for me. I remember a certain frisson of excitement as the room darkened and images, new and fascinating were lit on a screen, such naivety is gently touching now. Straightaway, I fell in love with the images from the Thoth Tarot. This was the first Tarot set I became familiar with and the image of The Fool still appears large in my mind as it did in that room on that first occasion, now unduly exaggerated in proportion and power by memory. I took my Tarot studies seriously, making notes from existing writers and then composing my own text. I was quite surprised at the ease with which ideas and words flowed. It was here I encountered the name of Isis for the first time. On a warm summer evening, as we studied Tarot Trump 11, The High Priestess, She of the Silver Star, Isis came into my life, along with Her outer manifestation, the High Priestess. In that single moment my life was changed. As I heard Her name spoken outside the confines of

THE BREATH OF ISIS

myth of historical novel, something deep within me awoke once more. I felt a resonance which I did not understand. Though I did not know it then, She had found me and I had found Her. Strange deep memories began to stir in me. My dreams became very intense even frightening. I now began to approach the idea of a Goddess in my own spontaneous and idiosyncratic way. One night I sat alone in a darkened room lit only by a single candle. My altar was the top of a chest of drawers. It was perfectly empty apart from the candle, not by some grand design, but because I simply had no knowledge of ritual objects. I found myself intoning out loud, "How ridiculous you are," repeated the left side of my brain over and over again until it was like a competing background chant. As the invocation continued and rose in power, so my skin began to prickle, the candle flame appeared, to my inner vision at least, to grow taller and I seemed to sense a presence enveloping me. At the time I could not explain my actions even to myself as I spoke the words aloud. I am She who is black. I am She who is white, I am She who is no-thing. I am She who is all things. I am She who contains everything. I am She. She is me, She and I are one. What had I done? Had I done anything other than sit in a darkened room and make myself ridiculous? Part of my mind drew me on in inexplicably while another part poked fun at my absurdity with a nagging rational voice. In the absence of any teaching or contact with a specialised group, I was forced back on my own intuition and intention. At that time, I had no contact whatsoever with any other women who saw themselves as priestesses. I was working purely alone, guided by instinct and the crumbs gleaned from esoteric writings. Nevertheless, though I did not know it then I had reached a turning point. I had opened a doorway in myself to renew a very old relationship between myself and the Goddess Isis. Driven by my own inner restlessness, I had made a space within myself for Her to enter. My invocations continued in the silence of my bedroom.

Hindsight now permits me to place this searing episode in the

THE CALL OF ISIS

greater context of my life, but even hindsight does not mitigate the difficulties of the transition. This was not in any way an ideal entrance into The Mysteries, yet its ferocity was in some way an indispensable part of my awakening. My plunge into the depths was a baptism of fire which left me totally changed as if a layer of my being had been totally burned up. Though it took me several years to recover and find a new equilibrium, this rough passage probably saved me years of gentle study. I crossed the threshold of that house as a seeker and when I parted company with that group, I was no longer seeking, I had found the direction home even though I still had far to travel. I did not leave empty handed though to all outward appearances, I left under a cloud. Labelled as a troublemaker, my tenure in the group had expired. It was a pattern to be repeated throughout my life. However, among the many who came and went, I made deep soul connections with five people who became lifelong friends. Between them and in different ways their friendship carried me from solitary isolation into the world of magic and Mystery School.

CHAPTER THREE

THE MANTLE OF ISIS

Having left the claustrophobia of the group, I began to make connections of my own. I found a group which met monthly for a talk in a public library in Clapham followed by lively conversation in the local pub. Arranged by a woman of true Aquarian spirit, these meetings provided a welcome antidote to the power-games I had lived through. The talks were interesting, the atmosphere was friendly. The organiser was a woman much ahead of her time. She ran a small psychic development group from her home, and I was invited to join. I have very fond memories of my time with her. She was a genuine voice for the New Age with no time for spiritual pretension or psychic one-upmanship. She was a magnet in her local community and her home was an open door for all sorts of interesting people both young and old. Here I met a pagan priestess, and an assortment of free spirits including Mary Caine who had published original work on the Kingston Zodiac. I felt quite at home in this company. Encouraged by the popularity of the monthly talks, my new friend decided to tackle a much bigger project and host a weekend festival. Once again, she was pioneering a path where others would follow. She envisaged a local Aquarian festival, way ahead of the large London Mind-Body-Spirit extravaganza. Organising the festival became a continuous process and eventually I was asked to join one of the groups and

THE MANTLE OF ISIS

take charge of the stage event programme. I was just thrilled to be asked to do something purposeful. One of the other regular visitors to the library was Jerry Ozaniec who was also asked to join the organising group and take responsibility for the lecture programme. Fate held much in store for the two of us. We worked together over several years organising Aquarian festivals at Battersea, Lambeth, and Clapham. At last, I felt useful and accepted. The template for mind, body and spirit gatherings is now familiar, but then it was all new and exciting. The normally quiet and reserved atmosphere of the local town hall had surely never experienced anything quite like it before. The main hall was a riot of colours and scents as incense wafted through the hall. Every stallholder offered something new and exciting: pagan jewellery, ethnic clothing, study courses, astrological readings, shelves of books, and a whole host of things I had never seen before. Tarot readers filled a side corridor, healers used the side rooms, there were workshops in an upstairs meeting room and lectures in a downstairs hall while performers took to the stage every hour; it was a spiritual carnival. But it was much more than a jamboree. Jerry had managed to book a key speaker, Gareth Knight. His talk was packed. Already an established author and noted occultist, he was on his way to acquiring a significant reputation. His presence was quite a coup and I dropped everything else to be in the audience. It was my first experience of hearing a lecture in the Mystery School tradition, it was not to be my last. During the weekend, I also attended a workshop given by Vivienne Jones, (later to become Vivienne Jones-O' Reagan). Despite first meeting under the strained circumstances created by our esteemed, 'teacher' in the Victorian parlour, we have remained friends for life and the sense of sisterhood that we experienced on meeting was greater than sense of rivalry that he tried to create between us. Though younger than me by about a year, Viv was already immersed in the world that I aspired to, well connected, well read

THE BREATH OF ISIS

and already studying with a School of Esoteric Science, Viv already had confidence and knowledge. When she had visited me for the first time, we found so much to talk about that we stayed up all night. Viv went on to give much service to the Pagan Federation and later in life she and her husband Chrys worked within the group Aurum Solis founded by Melita Denning and Osbourne Philips. But that is to rush ahead. Vivienne had been booked to take a workshop. Her guided meditation was my first experience of an inner encounter with the Divine Feminine. I remember this journey only too well.

Find yourself in a secluded place in a lush green wood of dappled shade. Nearby you hear the sound of water, a stream gushes down from the hillside cascading over dark rocks making a waterfall. The air here is filled with damp spray and the earth smells rich and green. You stand quietly taking in the natural beauty of the place. Suddenly you hear your name spoken and turn to see the figure of a beautiful unearthly woman standing before the waterfall. She holds a chalice in both hands and extends it to you.

In my mind's eye, we travelled through a wooded landscape until we reached a clearing amidst the trees where we found a waterfall. As we stepped towards it, the radiant figure of a woman stepped forward holding a chalice in Her hands. When I stepped forwards, Her gaze was penetrating. *"Drink deep, my child, drink deep."* She said, and I did. I am unable to fully convey the impact of these few simple words. As the visualisation proceeded, I began to shake, was overcome by tears and felt almost faint. Part of my disorientation was doubtless caused by my inexperience but these physical signs continued to accompany significant moments of psychic intensity for many years. This was certainly among my first such experience and quite simply, I did not know what to do with myself. When we returned to the main hall afterwards, I was ashen-faced and unsteady on my feet. I was so shaken that neither the hall nor the people seemed quite real, it took me several days to recover and to get my physical bearings again. The impact of the experience came as a psychological shock. Where had this experience come from? Was it an external event that I was experiencing inwardly? Was it an internal experience that I was externalising? Above all why did the experience shake me to the very roots of my being? How could an image in the mind produce an immediate physical and indeed emotional impact?

Thirty years later I am in a better position to understand the journey. Its apparently simple images offer potent seeds charged with psychic energy. The natural setting of wood and water, stone and earth set the tone, providing a composition of place tuned to nature herself. The water cascading into a pool conveys a dynamic vitality and a life-giving potency, it is attended by a figure representing feminine divinity. She offers the chalice, another symbol of the feminine divine. There is no obligation to accept but taking a draught from these sacred waters is to partake in an archetypal communion. Intellectual analysis is a useful tool permitting understanding but at the time my response was totally instinctive. The town hall may have been an unlikely setting for a personal vision, but revelation is no respecter of convention.

Viv and I continued to be friends and I through her I took my first tentative steps towards Mystery School. Despite being pulled towards joining the SOL (The Servants of the Light – School of Esoteric Science) I needed to be certain that it was, 'right.' Every night before I fell asleep, I offered up a little thought-form, if this was the right decision, then let it be confirmed by a sign. Looking back into my diaries, I see that I have done this often, asking for a sign before proceeding on a course of action even when action on my part would have been quite simple. So instead of applying to join the SOL, I asked whether I should join the SOL and I waited for an answer. I suppose my attitude carried some kind of implicit challenge too. Dion Fortune's magical view had already begun to take hold and I think I wanted signs that greater minds than my own were in some way entering my life. I also felt that I now carried a label as a troublemaker, the magical community was a small place. I even wondered whether an application in my name might be instantly rejected. So I waited and hoped that, 'the universe' might kindly open the way for me if the way ahead was my rightful path. When Viv and I next met some weeks later, quite unbidden, she told me that she had spoken on my behalf to The Director of Studies who gave me the green light to join. And so I joined Mystery School not knowing what to expect. When my first set of papers duly appeared, I set about my task with absolute commitment. I completed the meditation assignments on time and began to read widely and deeply in my attempt to become absorbed in the WMT, the Western Mystery tradition, now more often called the Western Esoteric Tradition. Time passed without undue disturbance. Viv and I became inseparable. There was a physical similarity between us and people often took us for sisters. We attended many events and conferences together and passed hours in conversation about magic and magicians, priests and priestesses.

This period was one of tentative exploration, mentally, through extensive reading, physically by attending various conferences which brought me into a new circle of like-minded people and spiritually as I came into contact with the metier of the tradition. At an annual SOL Conference, I heard Caitlin Matthews speak. I attended the annual Quest Conference, (remarkably it still meets today some 40 years later) and heard Marian Green give a public talk. She was down-to-earth and very amusing. Both Caitlin and Marian went onto to become prolific writers and teachers. Even as I write these words, Caitlin and Marian are still in service to the tradition. With hindsight I can see that this period formed a foundation which provided a rich seedbed for the rest of my life. Marian eventually took me under her wing for no particular reason, she does the same for many people. Although we had already met in that first group, it was not until the maelstrom in my life had subsided, that we became friends. We first met in the hallowed

THE MANTLE OF ISIS

green Victorian room where Marian had been invited to give a talk. I can still recall the simple exercise she set as a guided meditation: beginning at the tree in the centre of a field, turning down hill to walk to a white cross-bar gate. These first experiences with guided imagery still live in the mind decades later like imprinted patterns. I remember that when we shared our experiences, where others reported unclear or hazy images, my inner experience was crystal clear and fully vivid. Marian made a good humoured joke about my report. She must have spotted something in me then, just as I can now see a natural candidate for the Mysteries. She brought such a different atmosphere to that same green draped room, she was so full of warmth and laughter.

Nowadays guided imagery carries no novelty value, it is the stock-in-trade of holistic spirituality and the creative imagination is now employed as a tool for self-help. Yet looking around at its current usage a great deal that passes under the banner of the creative imagination is a complete misapplication of the term. Too often guided imagery is little better than a directed daydream filled with flimsy images and whimsical scenes: *"imagine you are walking in a bluebell filled glade, find yourself walking beside a stream, it is a beautiful summer's day etc."* Creating pictures in the mind is no more than an empty intellectual exercise unless the images carry some symbolic weight. Journeying in the hands of experts can be a shattering experience. I came to learn that the trained imagination is the modus operandi of The Mysteries but at that time I simply found these inner experiences totally astounding.

Another early inner experience is recorded in my diary: in a meditative state of mind, a scene arose spontaneously in my mind. I entered a cave which then opened out into an underground chamber filled with water and fed by springs encircling the pool. Everything was brightly lit, the waters were pale blue and warm to the touch. In the centre was an island of carved rock. I swam across to the island and found a casket with my name engraved upon it. As I opened the

THE BREATH OF ISIS

box, I heard the words, "Work and learn." This is what I did and decades later, I am still doing the same. This powerful injunction has supported me throughout life. The exhortation to, 'work' is not intended in the ordinary mundane sense but in the alchemical and magical sense. The lifelong process of transformation is often called The Great Work. Practitioners of the tradition most often refer to rituals as, a 'work' or a, 'working,' the term, 'pathworking' refers to 'work' undertaken upon the Paths of the Tree of Life now it is too often and incorrectly used to describe general guided meditations. The meditation took shape like a living mandala which I entered through the cave, a classical feminine symbol. The circular pool was fed by surrounding streams and in the centre an island provided both a point of focus and a place of stability. The underground chamber was not dark and cold but warm and lit invisibly from within. I felt compelled to make the journey to the centre by swimming across the waters. This engagement with the scene was an essential component, for the psyche was showing itself to me dressed in symbolic guise. The 'message' was only heard once I had crossed the pool, clambered onto the island and opened the casket bearing my name. Had I failed to engage with the tasks offered by the psyche, the images would have remained no more than pleasant but meaningless excursion. None of this was known or understood when the imagery arose long before I joined the Mystery tradition. During that single weekend fate once again had showed its kindly hand. Not only had the festival been a wonderful success, but I was given the opportunity to hear Gareth Knight speak as representative of the tradition that was beginning to call to me but I had been touched by a numinous encounter with the Divine Feminine through my dear friend Vivienne, the first priestess I met on my long and winding journey. The two themes that were to dominate the rest of my life were now present in seed form: the Divine Feminine and Mystery School, and the people who were to play such a large part in my life were now in place although of course I did not know it at the time. What of the rest of my life at that time? My husband showed no interest in my new activities, my new books or my new friends. My inner life was beginning to spill into my outer life. This is not healthy or desirable.

I had been introduced to a piece of music called *The Raising of Nefertiti* which was produced by The Nefer Ensemble created by Denis Stoll Dance and his wife Cheryl. I just could not hear this piece without being moved to tears, I only had to play the music to be inwardly transported back into an Egyptian setting. I was given a copy on a tape cassette and eventually transferred it to a CD of my own. Over the years, I had tried to locate a copy but without success, it worried me that I might lose my only copy and I knew I would be heartbroken in that eventuality. But today as I check my manuscript working of course from my laptop, I search for Dennis Stoll on the internet. To my utter delight not only am I reading about his life but I am hearing the beautiful music that I love so much and I am delighted to discover that a re-mastered version is currently available. Moreover, his wife Cheryl has continued and extended his work with her own inspired visionary work so aptly named Star Wisdom. So, through the good auspices of Aquarian communication, not only have I discovered that I can hear such beloved music on my laptop whenever I wish but I recognise another beautiful ancient Egyptian stream in full flow.

Returning swiftly to the past once more, I was introduced to the writings of Isha and R.A. Schwaller de Lubicz which I read and re-read over and over again in an effort to understand more about Egyptian spirituality. I began to dress differently and I began to take on a different appearance, I could not help myself. The pull of this new life was so overwhelming that it could not be ignored, I was magnetised by magic. My husband carried on as if nothing were happening, like the proverbial ostrich his head was deep in the sand. Our lives were separating and as they say, nature abhors a vacuum. I had begun to spend time with my new friends, my social

THE BREATH OF ISIS

life and my magical life were overlapping. I was invited to a meal at Jerry Ozaniec's home. We had a lot in common including partners who did not understand out shared interest in magic. I thought I had found my magical partner but separating magical involvement from personal involvement is an all but impossible task as many others have also discovered. The magnetic attraction between us was palpable. A new phase in my life opened and I did my best to keep an unsteady balance between magic and domesticity.

Although I had read widely about the Western Mysteries my understanding was not grounded in experience but only in book learning. My inner experiences felt potent but were quite solitary. I had no experience of group ritual whatsoever. So, when Marian announced a forthcoming weekend course, the opportunity was just too timely to ignore. To me Marian was the experienced and trustworthy voice of The Mysteries, I was a keen but totally raw recruit. We met in Buxton in Derbyshire and over one weekend my life changed again. It is worth repeating that I was completely an utterly a novice, but at Marian's weekends everyone participates fully regardless of experience. Marian assigned me a role as the Officer of the West. In her usual manner, the part was probably allocated by lot thought I don't really remember. Anyway, I needed to represent the western quarter and all the qualities assigned there. As I spoke the allotted words, I was astonished at what I felt and experienced, it was like standing in a waterfall of invisible energy that appeared as if from nowhere. However as the ritual proceeded, I witnessed something that I can never forget. We were working in a circle of about a dozen people. I was positioned in the West, Jerry was positioned in the East directly opposite me at the other side of the circle. As I looked towards him, I saw a ball of light emerge from his head and hover. It extended itself into a column of light at his side and instantly took on his shape becoming a complete replica in etheric substance. My mouth dropped open with shock, I was not watching this with my inner vision but with ordinary

THE MANTLE OF ISIS

physical sight. As if this wasn't enough, this full-size figure began to walk across the room towards me fading almost half-way across when it but began to dissolve as instantly as it had been created. I was utterly astonished. When I asked him about it, he told me it was a conscious act, though he had no idea that his projected thought-form had become quite so real to me. It was, he said the projection of his desire to be with me. It seemed to be an amazing confirmation of our magical bond.

Another year passed and during the following Quest Conference Marian announced a new project which she called The Green Circle. She envisioned a network of small groups linked by an interest in the many aspects of magic. The idea was soon translated into reality and many local groups came into being including the one that Jerry and I started. Even now I can look back on this as being a very constructive period. The group remained remarkably cohesive over many years and several of our members later went on to establish other groups around Kent. We established a programme which included tarot, astrology and Qabalah and spurred on by success, I began to write rituals. I foolishly thought I knew a thing or two about, 'magic' until I stepped out of the baby pool and found myself swimming with the real experts!

I think it was Vivienne who drew my attention to a forthcoming workshop. Almost before the words were spoken, I knew that I had to attend. Hosted by Gareth Knight, the subject of the weekend was Dion Fortune. I went with my friend Vivienne. The magical career of Gareth Knight is well documented, so I have no need to reproduce it here. Though I did not fully appreciate it at the time, Gareth Knight had positioned himself in a unique place: experimental, unorthodox and radical. As one of the magical practitioners of a previous generation, he was trained within Dion Fortune's, The Society of the Inner Light. Having left the embrace of the group mind he had begun to offer Mystery School training via a correspondence course. In the book, *Dion Fortune and The Inner Light*, Gareth

THE BREATH OF ISIS

Knight writes of his motivation at the time: "*Speaking for myself I retained the ambition to build an active group that would replicate the Greater Mysteries worked by The Society of The Inner Light, that I knew in my salad days ...When invited to lecture in public, I tried to introduce techniques I had learned within the grades of the society to a wider audience. This was to my way of thinking another aspect of what the Tibetan Master called, the Externalisation of the Hierarchy. In 1979 in a weekend devoted to The Tree of Life I conducted a multiple, 'path working' a 'rising on the planes.' It was the first time ever, as far as I know that such technique was tried in public. In subsequent years it has become almost commonplace in workshops around the world. In 1980 my subject was the works of Dion Fortune with a particular emphasis upon the novels, not least the figure of the sea priestess and here I introduced some public ritual work also, although somewhat in disguise, in plain clothes and more in the form of a play reading but with hidden dynamics.*" So here was a Mystery School weekend in the guise of a public workshop! This was a tremendous step and a radical break with tradition. It was a bold and pioneering move which also presented many challenges. The Dion Fortune seminar was the second in what became a decade of ground-breaking weekends, a masterclass in magic was about to open and I was in truth just a novice. It is not coyness that prevents me from describing the events of the weekend in detail. Nor have I been bound my oaths of secrecy in case you were wondering. I could offer a narrative but it would be meaningless. What I cannot convey no matter how hard I try, are the multi-layered dynamics of magic in the Mystery School tradition – better instead to recall The Four Magical Injunctions, To Dare, to Know, to Will and to be Silent, and to comply with the last of these I keep my silence.

Gareth Knight ran a series of annual workshops for a decade. They were held at Hawkwood College, an educational and conference centre in Gloucestershire. To a novice like me, the series became an on-going process, an alchemical slow cooking and a

THE MANTLE OF ISIS

baptism of fire as we were immersed in The Chemycal Wedding of Christian Rosencreutz, the Mysteries of Isis, and much later the mythology created by J.R.R.Tolkein. Mature reflection and the detached space of hindsight however does permit me to make some pertinent observations. The events at Hawkwood College were soul-searing and often incomprehensible to the rational mind. Although the weekends were open to the public, Gareth Knight's students held the centre ground. Perhaps they were privy to the purpose of the weekend, perhaps not? Perhaps Gareth Knight himself was following his own inner guidance moment by moment, this is often the way but in actuality, the real inward purpose of the weekend was never made explicit at the time. This too may have been unavoidable since the participants consisted of his personal students, some SOL students, some unaffiliated esoteric folk and even a few members of the public. From this unbalanced mix, Gareth Knight needed to weave a group-mind able to bear an extremely high-level impact of particular energies. It would not be untrue to say that there was some feeling of being used as psychic cannon fodder for purposes unexplained. I am indebted to the book *I Called it Magic*, Gareth Knight's magical autobiography which at last provided an explanation. I heartily recommend the book to the curious reader. The magical and private agenda of the weekend so often bore little relation to the programme title. In 1980 the weekend, *The Occult Work of Dion Fortune* culminated in sending away the figure of Lilith Le Fay. It was explained much later that she was perhaps even an independent entity of doubtless Atlantean origin rather than a figment of Dion Fortune's imagination. This troublesome force, intelligence, personality, or whatever had seemed just to become larger than life. I suppose such things are not impossible. So, her image, presence, essence, again I am struggling for words, was rowed back out onto the cosmic seas. Apparently, she re-emerged at a later date in a more softened form. My understanding of such explanations might still be incomplete and totally flawed.

THE BREATH OF ISIS

The weekend entitled *The Mysteries of Isis* again proved to be something else entirely. Once again using the same dynamics, the difference between those 'in the know' and the rest of us was stronger than ever. We the participants had gathered to perhaps understand the historical-classical living Isian mysteries more deeply, Gareth Knight, assuredly at the behest of the Inner Planes was dancing to a different tune, as must be the way. The unspoken and unrevealed intent of this weekend, presumably known to some or just the few, was to clean, clear, release, empty, sever, or otherwise purge an Atlantean substratum consciousness. In his own words, "*What we realised about this weekend as a whole was that the Atlantean powers, so beloved by occultists of previous generation, need no longer be regarded as the root and power base of traditional wisdom. They could be sloughed off from the bottom so to speak, to give way to a new foundation – one that was based on Celtic myth and legend.*" Apparently, Gareth Knight believed that some of the ancient Atlantean forces has been locked up under the ocean yet seemed to have been seeping through from time to time – possibly even the source of master-race theories. Incidentally although it may be said that the native tradition of the British Isles draws it vitality from its Celtic source, the fuller western esoteric tradition is undoubtedly drawn from Hermetic philosophy which most scholars maintain is derived from the ancient Egyptian wisdom passed down to Greek philosophers such as Plato and Pythagoras. But back to the events of 1981. By his own reckoning given in the book, "*The work in hand was to make contact with these ancient powers to re-consecrate the sub-marine temple of the goddess and link it with the stars typically the constellation of Corona Borealis.*" The intention to undertake this working with motley participants unprepared might indeed be questionable. "In the event, towards the end of the working, the circuits blew wide open to startling effect, causing many afterwards to say that it was the most upsetting rite in which they had ever taken part." There was a general feeling

THE MANTLE OF ISIS

that something had gone wrong. Dolores (head of the SOL) was taken over by a dominating male figure and rushed out from the hall and the ritual was immediately closed. These kind of psycho-pyrotechnics became a feature of the weekends 1980 – 1982, after which Dolores withdrew to concentrate on her own school The phrase, 'wildness in the blood' rises in memory for some reason. After the event, several people reported difficult contacts with Atlantean figures, presumably the result of dropping a stone into a pool of decaying matter. I will say no more here about the personal ramifications of being part of this event, being willingly present but unwillingly utilised. Other memories of events are perhaps too hazy to be serviceable. However the emotional and psychic feelings of an intensity close to breaking point remain indelibly imprinted. Every year without fail there were casualties and scapegoats, the walking wounded as we laughingly called ourselves! Apparently, we served as the footsoldiers in some rebalancing, realignment and 'redeeming' of vast and deep psychic structures revealed only to those with an ear to the veil between the worlds, happily I am not one entrusted with such plans.

Concurrently during this period, Jerry and I also attended a series of weekends hosted under the aegis of SOL, it was a heady time. Gradually through exposure to the dynamics inherent within the tradition, I ceased being a novice. I stopped feeling faint and lightheaded as the energies of the group lifted, I stopped weeping as emotion overcame me, I ceased being among the psychic casualties, and the faint glimmerings of understanding began to take shape. However, by the end of the eighties, I experienced what can best be described as, 'magical fatigue' and I was looking for a less strenuous outlet for my magical passions and once again following in Viv's footsteps, I joined the Fellowship of Isis. By this time, I had been involved in things magical for just over a decade. I had seen many extraordinary things, quite beyond the ordinary, such things are not foreign to nature but a reclamation of the natural

THE BREATH OF ISIS

powers embedded in the human soul. I had seen things magnificent, glorious and exalted.

In 1987 my first book *Meditation – The Inner Way* was published. Like so many things in my life it happened not through intent but through happenstance. It had never occurred to me that I could write or that I should write. Now, I write every day. I have described the first period of my magical life as the laying of a foundation, but the second period was not one of construction but of destruction. I am here reminded of something Dion Fortune said to answer the question, *"How shall I know that my application to serve The Masters of Wisdom has been accepted?"* Her answer was not comforting but it was succinct. Quite simply – the fabric of your outer life will come apart seam by seam! Like others committed to the Path of The Mysteries, I know this to be true. Sceptical minds may just say that we are all subject to change and to the storms of life, this is undeniable. However DF was referring not to random change that we all experience but to a process of pruning away all that stands in the way of soul-service. This may seem harsh to anyone who regards the spiritual life as a comfort zone, actually it is more like placing yourself in the firing line. My life had gone through a searing process, none of it pleasant. My marriage had inwardly imploded, it could not contain the magical time-bomb planted within it. I had lost interest in my teaching career long ago. I nursed other aspirations, but aspirations alone do not pay the bills. My daughter had been borne in 1982 and my son was born in 1987 and in-between I had a child who was stillborn. After my son was born, the house of cards which constituted my life collapsed. I went to my mother's house with my children and stayed there a year living in the spare room which had just enough space for a double bed and a cot. My son was five weeks old and I went back to work. Throughout everything my family, most especially my mother gave me unconditional love and support which was my refuge. The house where we had held so many group meetings was put up for sale. I had become a single parent on the way to divorce. I could not have felt worse, broken as it were by my own hand, magic had indeed wrecked the appearance of my life. Time does not stand still, the house was sold, I moved into a small house with my children and just went to work. My life had become mundane and humdrum, while in my heart, I yearned for things magical, spiritual and divine. I felt completely estranged from Mystery School now, it had seemingly broken me. When Viv suggested we go to Ireland together and spend time with Olivia Robertson, (in later years always known and addressed as Lady Olivia, but not so then), I was delighted. We travelled with the children and stayed with friends of Viv's in a cottage called The Bridge House just a few minutes away from the castle. It was a wonderful interlude. My children played with their children, romped around with dogs, goats and chickens, were well fed and looked after while Viv and I went to the castle by invitation. My informal tone might appear a little surprising to those come to the FOI more latterly. But in those days, it was possible to sit with Olivia and her brother Derry in the rambling conservatory, to share a meal in the dining hall or to make tea in the kitchen. I suspect that such informalities are long gone, the price to be paid for worldly success but then things were quite different. I have memories of Derry who passed peacefully into spirit some years ago. When I met him, his health was waning and he did not speak over much. On one occasion he had a very severe tooth-ache and I did my best to provide some healing. I know that at the appointed time, he passed easily into spirit while just sitting in a chair in the library. Several years later, during one of my own residential weekends, in meditation he seemed palpable to me, he took me to the temple which I knew well and standing beside me said, "*I grant you a new dispensation.*" And to accompany these words, he traced a sign over the ground with his extended hand. It was only recently that I recalled this fragment of memory.

At Olivia's suggestion, we took the children into the temple.

THE BREATH OF ISIS

I have wonderful photos of my children sitting at the foot of the high altar to Isis. My daughter even had an extraordinary dream which she shared with me on our way to the castle. She told me that in her dream, Olivia had appeared and opened a great book and then invited the whole world to come to the castle. It was an extraordinary insight which proved to be prophetic for the world did come to Olivia and also Olivia went to the world. The FOI has provided an avenue for the longings of the collective heart for the returning Feminine Divine. So, to Lady Olivia Robertson, Archpriestess of the FOI, I offer salutations and greetings. While at the castle, I undertook a Rite of Rebirth. The seeds planted here did not take long to ripen.

The modus operandi of the FOI was different from Mystery School. It offered a curriculum based on a series of sacred dramas but did not offer any metaphysical teaching or training. Its appeal was broad, its door was open to anyone drawn to uphold the name of the Goddess. Sacred drama when undertaken in the right spirit is a meditation. Temple skills were imbedded in the FOI curriculum, not explicitly stated but implicitly encoded like a spiritual DNA. Sacred drama is itself an ancient vehicle of spiritual power. The fabled Mysteries of Egypt were expressed through sacred drama, story was made real and embodied through its priesthood. I returned from Ireland with spirits uplifted, I was done with Mystery School which had broken me. My outer life unexpectedly changed once again. Jerry returned to live with me, and we made plans to move. My heart was contented, but the process of becoming is one of continuous birthing and dying, I had merely reached a plateau where I might rest awhile. Once in our new home, I turned my attention towards Goddess Isis and the work of the Fellowship. At last, I felt blessed with a magical and domestic partnership. So, when I heard that Caitlin Matthews was hosting an event to be called Isis of Ten Thousand Names, I was thrilled that we would be sharing this together. I had a meeting with Caitlin and other key participants

THE MANTLE OF ISIS

to discuss the ritual drama. To my surprise Caitlin had allocated me the role of Isis. She had taken one of Lady Olivia's rituals and added a new ingredient. The Goddess Isis would make a timely but unexpected entrance to deliver the classic words given by Lucius Apuleius in *The Golden Ass*. The cue for the entrance of Isis would not appear on anyone's script, other than those of us sitting in that room on that day. The sacred drama revolved upon the theme of Gaia's initiation into a higher state of being. Unusually the drama contained a second drama, a central section called The Trial of Earth. Planet Earth was not on trial, but the trial format permitted people to speak either for or against the proposal, namely that the planetary body of the earth should proceed towards its own rebirth. In this section, the participants were asked to speak freely and to express a purely personal view.

During the preparations in the weeks beforehand, I remember being quite unnerved by the unscripted structure, wondering how it might work effectively. Curiously just before I was asked to take on the role of Isis, I dreamed I was flying among the stars. The blessings of divine intervention cannot be timetabled, the entrance was known only to a handful of organisers. It is very difficult to describe the build-up to a ritual in the preceding weeks, slowly and almost imperceptibly, things, 'drop into place,' synchronicities flow, dreams intensify, sensitivities sharpen as the inner mind opens and subsumes ordinary temporal thinking like a great fish swallowing a minnow. This period can be very difficult; the ordinary tasks of life must continue even while the inner tension continues to mount. As the event draws close, the practical things become paramount, packing always provides a distraction and the inner tension must move to one side. By this time, I had participated in many such events, dealing with pre-ritual-tension, fondly referred to as PRT was nothing new. On the journey, however I distinctly remember that my scalp felt itchy, it was so noticeable as we travelled that I wondered whether I had become suddenly allergic to the shampoo I

THE BREATH OF ISIS

had been using, it was the only explanation I could muster.

The next day while listening to a morning lecture, my scalp itched so much that I was convinced I was experiencing some kind of allergic reaction. As the weekend unfolded, I continued to feel the sense of tension building. This period before the actual ceremony is much like surfing a giant wave, a dynamic momentum that carries the group forward. The skill lies in moving with the flow while maintaining personal balance. On the Saturday evening not only did my scalp itch mercilessly but as I got ready for bed, in the mirror I saw red streaks down my back. Isis spoke to me in deep meditation and told me not to be concerned and that all was well.

These weekend events had fallen into a pattern familiar to me. The first session on Sunday morning always consisted of a rehearsal, a walk-through without words and with plenty of good humour to keep the energies contained. Such formalities may seem strange but a ritual with many participants requires choreographing just like any drama. Building this shared confidence enables the actual ritual to flow with much greater ease and facility; the outer dynamics are one thing, but the inner dynamics are quite another. Since report writing remains standard magical practice, I am able to draw upon my own report written at the time. It also appears in the book *Daughters of the Goddess*.

> *As the rehearsal proceeded, it became impossible for me to stay in the room. The energies in the hall were accelerating too fast for me. I stepped outside into the ante-chamber. I was quite unable to sit still while the energies in the hall were still mounting. Like an expectant parent pacing a hospital corridor, I needed to move. I began to dance, with slow yoga-like movements. As I danced, I felt a great descent of power. A winged mantle was placed about me. Contact was opened. I cannot adequately convey my sense of surprise and wonder; I was both amazed and quite unprepared. No-one had prepared me for this.*
> *There was now a short break for tea and robing. Others left the*

THE MANTLE OF ISIS

hall chatting in small groups. I found it difficult to even speak. I went straight to my room. Time seemed to hang. Mentally I walked the tightrope, holding on to physical reality and my sense of self while not losing contact with the presence in which I was immersed. Finally, I was ready, robed in swathes of shimmering green deep rich brown and gold, a sistrum in my hand. I looked into the mirror and saw the face of another. I left the room and made my way slowly to the hall. Walking was not easy, I felt unsteady on my feet. The participants were already seated. My entrance was not scheduled. It was to be a surprise, symbolic of divine intervention. I sat on a great throne-like chair in the ante-chamber facing the closed door to the hall. As the ritual commenced, my mediation deepened. As the group opened and called upon the deities to be present, I-She answered aloud in the silence of the ante-chamber. This continued throughout the opening sequence. I-She answered with word and gesture.

Although I was seated beyond the hall outside the closed door, it was as if the door had become transparent. It was no barrier. Within the hall planetary energies were mediated through a group dance. I saw the planets amidst the heavens. When the Maze Dance of the Zodiac was performed, I saw the living starry constellations as great beings. As each one passed before the throne beyond the closed door, salutes were given.

With the planetary energies in attendance, the group enacted the Trial of Earth, more properly the trial of humankind. Gaia was not on trial. The trial was called to assess whether the Earth's planetary body and human consciousness together were ready to take a cosmic initiation. Unusually in this highly structured ritual, participants were at this point free to speak as the spirit moved. Voices weighed responsibilities, understanding and destiny. Individuals spoke of past failings, of present crises and future possibilities. Finally, after long and careful debate, the

THE BREATH OF ISIS

decision was unanimous. The Earth would proceed towards its own initiation. I-She was filled with joy. The time approached for my entrance. I stood in readiness. A crown was placed on my head with a mantle of stars. I-She was called from within the hall. The doorway became a star gate.

It was planned that I should walk around the hall and finally come to stand before the person enacting the role of the Earth. As I-She entered, the assembled company, each appeared like a shining beacon. Though I had expected to simply walk around the hall as planned, this was impossible. As I stood before each individual, I-She responded, to each a blessing, a phrase, a touch, a word, given totally spontaneously, mediated moment by moment, attuned to each individual person. My step was unsteady. Every footfall was placed slowly and with great deliberation, I felt as if I was wading through the collected energies of the room. At last this unplanned circuit was completed, all had been touched by the Isis light. Finally, I reached my appointed place and at last stood before the representative of the Earth. It seemed as if I stood before the whole of humanity, confused, bewildered, child-like and vulnerable, reaching out for that only dimly sensed and not at all understood. I was wracked by a compassion so intense that my whole body shook. My sight was blinded by tears. The immortal words of Isis were spoken: "Behold I am come."

The sistrum was raised above the Earth with a suddenness and force that surprised me. It felt as if humanity was being roused from a deep slumber. The words of Isis were spoken. Finally, my role was complete. I-She left the hall to sit again on the great chair in the ante-chamber again. This time the door was left open. I sat and looked upon the harmony of the spheres enacted in dance by the participants. The joy within the room was palpable. I-She sat at the gate, the participants danced in a circle and passed

THE MANTLE OF ISIS

before the throne. I-She acknowledged each one with salute or gesture. The sense of rapture was so intense that my body began to shake violently. I felt that the mediation had reached a critical level. It was time to withdraw. In one sharp gesture, I reached up and pulled the veil down over my eyes. Contact was closed. My work was done. I stood and turned leaving the ante-chamber. The participants still danced. I withdrew. I did not look back.

When I read the words of my own report so many years later, I am still moved by the memories it evokes in me. I still feel a sense of awe and complete wonderment that the Mantle of Isis had been laid on my shoulders. I understood for the first time what it might mean to be a Garment of Isis. This weekend was a turning-point, it was a momentous and extraordinary landmark in my journey towards Isis. I now understood why my body had become so agitated, it was another kundalini episode but this time it was constructive and focused. The itching scalp and the red streaks on my back were manifestations of the intense energies circulating through my system. Needless to say, when I returned home, I was quite exhausted but suddenly attempting to slip back into twentieth century life was not easy. My energy system was still wide open, perfectly attuned for ceremonial work but a totally unsuited to ordinary life, everything had become too sharp and too magnified by the ability to perceive the imperceptible. My scalp had ceased itching but when I washed my hair, white flakes of dead skin visibly washed out. Two friends arrived unexpectedly that day and I was thankful for their company. One friend had bought a gift of rose scented soap, how curious considering that it is through eating the rose that Lucius is restored to human shape. Such classical thoughts were far from my mind at that moment. I asked my friend, a hairdresser by career to kindly look at my scalp. She said she had never seen anything like it, the whole scalp was red raw. She bathed my scalp with olive oil, wrapped my head in a warm towel and put

THE BREATH OF ISIS

me to bed. My two friends whose arrival was quite unexpected, took care of me and looked after my children while I rested. My scalp was burned, my crown chakra had been opened, Isis had entered. Within a week I had received a letter from of the participants who had taken on the role of the Planetary Being during the ritual. His words are as follows:

> *I participated in a powerful ritual and played the part of a rather rebellious and totally disrespectful earth. I was to stand before the gods who were to judge whether the earth was ready to partake in a cosmic initiation. The most powerful part of this ritual was when Isis, mediated by Her priestess addressed me. It was as if Isis herself was talking personally to me, at that moment it seemed as if no-one else existed in the room but the two of us. The words of Isis, 'From now onwards until the very day last day of your life, you are dedicated to my service,' struck deep inside me.*
>
> *The following evening back at home I had gone to bed, and I was relaxing prior to sleep when Isis in the form of her priestess appeared by my bed leaned over and took my right hand in hers. I felt a distinct jolt. Her presence and physical contact left the most vivid impression. It was not a dream. I was clearly in my own room and the experience was very real and intense. Now I feel a deeper bonding with Isis.*

When I received his report, I was dumfounded, I enclose it here as a faithful reporting of the events of that weekend. This is an encounter with Isis of the Mysteries but She has Ten Thousand Names and acts through all of them. I have always experienced difficulty with the process of, 're-entry,' the descent back down the planes, the reintegration of the physical and subtle bodies. The return after this particular event was especially difficult. I have no glib answers, no short cuts and no easy solutions, perhaps there are none to offer. One of the participants wrote glowingly of the event to Olivia who kindly invited me to be take ordination in the FOI.

AWAKENING

NOTES

1. Gareth Knight: occult writer and leading exponent of western esotericism. Hs spiritual journey began in 1953 in Dion Fortune's Society of the Inner Light where he became its librarian for a time. Later he edited the magazine *New Dimensions* and co-founded Helios Books. In a long career he has written numerous books. In 2013 he started his own publishing company called Starlight Press. He died in March 2022.

2. The Servants of the Light – School of Occult Science was founded by Dolores Ashcroft-Nowicki. The school teaches throughout the world with over with over 6000 students in 23 countries. In 2024 the school was passed into the hand of Dr Steven Critchley.

3. Caitlin Matthews: author, harpist, shamanic practitioner. Caitlin has written numerous books, created new Tarot designs and given courses in Europe and beyond to share the ancestral spiritual wisdom of the British Isles. Together her husband John and co-worker Felicity Wombwell founded FIOS, the Foundation for Inspirational and Oracular Studies dedicated to preserve and explore sacred oral traditions. Caitlin is one of the custodians of the Fellowship of Isis. She offers a shamanic soul service from her home in Oxford.

4. Marian Green: writer, teacher, magical practitioner. In 1968 Marian founded The Quest Conference which is still held today. In 1976 she founded The Invisible College to offer short courses on a variety of esoteric subjects and in 1985 she began The Green Circle as a grassroots network for esoteric teaching. Marian is an expert in folklore, the traditions of witchcraft, natural magic and ceremonial magic.

5. Dennis Stoll: musician, composer, conductor. Dennis Stoll studied with Sir Henry Wood, Sir Eugene Goosens and Sir Thomas Beecham who appointed him as his deputy with The London Philharmonic Orchestra. Beside his long career in music, he had profound interest in ancient Egypt. He founded The Ancient Egyptian Arts Association. In 1969 he and his wife Cheryl founded The Nefer Ensemble, a group dedicated to restoring the dancing art of the temple tradition. She continues their work through the aegis of the Star Wisdom

6. René Schwaller de Lubicz: writer, alchemist, philosopher, visionary. During the 1920s he and his wife Isha, established the Station Scientifique Suhalia, a centre consisting of laboratories for physics, chemistry, micro-photography and the manufacture of homeopathic tinctures, an astronomical observatory and workshops for practical skills such woodworking, blacksmithing, printing, weaving, rugmaking and glassmaking. The project was inspired by the Kemetic Sacred Science. He is best known for the survey of the temple at Luxor which revealed the Pharaonic Wisdom and his subsequent book The Tempe of Man.

CHAPTER FOUR

THE RITES OF ISIS

After the Isis event at Hawkwood College, I was invited to take up the role of priestess-hierophant in the FOI, I was delighted and set out to be married at the same time in the castle and according to the Isian rite. We travelled with the children and were duly married in the Temple of Isis. I had become a priestess to the deity of my heart, I had married the priest of my heart, but still domestic harmony eluded me. I wanted to extend my service, to move forwards in the name of Isis. Yet I sensed a deliberate withholding of energy and commitment from the man who not so long ago joined me in the Isian wedding rite. He came grudgingly to sacred space, seeing it as some kind of afterthought when all other tasks were complete, for me it was the centre from where all things flowed. Nevertheless, I had little choice, I ploughed on, following my inspiration but once again my heart was becoming darkened by fear. I wanted to set up a shrine to Isis in our home following a rite in the Fellowship's liturgy. We duly performed the rite and were just upstairs disrobing when there was a knock at the door. My friend's daughter stood there offering me a newspaper cutting. "*Mum thought you might like this,*" she said. I opened the cutting and to my astonishment, it was an article about Lady Olivia and the Fellowship. When, I asked my friend about it a few days later, she simply said she had come across the article in a magazine and had saved it for me. When working magic, 'signs following,' that is

THE RITES OF ISIS

synchronistic occurrences would be taken as positive confirmation. I took this as an extraordinary confirmation of the rightness of our action.

My desire to spread the Isian current never diminished, yet I so often felt dismayed by the range of options and opportunities available to me in the contemporary world. I observed the rise of the media priestess quite unmoved, the role of queen bee held no fascination for me. Expensive workshops likewise filled me with dismay. I have never understood how the brevity of the weekend workshop could serve genuine aspiration. For me this is a matter of dedication and commitment, of steadfastness and endurance, of quiet revelation and inner knowing; this is a journey for a lifetime, a relationship built deep in the heart. This is not the stuff of weekend workshops, overnight infatuations or flimsy interests. I have offered a number of courses over the years, but these have been primarily for people I have already worked with in close and deep association. In my attempts to open a door into The Mysteries, I have attempted to create an avenue for dedication. It has been my wish to work with a small group at depth over an extended period of time while still holding the space open for newcomers. The first Green Circle group worked together for some five years, the second group worked together for some four years. Students have become lifelong friends and they in turn have brought friends into my orbit. This slow and organic development permits the existing group mind to gently embrace and include incoming consciousness. I have often viewed my own absence from the lecture circuit as a great failing, but it is only now that I really understand. The Way of the Mysteries is not conveyed in a weekend or even through a course of months but over years. By its very nature, the work that I love does not call the many but the few, building a group takes time. Curiously now in 2013, at the time of finally writing this book, I am again closely in touch with several friends from earlier decades.

The next episode in my story opens with a curious piece of

THE BREATH OF ISIS

synchronicity. Marian dropped me a note saying that she had received a letter from someone in Hampshire asking about Tarot courses, nothing very unusual in that. Hampshire is a pretty big county, but this letter had come from someone living in my street, just two doors away to be precise! We didn't know each other at all so clutching Marian's note I tentatively knocked at his door and the rest as they say is history. What machinations of fate can produce such timely intervention, I really do not know but I remain grateful for such extraordinary blessings. Steve was keen to learn Tarot and I was keen to teach. I had no space in my house to run a group but my neighbour Steve had plenty of space. I had already made some interesting connections in the area. Now I had a place where we might meet on a regular and deeper basis. A new group assembled itself. We began to meet in Steve's house and later a core group consolidated. Our host Steve proved to be a wizard of practicality. He could build anything without fuss or difficulty. He duly converted a suburban bedroom into a temple, including a shrine recess and starry ceiling fitted with tiny dimmable lights in the shape of Orion. The physical creation of the temple was a great joy to me: gilding the wood and painting the ceiling was a labour of love. We turned a room into a temple painting it midnight blue and gold.

Creating the temple was one thing, creating the group-mind was quite another. Building a group-mind takes time. Looking back, we were blessed with a wealth of talent belying our small numbers. We were blessed by the company of a gifted dancer, who had been trained in the Royal Ballet School. Her husband was an actor who had a wonderful speaking voice. I can still hear him delivering his lines with wonderful gravitas. We were blessed by the talents of two wonderful professional artists, both well known as Tarot illustrators. As if two artists were not blessing enough, we also enjoyed the company of a graphic artist who had long moved from paintbrush to computer keyboard. On the psychological and emotional front, we were blessed with two highly skilled therapists, the first was a

THE RITES OF ISIS

hypnotherapist with other skills in radiaesthesia and feng-shui, the second was a professional counsellor specialising in relationship work. Other more far flung members included an experienced ritualist and bard, a highly gifted computer programmer and who went on later to design software of global renown for star astrology, three highly accomplished priestesses of long standing, various magical friends from earlier years including Marian Green and her partner who often joined us for annual events and a most courageous woman under a life sentence from a degenerative condition who found enough strength and hope in the magical alchemical process to claw her way back to the survival zone. Study groups abound but a group no matter how small, working fully under the aegis of the Mystery Tradition is not merely a study group. It is as Dion Fortune says, the outer manifestation of divine intent. It is birthed and guided from the Inner Planes through inspiration and direction. All groups begin as a collection of individuals bringing a variety of experiences though even this multi-coloured pool of talent has to be shaped and orchestrated if a single group mind is to emerge from the many. The process is organic and developmental, it cannot be rushed. So little by little we moved our way slowly forwards. Through mutual co-operation, shared meditation, discussion, dialogue, reading, listening, personal contribution, individual work and some specific teaching, we began to attain a blended harmony of intent and understanding finding meaning in the words, To Dare, To Know, To Will and To Be Silent. The group members showed great trust in moving beyond a personal comfort zone to a new shared place. The maxim, Make Haste Slowly serves to balance the desire to know with the need to integrate knowing; without time for assimilation and integration, psychic indigestion will result in disaster. I have seen this manifest in a variety of ways: unresolved issues grip the heart and freeze the mind, insecurity swings into the group like a demolition ball, inadequate preparation turns macho-man into a simpering idiot and repressed triggers take in disguise as

THE BREATH OF ISIS

personal demons. It is difficult to explain dynamics which straddle psychological-spiritual boundaries. There are no compartments in this holistic framework where rituals serve to drop pebbles into the waters of daily life and repercussions spread out in concentric circles showing that everything is interconnected.

Seasonal celebratory rituals rarely disturb the peace of the psyche, such joyful events do not impinge deeply but rather provide a feeling of well-being and personal attunement with the season. However, when sacred drama replaces celebration, a monumental shift in emphasis takes place. Sacred drama, always the modus operandi of The Mysteries, permits and indeed demands a certain shift away from the personality, just as an actor takes on a role and adopts a new persona. In sacred drama, the roles are those of the gods and it is through these transpersonal identifications that the small localised egoic self begins to lose its foothold. Ritual as sacred drama, not seasonal celebration is an agent for deep and powerful transformation. The interface between sacred ritual and psycho-drama has now merged, the one offers transcendent spiritual experience, the other offers a psychological tool but the modus operandi is essentially the same. In the process of re-identification, the personality, always engrossed in the consciousness of familiar tasks, habits and routines is bypassed and a transcendent level of being is provided with a space in which to experience the non-personal. This shift from the local and individualised self towards a universal and collective experience of the human experience grows only slowly but with certainty and inner purpose. Ritual dynamics invariably find personal sorespots in the unresolved issues of childhood, the woundings of life and love, the rough edges of the personality. Magical groups are notoriously volatile, it cannot be otherwise, for the dynamics of the process probe relentlessly into the psyche. This on-going process is always challenging and its demands produces personal resistance in many forms, unresolved pains appear and will not be silenced

THE RITES OF ISIS

until they have reached the light of conscious awareness. Rituals which incorporate and externalise archetypal templates provide an on-going psychotherapy. No wonder then that Jean Houston calls this process, Sacred Psychology, others have called it magic, Gareth Knight's autobiography published in 2013 bears the title, I *Called it Magic*. The interface between magic and psychotherapy is so close that the same personnel often straddle both fields. It is curious to note that one is a respectable profession while the other is apparently a dubious occupation. Without active engagement in the process of self-knowing, ritual is reduced to theatre and dressing up, it is nothing more than an empty vessel but engaged ceremony become theurgy, meaning divine acts, and its purpose is to join consciously in the renewing cycle of deconstruction and, reconstruction. The injunction To Dare is not an idle challenge, for it takes tremendous courage to Know Thyself.

The group worked intensively together for a number of years. We produced a magazine and wrote an enormous variety of rituals, seasonal, magical and initiatory. Although we had set out under the aegis of the Fellowship of Isis as the Lyceum of Isis Urania, the lodestar of some deeper consciousness was never silent and through a process of continuous metamorphosis, we changed names, first becoming the House of the Net, next The House of Isis and Osiris and much later The House of Life. These refinements of direction reflected an evolutionary impetus to redefine the relationship between two quite different magical-spiritual currents, that of Mystery School and that of the FOI. Devotion generates love, metaphysical skill generates precision. However, this persistent tinkering was far less conscious than it might appear. I was as yet unaware of the forces awakening in my being. In retrospect I can see that I already possessed the two keys that were to remain and deepen, the connection with Isis and the Kemetic temple tradition. Hindsight clearly shows me that the marriage of these two currents was not congruent with the living stream running within the

THE BREATH OF ISIS

Fellowship and though I could not know it, I had not reached home, I had instead found a familiar territory. The Lyceum Isis-Urania, took its inception as 3.30pm Sunday 22nd January, 1995. The group met to perform an extended version of an FOl ceremony, The Dedication of a Shrine. Everyone brought gifts to symbolise their personal aspirations and the inaugural horary chart was read to the assembled group.

MC. Pisces
This represents the direction which the group will take through its natural growth. Pisces brings sensitivity, mediumistic abilities, creativity and artistic expression.

Ascendant in Cancer
This represents the group personality. Cancer is another water sign. This reinforced the strong 'watery' nature of the group giving emotional depth and developed sensitivity.

Sun in Aquarius, 7th House
This placement brings a desire to interact with others to establish harmonious relationships. This is expressed as a need to feel part of a family. Karmic relationships will either make or break this new relationship.

Moon in Libra 4th House
This placement brings a desire for peace and security. It also brings artistic sensitivities and indicates the possibility of redecorating the environment to suit inner foundations. The Mother is a strong influence. There is a need to develop a coherent programme to avoid indecisiveness.

Mercury in Aquarius 8th House
This placement brings a talent for analysis and insight. It brings the mark of the born investigator and the ability to penetrate the mask worn by others. Watch the tendency to dissipate this energy through

gossip. Your progressive ideas may be too progressive for the general group mind to which you belong.

Venus in Sagittarius 5th House
This placement brings inner strength, idealism and the possibility of philosophy. Talent is available especially through art and music. Self-expression will be of great benefit.

Mars in Virgo 2nd house
This placement brings considerable energy and some reluctance to accept the responsibilities that accompany this work. Money will come and go to de-emphasise its importance, instead focus on the development of talent.

Jupiter in Sagittarius 5th House
This placement brings an interest in religion, philosophy, prophecy, inspiration and creativity.

Saturn in Pisces 9th House
Philosophy and beliefs are approached in a serious manner. This placement is excellent for teaching and lecturing.

Uranus in Capricorn 7th House
This placement represents the need to accept karmic obligations. It brings unusual relationships.

Neptune in Capricorn 7th House
This placement represents the quest for a soul mate. Through this placement many evolved souls will elect to come at this time to serve humanity as leaders and educators in the quest to establish a more spiritualised world.

Pluto in Sagittarius 7th House
This placement brings prophetic ability, faith in human nature and unusual talents. It brings a need to express inner creativity. This placement is deeply transformative.

THE BREATH OF ISIS

THE ASPECTS

Sun conjunct Uranus
This placement is magnetic, intuitive creative and independent. It brings an ability to see ways of improving things.

Venus conjunct Jupiter
There is an appreciation of harmony and beauty. This aspect brings a material abundance.

Uranus conjunct Neptune
This placement brings a deep intuition and a sense of the spiritual and mystic.

ASC opposition Neptune
This placement brings creative individuals who are attracted by spiritual leaders.

ASC Sextile Neptune
With this placement you will not wish to be successful in the outer world unless your efforts have some benefit to humanity.

ASC Sextile Pluto
This placement brings the opportunity to transform the conscious personality through intuition and perception.

Moon Sextile Jupiter
This placement brings the opportunity to dissolve negative traits through the development of a good philosophy.

Uranus Sextile Pluto
This placement brings creativity and innovation.

Mercury Sextile Venus
This placement brings harmony through mental expansion.

Venus Square Saturn
The challenge here is to accept those difficulties which are spiritual lessons.

THE RITES OF ISIS

Mercury Square Pluto
This is the placement of the doubting Thomas. It asks you to keep an open mind when experience outstrips comprehension.

Jupiter Square Saturn
The challenge here is to complete the objective.

I have not looked at this analysis for many years, but hindsight shows me that this astrological template became manifest in our intentions, goals and experiences. Choosing a propitious astrological moment to in which to begin a new venture was once considered to be important, though it is all but a forgotten art, our tiny experience somehow shows that it is not an irrelevant one. On reflection, over time the group came to fulfil this template in a quite extraordinary manner. We did indeed develop a coherent programme without which the focus and aspiration of spiritual intention fades into just another social meeting. We certainly attracted creative minds and our shared quest represented our desire to be of service in the creation of a more spiritualised world. We came into being on a deeply intuitive wave with a real sense of the spiritual and the mystical. The group certainly provided opportunities for personal transformation through the guidance of intuition and perception, indeed that remains the raison d'etre of a spiritual curriculum. We saw the development of prophetic ability, unusual talents and inner creativity, all placed in the service of deep transformation. We were all deeply engaged in the process of first recognising and then dissolving personal negative traits under the aegis of philosophy which is after all, the love of wisdom. The comparatively rare qualities of emotional sensitivity, mediumistic ability, creativity and artistic expression were just natural expressions of who we were as individuals. We continuously plumbed emotional depths and in consequence developed great sensitivity not merely towards each other but more importantly as a quality for life itself.

As the group philosophy became clearer so teaching, lecturing and

THE BREATH OF ISIS

especially writing became increasingly important. Talent overflowed and in bringing gifts to the group mind, individuals developed their own unique creativity, art, theatre, dance, performance, books, study papers all appeared naturally and spontaneously in the service of the beautiful and for the love of wisdom. The mental skills of analysis and insight, so often disregarded in the new quest to be ever so touchy-feely, were never put to one side, intellectual skills always have an important role to play in a curriculum of personal development. Mental acuity combined with both the desire and ability to investigate and penetrate the various masks of appearance whether personal or institutional, is a powerful and indeed unusual drive. It provides the propulsion towards self-understanding through stripping away the false and redundant wherever it is met. There were indeed times when we floundered for explanations and the means to understand the experiences we had generated, especially by creating sacred dramas based on authentic Kemetic texts. It is only with hindsight that these significant themes have made themselves visible as if appearing from some invisible disclosing fluid but at the time we more saw ourselves quite simply as friends on an adventure having creative fun, sharing interesting discussions and making quality time for each other. These astrological phrases are in certain instances so accurate as to be amusing. We drew upon our combined artistic sensitivities and quite literally redecorated the environment to suit our new inner foundations. The Mother was indeed a strong influence, Her name is Isis, the beautiful mother goddess.

The group produced its own emotional dynamics as all groups must and in time two members became one household and were married. The word, karma, is relevant here but perhaps not very helpful. Crossed between its Buddhist origins and New-Age-Speak, karma seems to point to past lives, to hidden interconnections, to veiled soul agendas and even to forgotten romance, such ingredients can easily destabilise a group without a firm footing; magical-

THE RITES OF ISIS

spiritual excursions so often whisk the carpet away from underfoot at an instant. We neither set out to explore such deep personal connections nor encouraged them to arise, but deep resonances of tradition and place were certainly felt and by definition all our interrelationships were somewhat unusual. Finally, it remains true that our ideas of dynamic creativity, in-depth personal engagement, philosophical underpinnings and heavy-duty ceremony were indeed out of step with other contemporary magical-spiritual currents. We were neither Wiccan nor Pagan, neither New Age nor Goddess worshippers, not fully Western Mystery Tradition, not even FOI. Our apparently 'progressive ideas' dropped me into the hot waters of contention more than once. We were on specific occasions indeed found to be, 'too progressive for the general group mind to which you belong.' It has taken me a further two decades to understand where my real place is and what I must do to keep the tradition of my heart alive.

When I now review the programme that we created, I am quite astonished at both the quantity and quality of the projects we undertook. We held three Isian Assemblies. These were open to a wider but invited audience. The group was formed in January and in the May we enacted *The Ascension of Osiris*. I was invited to take part in *The Way of the Priestess Conference* held on June 11th 1995 at Mallet Street. In 1996 we took The Sacred Marriage as our theme. By 1997 other group members were inspired to write and *Isis Ecclectica* was performed. I remember that this was an especially beautiful event, the hall was hung with garlands of artificial roses, and the altar draped with cloths of velvet and gold. We produced magazine, *The Veil of Isis* with issues on Hathor, Sekhmet, Sophia and Chartres. The group met monthly and then once in the year we met for a residential weekend. Over time, we held weekends dedicated to Osiris, Neith, Isis, and Sekhmet. Our weekends were always experiential. One year we processed around the conference grounds in imitation of the Isian procession described in *The*

THE BREATH OF ISIS

Golden Ass. Four of our priests carried a statue of Isis shoulder high on a palanquin, we assembled on the terrace and lit a brazier.

During the life of the group, all members undertook some level of ritual re-identification. Two members took Rites of Rebirth to coincide with their Chiron return. Four members took ordinations and one member was raised to Heirophancy. During this time, I wrote, *Teach Yourself Meditation*, currently going into its 5th edition, T*he Essential 101 Tips to Meditation* and *The Elements of the Egyptian Wisdom*. In November 1997, Marian Green and I jointly facilitated the course *Women and The Golden Dawn Tradition*. In September 1998, the group met for a weekend seminar *The Priesthood of Aquarius* at The Runnings Park Conference Centre. While working on the book, *The Elements of the Egyptian Wisdom*, I was inspired to write a meditation, which I called, The Beauteous Ones. I sent a copy of it to Debbie Nix (now Deborah Merwin) who I had met at the World Parliament. She replied by sending a tape of a chant which she wrote almost immediately upon reading the words. This chant in turn has continued over the years to send out ripples of recognition among those who resonate to this tradition. On hearing it, I knew that I wanted to create a presentation in Hathor's honour, to be called *The Blessings of Hathor*. The outline was duly offered to the FOI annual convention in the UK and accepted but later the presentation was turned down. The arrangements were already well in hand, so I hired a hall on the outskirts of London and continued with the preparations. Debbie's chant often seemed to awaken the sleeping Hathor-seed as the following report shows.

> *I am sitting in an ordinary room in an ordinary house in the suburbs of Southampton. There are four of us. Naomi has invited us to take part in a guided visualisation. She sets the scene on the banks of the Nile, a boat is arriving carrying a precious cargo, priestesses of Hathor - The Beauteous Ones. As*

THE RITES OF ISIS

I listen my heart swells, my pulse starts to race, tears come to me eyes in deep knowing and recognition. I know this place, I know these women, I was one of these women. I feel such longing and poignancy that I can hardly contain myself and at the same time, I have a sense of relief, of coming home. At last, we have found each other again.

At the end of the visualisation, I share something of my personal experience with Naomi who tells me she is planning a day in London to celebrate the Goddess Hathor and invites me to take part as one of the priestesses. I don't know what that means. and I feel afraid but despite this my instant response is 'yes' – it feels absolutely right. In preparation for the day, I begin a practice to help me connect with the energies of Hathor. I make a shrine, read whatever I can find and make a list of Her names. Every morning and evening I light a candle on Her altar, call her name and sing her song and inviter her into my heart, asking for her help and guidance. Most days I think I am crazy, some days I feel nothing, other days I just cry, on other days I feel a lightness of spirit. I stay with the practice. It seems that one of the ways that the beautiful ones bestowed their blessings was through the sacred beaded necklace – the menat. Naomi and I meet for craft sessions and set about making one. I thread the beads making a crescent shape for the front and mould a phallic shaped pendant for the counterweight at the back of the neck - we copy our designs from ancient engravings.

As Hathor is also known as the Golden One, I decide to make a dress using golden raw silk, to be tightly fitted all the way down with a pleated sash. I can just squeeze into it and when I put it on it, I feel a shift in my energy. I sense it is important to save the energy for the day, so I try on the dress for the shortest possible time. Naomi has given me a tape of the chant written by Debbie Nix which was inspired by the visualisation. As the day draws

THE BREATH OF ISIS

nearer, I am becoming more nervous, but something is carrying me on and in trust in Naomi's trust in me.

It was such a relief on the day, meeting with the other women who were equally nervous. We share a meditation together and the dressed. I felt a change as I put on the dress and the menat necklace – a kind of inner strength and authority. The menat seemed to express the balance of masculine and feminine energies through the soft curve of the beads at the front balanced by the counterpoise at the back. The beads felt alive, warm and glowing, radiating the pulse from my heart. I felt a great sense of sisterhood, of tenderness and affection. I marvelled at their beauty and radiance. I felt radiant, alive and full of love which I longed to share with everyone present. I was suffused with an energy so much greater than my own. I surrendered to her bliss, it was not difficult.

Debbie N. had arrived, and she led a procession into the main hall chanting her song as she walked. We walked through the hall greeting people and offering blessings. I experienced the simple desire to take people by the hand, and looking deeply into their eyes, open myself to the divine presence shining through me. The little 'I' had no idea what was going on.

The next day my ego mind would not be silenced telling me in no uncertain terms that I was quite mad, vain, self-important and utterly deluded. I now know that this is how the mind reacts to things it is afraid of and cannot understand. Now I am able to observe it at play, while staying centred in my heart but at the time I felt confused absurd and stupid. But later, I was especially touched by the feedback I received, one of the members of the group said that he had felt naked, defenceless but totally loved in Hathor's presence. Another person said that she saw the flow of unconditional love flowing through me.

Lynn-Amanda Brown

THE RITES OF ISIS

On the day we numbered almost forty people, the big hall was filled by our presence. As part of the preparation, the priestesses shared in a meditative session which put them in touch with the Hathoric nature through the emblems of her authority, the menat and sistrum. The outline of the day was kept as simple as possible. A beautiful altar was established to honour Hathor. The event began with a procession, her statue was carried on a palanquin by four members of the company and finally placed on the altar surrounded by images and statues set on golden cloth. The company wore white robes, and the six priestesses were dressed in robes of gold. After the procession, the company sat and listened to a talk which provide an intellectual framework and served to focus the group as one mind. Solo dance and drumming, followed by group dancing and then wordless sounded chanting, all served to shift the atmosphere from intellectual focus to emotional openness. Invocations, individually and spontaneously offered began to shift the energies of the room and Hathor's presence began to draw close. This dynamic energy was focussed through a guided visualisation which took the participants deep into the temple structure so that each person might make their connection with Het-Her. The experience culminated in the sharing of blessings among the company mediated by the presence of the priestesses.

The period of intense and beautiful creativity in the temple was marked by increasing despair at home. How could this be? The man that I had married in the Temple of Isis had turned his back on the Goddess of my heart. The strain was unbearable and devastating to me. He became increasingly less willing to undertake the work of his own reconstruction. His example could apply to anyone entering the Way of the Mysteries with unprepared motivation. The unwillingness or inability to process the feelings or realisations that arise, becomes the greatest stumbling block to personal integration and union with the soul powers. As devastating as such realisations might be, the same realisation also offers the remedy and cure for

THE BREATH OF ISIS

the soul which is the real meaning of the word, psychotherapy. This unwillingness to process can hide itself quite subtly in the many convoluted ways of the ego. On the Tree of Life, the final path of return carries the title, The Intelligence of Transparency. It is a timely reminder that anything that blocks transparency will cast a shadow.

The Way of the Mysteries offers a route into the depths of being, 'deep mining' as one of the group used to say. It is a good analogy. The opening to the soul created by the intense ritual, meditation and deity magic, is deep. It cuts right down into karmic layers like a hot knife through butter releasing what has been forgotten. Often such things have been forgotten with good reason. Sometimes these memories burst out fully fledged and complete, at other times, they spill like poison back into the personality. My quest to comprehend the ills in my relationship led me where I had not expected to go. My disappearing relationship was like an infection consuming my every thought and scrap of spare energy. What lay behind the inescapable magnetism that had drawn us together? Like a dog with a bone, my mind would not release the question without an answer. I had reached boiling point in myself, a state of intense physic agitation, emotional distress and relentless mental activity. In a state of utter despair, I went to a therapist with training in far memory work, I needed to understand what lay at the nub of our relationship charged as it was with extremes of both love and even hate.

It was easy for me to slip into an altered state of awareness but what appeared in my mind was most unexpected. The heat of the sun filled my mind, but then the blackness of a darkening sky and terrible sounds filled my hearing. Reporting what I was seeing, I was asked, 'Is this Atlantis?' After a few moments of reflection, I knew that this was not Atlantis but I still did not have my bearings. Then in a horrible flash of recognition, I knew I was in Pompeii, caught in its death throes and reliving my own. When this crescendo was behind me, I was asked to see if I might find any links with my

THE RITES OF ISIS

present partner. At once I find myself in the Temple of Isis and news is brought to me, a gladiator has been killed in the arena. As the thought arises, I dread the idea that our love might be based on a soppy re-run of some overblown romantic nonsense. But no, I instantly realise that we never even met. Instead, the story unfolds in my mind to reveal a gladiator trapped into a vicious life, kill or be killed, that was his allotted fate. In Pompeii the barracks are close to the Temple of Isis. In some way, he saw or came to know that another life was possible. He called upon Isis to bring him salvation and in a dream she promised that a priestess would come in the future and take him to The Gates of The Mysteries. Trusting this, he allowed himself to be killed without resistance. When news came of his death, I knew we were destined to meet again. So did I rush home with the answer to our problems in my hand, No, I kept my silence. My newest revelation would have been treated with the same contempt as all the others. He had long inured himself against the voice of Isis. The turning point came in Chicago when he was rebuked for not listening to Her words and taking closer care of Her priestess. He screamed in my face. *"That's not Isis, that's Naomi."* But I had already spent many years distinguishing Her voice from my own and I knew he had screamed at the face of a Goddess.

I have often mused on my Pompeian story over the years, did it have any validity? Was it merely a symbolic representation of a natural belligerence or was it all just pure invention? As I write these words again, with Isis so close in my mind, I am instantly overcome with paroxysms of emotion. I weep because I did all I could, and it was still not enough. She reminds me that I was pledged to take him to the Gates of the Mysteries and that promise was fulfilled. She says gently that She can find him again if needed. There is much that this account does not contain, events too personal and painful to share, times too devastating and despairing to share. I have chosen sufficient episodes to provide a narrative, I have spared you details of the growing pains along the way which are relevant to no-one but me.

BREATH OF ISIS

The group continued until about 1998 but under the strain of a failing marriage, my input became less constant. The group also changed, Steve was married and no longer the single man in a big house, he now needed his space back. So, sacred space was returned to domestic space. Eventually my marriage broke down completely and I was forced to abandon all magical-spiritual work and concentrate on my own recovery and renewal. But the group's achievements still stand: a number of life changing ordinations, the forging of personal friendships which still stand, deep healing through the group's willingness to engage in process, a series of annual events, the Isian assemblies and many wonderful rituals. After I left my home and husband, my life changed dramatically. Group activity ceased, I had other more pressing things to deal with. During this time, I wrote *The Aquarian Qabalah* but in contrast to the previous seven years which had been rich and creative, this interlude which lasted almost seven years was stone dry. I did not become involved in magical work again until 2006. One incident, stands out from this time and even now so many years later, I still have no explanation for it.

In the summer of 2000, I went as a volunteer to a summer festival at Gaunt's House in Dorset. For the most part, my time was taken up in the children's area but one afternoon I went walking around the camp with a new friend I had made. We spent some time in the marquee where books were on sale. On one side, something caught my eye, a series of copper spirals, apparently designed to counteract the electrical output from a computer. The spirals were attractive and without a second thought I passed my hand over it. Instantly, I screamed aloud, I felt as if the palm of my hand and the top of my head had been burned simultaneously and I felt as if a spike had been plunged into the top of my head right down into my brain. Such words seem ridiculous, melodramatic and absurd but try as I might I can find no other or better words to use. My companion took my arm, I had turned ashen. He did the sensible thing and

THE RITES OF ISIS

took me for a warm drink. But it didn't really help, I knew that my energies were, 'coming undone' – a silly phrase, but it explains exactly how I feel at such times. My own tent was on the far side of the field and I knew I could not walk that far so my friend kindly helped me to his tent where as a seasoned camper he had made good soft bed on a sheepskin. I lay down shaking and crying quite involuntarily. I was not crying about anything, merely responding to the fact that my emotional body was in trauma. I knew I was in trouble, and I had no idea what I might do. My friend left me for a while to organise someone to cover for my shift and I tried to get some self-control back. Taking myself to a deep place of quiet, I called on Isis to help me. I had a horrible pain in the centre of my head and no strength in my body whatsoever. In meditation, Isis appeared and said she would drop soothing oil into my brain at the bridge between the two hemispheres. She said that all would be well, but I should continue to rest. I passed from a deep meditative state into proper sleep, waking later to discover that two hours had passed. I was however recovered and able to walk back to my tent and later returned to my volunteer duties. Next day, I visited the stallholder who was pleased to see me recovered. Since he asked me what had happened. I told him. He was quite astonished and did not know what to make of it all. I reassured him that his product was perfectly safe, there was no problem with the delightfully coiled copper, only with me, it is a repeating and enduring pattern in my life.

Engagement with the process of transformation is vital and holistic, it is not merely a matter of mental reorientation, it encompasses the energy bodies and the physical body too. I have learned over the years to carefully guard the etheric and subtle bodies that I inhabit. Once very early on in my magical life, I volunteered to be a guinea-pig at a friend's Touch for Health workshop. I lay on the massage table while he ran energies through various meridians by holding the two end points of the pathway, a simple enough procedure. On the next day I could hardly stand, my stomach was

THE BREATH OF ISIS

bloated, the glands of my throat were swollen. I could hardly crawl out of bed. I needed to realign my energy field to return myself to a place of stability, it took a couple of days before I felt recovered. Later on in life, in the weeks before substantial rituals, I would receive strong impressions about changing my diet or perhaps even avoiding other activities. Over the years I thought I had learned well enough, but the copper coil caught me quite by surprise. Like the caterpillar, you too may enter the cocoon of being and emerge a new but unlike the caterpillar rebirthed at nature's behest as the beautiful butterfly, you must become the agent of your own divinity gradually shedding all that masks your divine light. What are these Mysteries that reveal who we are, what we have done, where we have been and what we might become? These are the Mysteries of Isis.

CHAPTER FIVE

THE GARMENTS OF ISIS

When I first heard the Priestesses of Isis described as the Garments of Isis, in a talk by Dolores Ashcroft-Nowicki a flash of recognition passed instantly through my mind, a light-switch long unused was suddenly switched on. Although the phrase hinted at much, for my part it was still only an intellectual appreciation without any substantive experience. I had no idea how such a communion might come about. I was already familiar with the magical diaries of Christine Hartley and Charles Seymour published as *Dancers to the Gods* and I knew it contained reports of such experiences. Now these diaries hold a special place in esoteric history as Charles Seymour was the inspiration for the Priest of the Moon in Dion Fortune's novel *Moon Magic* and Christine Hartley enjoyed a magical career of considerable note. She wrote the book *The Western Mystery Tradition*. In the diaries, we read first-hand accounts of experiences which cannot be contained and described in psychological terms. Here are personal accounts of dynamics which stretch both the mind and the imagination. The following extracts typically convey untypical experiences.

> **Account by Seymour – Friday, October 15th, 1937.**
> *Banished as usual and then invoked in the name of Isis. Up came the power at once. Built Malkuth in the aura, then Yesod in the form of the horned moon. Up came a great silver star which*

THE BREATH OF ISIS

filled the whole room. CCT took charge – journey in the silver litter, past the lotus pool into the hall of the sphinxes and then into the sanctuary. CCT sat on the knees of the goddess with her head between the breasts of the image. Then came a tremendous head of power. I could see CCT bathed in a sort of silvery mist with the physical eyes, she got up and held out her hands as if in blessing and a stream of pale silver light came off them and on to me. It was so clear that I could feel it physically.

Christine's report of the same experience adds another dimension to our understanding:

Then at one time the Goddess came right down and I was her mouthpiece and spoke as she dictated, and then I was the priestess giving the responses. It was most strange and very wonderful. I seemed to be carried on without deliberate volition on my part and all I had to do was to keep myself well held in so that the power should flow freely.

Account by Seymour, Thursday, October 21, 1937.
Then with a burst of power that shook me, the Goddess took possession of her priestess – there was not much said – a sort of chant of the names of the Goddess which brought a rush of power and then she gave her blessing. It was like sitting in a blast of hot air.

Christine reports the same event:

Then the power began to come through and I got carried up because the Goddess came down and used me as a vehicle. I cannot remember what I said but she spoke through me, and I kept trying to get the right words as if I were translating.

Whenever I read these accounts, I felt a little like a voyeur intruding into the most intimate and sacred of moments, yet I could not avert my inward gaze. I simply wanted to understand, but of course understanding, as in all things, only comes with

THE GARMENTS OF ISIS

doing. I wondered what it meant to translate the words of Isis, I wondered what it meant to shake with the force of her power, I wondered what it meant to bless in Her name, something inside me recognised the veracity expressed in these extraordinary reports. Magical diaries are often kept, indeed it is part and parcel of a magical training to do so but such private diaries are rarely published. Reading such personal words, never intended for an audience is truly a rare privilege. In their reports, we glimpse the comparatively rare experience of genuine mediation, known in the Western Mystery Tradition as The Assumption of the God-Form. However, this terminology is not to my liking. I like it even less now that it appears often in magical workbooks as if it were something to be notched up as just another magical experience. This divine possession, this merger between the mundane and the transcendent, this mind-meld between the devotee and the divinity comes only after a long relationship of attunement and personal refinement. It is a communion bestowed through grace not commanded.

Religious experience in its broadest and most varied sense devolves upon the possibility of forming a bridge between human and divine consciousness. The shaman or mantic priestess in all ecstatic traditions achieves this through entering a temporary altered state of consciousness variously described as trance or even possession. The priest in a monotheistic tradition enters no such direct communion but takes on the role of mediator to the mediating figure or even to mediating articles of faith. However, outside the borders of monotheism, a direct mediation between the divine and the human has always existed in various forms. Possession is a common form of mediation usually between a cult divinity and its congregation. It is still found in Voodoo traditions and historically this state of consciousness has a long history, possession by spirits or even cult divinities is most often a blunt and broad form of shifted consciousness. Commonly the one entranced or possessed has little memory of what has transpired and though the ceremonial form serves as an invitation to otherworld presence, the emphasis is upon a sense of contact rather than its specific content. All forms of trance are altered states of consciousness which permit access to non-usual sources of information but typically a trance state is also separated from what is normally understood as waking consciousness.

In the Western Mystery Tradition mediation also plays an important role but it neither characterised as possession nor trance but as a fully conscious present and instant translation of an inspired and immediate indwelling presence. As Christine notes in her diary, she became a, 'mouthpiece and spoke as she dictated.' The experience was, 'most strange and very wonderful.' Her words contain a subtle but significant clue. She writes, 'and all I had to do was to keep myself well held in so that the power should flow freely.' The few simple words, 'keep myself well held in,' veil such an important esoteric truth, namely that Christine, as mediator is consciously able to place herself and her own conscious personality, out of the way. Not only does she consciously open her consciousness to the transpersonal voice of the goddess but she simultaneously closes her personal consciousness and maintains this fine balance throughout. This is mediation, neither trance nor possession but a fully conscious state of awareness. This might be viewed on the Tree of Life as the transfer of consciousness from Malkuth to Tiphareth, from the place of ordinary daily consciousness to the place of mystical consciousness which is the level of mind from where most western esoteric ritual takes place.

The Assumption of the God-Form is a ceremonial means of bridging the gap between the planes of consciousness. It is a means of, 'bringing through' information or perhaps teaching from a dedicated and divine source. It is not the same as the popular practice of channelling which in the absence of a spiritual discipline is most likely to draw upon the personal subconscious mind. Alice Bailey who knew a thing or two about conscious mediation

THE GARMENTS OF ISIS

considered that only about two per cent of so-called channelled material was in fact a genuinely connected to an external and wise source. Externalising the personal subconscious is easily effected, and quite impressive but this essentially self-referencing circuit will lack any sense of indwelling presence. On The Tree of Life this might be viewed as a transfer of consciousness from Malkuth to Yesod, from daily personal consciousness to a collective shared consciousness. The Hermetic use of the assumption ritual may be derived from ancient theurgical roots, but it remains quite unlike the Kemetic tradition wherein the divinity incarnates in the hm-ntr, the servant of the god. The Assumption of the God-Form creates a local, time-based connection to a discarnate source of wisdom, incarnating the ntr creates a lifelong embodiment.

I remember receiving a copy of the Isian News with the forthcoming announcement of the Fellowship's presence at the Parliament of World Religions. I had just returned from taking the children to school and as I sat quietly reading the words alone in my dining room, I experienced what on reflection I called, The Shower of Gold. Such experiences, always intensely personal and subjective never render well in the telling, yet another reason for the traditional sign of silence over the gate of The Mysteries. But it was as if briefly and momentarily I was immersed in a shower of golden light, dynamic, descending upon me, dancing around me. It felt like a moment of pure blessing. I offer no explanation. Literally at that moment, I knew I was called to be part of the delegation. When J. came home I told him that I wanted to go to the parliament. I did not tell him of my experience. He simply replied that we could not afford it. I knew otherwise. The feeling did not subside and later in the morning, the presence of Isis came upon me strongly and unexpectedly while I was out shopping. The presence was so distinct that I could not be silent, so I spoke up to again only to receive the unforgettable reply, *"I would rather you kept this house in good order before mediating any deities thank you."* Well, I had

THE BREATH OF ISIS

my answer, but in fact we did go to Chicago. We took the children and stayed with my American in-laws.

The first Parliament of World Religions was a centennial celebration of a gathering that had taken place one hundred years earlier in1893, an extraordinary assembly of forward looking individuals met across traditions and traditional divides to find common ground and shared goals. The second parliament of 1993 shared the same goals but its scale would have amazed the original participants. Some 6,000 delegates covering the major and minor religious traditions of the world took over the Palmer House Hotel. The emerging Goddess traditions were represented by The Covenant of the Goddess and the Fellowship of Isis. Our delegation was scheduled to present its own mystery drama midweek, the participants had never even met so rehearsals began straightaway. I was assigned the role of the Oracle of Isis. We met daily to create sacred drama from a shared script. My role however was unscripted.

Within a day of arriving in Chicago, I began to experience lower back pain for no particular reason. I was having trouble sleeping and by the Monday morning my legs and thighs were itching ferociously. The back pains continued intermittently I did not know what to think, my in-laws suggested I had developed an allergy to something but that did not explain the pains in my back. It was all very peculiar, red streaks had begun to appear on my legs, and I became increasingly aware of energies moving through my body, I needed periods of quiet meditation to remain calm. We travelled to the Parliament for the Opening Ceremony and queued with the other delegates outside the hall. My back pains became quite severe and my period began quite unexpectedly and quite out of sequence so I just assumed that the pain, though unusual was related to the onset of my period. However, the lower back pains continued, the itching continued, the red marks spread. Finally, the penny dropped. and I recognised that I was having rushes of Kundalini energy. I am using this word as a suitable shorthand for a complex spiritual experience

THE GARMENTS OF ISIS

obviously known to the ancient Egyptians. The rehearsals for our Mystery Drama commenced and I began to tread a most peculiar tightrope, navigating between the extraordinary spiritual bubble of the parliament and the domestic world of suburban Chicago with my American in-laws in the most apple-pie of households. My strange symptoms continued while I did my best to appear perfectly normal. We travelled daily into the parliament and usually had a little time outside the rehearsal schedule. On the following morning however with some time to spare, we walked around the Exhibitors Hall and I stopped to talk with a young woman selling some beautiful Russian icons. I told her that my grandmother came from Russia and curiously she said that she had been watching me as I walked through the hall. She said that I looked very familiar and Russian. This was very strange to hear as I do not often think of my Russian connections. However, as we talked. I began to experience the same back pains again. I knew that for some reason Kundalini was stirring again. I felt that this reaction was linked in some way with our shared genetic inheritance, but I knew that I dare not explore it further in so public an arena. I had to excuse myself as the pains became stronger. The hall, massed with spiritual energies seemed to send me reeling, I knew I had to leave. Outside the hall, I sat on a chair pressing the palms of my hands deeply against my lower back. A security guard even came over and kindly asked me if I needed assistance, actually I did. Fortunately, J. came over and escorted me upstairs to the FOI suite.

The room was a sanctuary of peace and quiet away from the bustling minds and frenetic energies in the hall downstairs. But I knew that I needed help. I went straight to the priestess who was to be mediating Isis in the ritual. The moment we had first met we just gelled like friends who had not seen each other for a while. I trusted her implicitly from that moment. We went straight to side room where I lay down on the bed. She positioned herself at my feet and as soon as she held my feet my energies began to

THE BREATH OF ISIS

stabilise. It was as if someone had used a dimmer switch to kindly adjust the brightness of an intrusive light. My energies were totally harmonized with hers but someone else walked into the room and immediately and instantly my energy field responded by flaring into chaos. As she walked close to the foot of the bed a different life energy rippled through me like a tidal wave. At one point Lady Olivia walked into the room and at the instant Kundalini power flared up like a fire on an oil field, fierce but without focus, the Isis light in her had magnetised the Isis in me. My new priestess-sister finally asked that no one else should come in for a while. She finally stabilised my energies by placing a large quartz crystal beneath my feet. It acted like a magnetic safety-catch placing my energy field in a holding pattern. It was perfectly clear to me that I was a clumsy novice in the service of Isis as a mediator and despite many years involved in Mystery School, no instruction in this most ancient and sacred art had ever been given. As a result, I had always experienced great difficulty with all the roles I had been allotted in a succession of ritual dramas. I simply did not understand what was required in the preparation period before mediation, nor in the winding down period immediately following mediation. A temporary bridge to a god-form is relatively easily dismantled but this is not the Kemetic way. Here the ancient phraseology is key, for all god-forms are indeed as garments placed completely over the mediating mind like an encompassing and greater costume. The long process of attunement between the devotee and the deity is in part the story of this work, it cannot be hurriedly told or hastily lived. My previous experiences of mediation had always proved to be most difficult on the return to normal consciousness, the final and essential closing of the circuit of the journey into exaltation. When my experienced sister-priestess explained that I needed to mediate right through to my feet using minor chakras too, it was a startling revelation and I knew at once that she was correct. My energies finally stabilised, and we returned to the main room and prepared for the next rehearsal.

THE GARMENTS OF ISIS

I knew that something intense was happening to me. I knew it was all related to the forthcoming Oracle of Isis. Instinctively I knew that I could not control anything, it was a question only of trust and surrender. Throughout this time, it felt like riding an incoming powerful wave while still holding my balance in the very physical world of children, my in-laws, American television and trips on the subway.

On the Tuesday evening, I began to iron the robes for the following day. As I stood at the ironing board, the pains increased with such ferocity that I was forced to stop. I spontaneously began to utilise movement, creating a personal mixture of yoga, dance and Tai-Chi like motions to give me temporary relief. But the pains continued to increase, and I found myself spontaneously stretching forwards on hands and knees, stretching to relive the pains which had become exactly like the pains during the first stage of labour, rhythmic and rippling. I reached out for a chair in front of me burying my face in the cushions. My hands gripped for support. I realised I was in a kneeling birth position. Suddenly and without warning, the pains increased. It all felt exactly like the second stage of labour, and I began to let out the sounds familiar to any mother giving birth. I knew exactly what was happening to me. The Isis current was both entering and opening the base chakra.

Now the sensations changed, the intensity remained but the actual pain stopped to be replaced by a relentless pressure which passed through me in spasms. I saw an image of a great rod stamping down through all my centres, it reminded me a huge pestle and mortar, more pushing, pushing, pushing until finally I experienced the crowning of my own base chakra. The sensations stopped instantly. I stood up unsteadily, "She's locked in," I said aloud to myself. I was now too weak to stand and went straight to rest, laying down on the nearby bed. I knew the process was unfinished. Isis began to integrate this new energy. As I lay perfectly still, She worked upon each centre in turn. I felt very weak as

THE BREATH OF ISIS

the energy circulated my lower centres but as the power moved upwards, I became more physically comfortable. Finally, I knew that the process was completed. I knew that my energy field had been expanded, it was as if Isis had breathed into me and filled my energy field with Herself. J. was around for some of these metaphysical callisthenics. At the beginning of it all I had asked him to look after the children upstairs. I do not remember at what point he returned but from his demeanour he was clearly bewildered. His lack of comprehension was almost physically painful to me. Not only did I need to manage my own process with calmness, but I now needed to offer a full commentary and explanation of the unfolding events moment by moment. His confusion might be thought understandable in the circumstances but real metaphysicians know that magical work is not a game of dressing up but a continuous transformation of dynamic living energies. This truth was now being amply demonstrated and revealed. When I quietly asked him not to step into the space close to me, he just ignored my words and almost as if to test me he stepped into the newly prepared energy field. At once all his feelings of confusion, even blind terror rolled through me like a hot wave. I had to integrate this energy into my own process until I was calm again. The process finally felt complete. Although I was extremely tired, I had not yet finished preparation for the morning. I still needed to shower. I got up and crossed the long basement towards the bathroom. As I did so, I could feel the chakra between my legs, I waddled across the room like a newly delivered mother. When I reached the bathroom and stood in front of the mirror, I saw six raised red spots lying in a crescent formation around my neck like the shape of an Egyptian collar. I showered and returned exhausted to my bed. J. followed me into the bathroom and showered too. When I climbed into bed, he told me that I had not hung my flannel back in the proper place. I struggled up walked the length of the room, placed the pink flannel on its white hook and silently returned to bed. I was

THE GARMENTS OF ISIS

not going to cross swords; thoughts had become too visibly real. Instead. I placed my trust in Isis and extended my hand out to Her. Despite the extraordinary, even bizarre events of the evening, I awoke the next day completely restored and totally invigorated, the ordeal of the previous night had already moved into the past, what was important was the day to come. On the morning of the presentation, we travelled in by train as usual but while standing at the station platform, I unexpectedly experienced a tremendous flow of power which passed right through me, even down into my feet. It was such a strong sensation that it was something of a physical surprise. I felt momentarily as if my legs had turned to stone. It was however a good feeling. I felt very secure and well grounded. As we approached the Palmer House Hotel, it seemed to me that like a beacon it was summoning great beings from invisible realms. That same evening, I noticed that the tops of my feet felt suddenly hot and itchy. I looked down and saw a bright red marks, one on each foot in matching places. I suddenly realised that the chakras in my feet had opened, it was such a bizarre moment that I even took a photograph which I recently found after so many years.

In the afternoon, we offered our performance. It was very beautiful and well received. Even now after so many years have elapsed, I can still recall the unprecedented potency of this mediation, yet I am unable to fully speak about it. Descriptions are meaningless and words are empty when stripped of reference points. All I can say is that I knew what it meant to become a Garment of Isis. Once again, my difficulties did not arise while the connection with Isis was being forged but only afterwards when it was needful to disconnect from Her. I am familiar with a state of being that I think has elsewhere been called, 'being strung out on the planes.' I doubt if these words convey very much but it has both a feeling and a physical component. It is extremely uncomfortable. It usually does not last too long but here back in the official FOI suite, I knew that I was in trouble. I could hardly stand. My dear

THE BREATH OF ISIS

sister-priestess held my feet and worked with the crystal again, but this time it made no difference, I could not reconnect with my own physicality. Other priestesses came and massaged my feet, but I still could not, 'earth' myself, as the saying goes. Rising on the planes of consciousness is vital indeed essential if a ceremony is to make a spiritual connection. But being, 'strung out on the planes' afterwards is an extremely uncomfortable and unpleasant. The moment of, 're-entry,' or reconnection is palpable. It is very difficult to describe but as it takes place, everything becomes realigned at the instant. Up to that moment, there is increasing distress and discomfort. The process might be likened to the turning of a Rubix Cube, only with the one last and correct move can everything fit into its allotted place. Experience has shown me that neither rest nor sleep effects the reconnection. Where the oracular tradition still lives, proper attention is given to the person of the oracle who on occasion needs skilful care.

Despite the best efforts of all concerned and the statutory warm drink, I knew that I was still not aligned, and I did not know what to do. A young man, an appreciative member of the audience had come backstage to visit. As he waited to speak with someone, he began to spontaneously to drum, in response, I stood up and began to dance, as I did so I could actually feel myself being realigned, as if all my energy bodies clicked back into one another like the classical Russian dolls. It was a moment of great relief. In the evening we visited friends. During that time, I became aware of a burning sensation on the tops of my feet. I bent down to look and saw that I had two bright red spots one on each foot, now the minor chakras had opened. During the FOI presentation, I remember only pacing in the wings waiting for my cue. Unlike other members of the company, I had no script, and no-one knew what I might say. The Oracle came through with both authority and compassion. It carried great emotional force.

THE GARMENTS OF ISIS

Beloved Family, Sons and Daughters of the Divine One.

Happy am I that you call upon me even at this eleventh hour. For, know that this is truly the eleventh hour for your world. I implore you to answer to the call to action from the heart. Look first to the past. For the past and future are one. The injustices, miseries, and oppression of nation upon nation have scarred and divided the human family. Hold up the mirror to the collected reflection of you all. Gaze deeply and see what you will see. When you have looked upon the consequences of past actions and deeds, seek forgiveness one from another. Seek forgiveness nation from nation. Seek forgiveness from the earth for you are all at fault. Hardest of all beloved, be prepared to forgive those who have wounded you deepest. Begin the work of reconciliation with a good heart and Divine Grace will be bestowed upon your labours. You cannot carry the burdens of the past; ego, violence, cruelty, oppression, lust, power, and hatred into the future. These may not pass through the portal. All must be reconciled here by you.

The door to your common future is open. Beyond it shines a light so brilliant and dazzling, that none have seen its full glory and splendour. The light will lead you. Let it be shared by all, it belongs to all, for you are all Divine. Extend the hand of love across race, creed, colour. Let nothing divide that which is already whole. Come, cross the Great Waters, to your future. It is your destiny to arrive. There is a blessing on all who serve.

Although the oracle was behind me and now suitably reassembled, I still had the presentation to deliver. I was not anticipating anything than delivering a prepared lecture to a small group. The presentation took place in one of the smaller committee rooms and it was packed. I gave a presentation followed by the meditation *The Roses of Isis*, its key theme was transformation. During the talk, a member of

THE BREATH OF ISIS

the audience left suddenly. She returned later to explain that she had suddenly experienced a violent loss of blood even though her period was not due. This kind of synchronicity is not unknown when working with Goddess energies. It had happened to me during the parliament but also most notably in 1982 when I was part of a large group working to free the group mind from a particular substratum. I too had passed bright red blood unexpectedly and out of sequence. In that particular context, it felt like a karmic release, a transformation both personal and collective. After the presentation session was completed, we were joined by the group who had attended Lady Olivia's workshop. The young man who had drummed with such good effect was present. Lady Olivia was in charge, my work was completed. The tone of this session was quite different. A priestess sang a beautiful evocation which I found deeply moving, another danced with movement and gestures that took me straight back to the Temple. As we danced, altogether, I could feel the Kundalini current begin to twitch and move in my lower centres. It wasn't destabilising but strong like tongues of flame. The energy in the room was palpable. Lady Olivia asked the Lyceum leaders to simply speak in the name of their own group and give a blessing or invocation. I had risen from my seat and stood waiting for a suitable space between speakers. I was standing close to a young man who surprised himself by giving an Oracle of Osiris. As he spoke, I felt power began to envelope me, it was as if Osiris was summoning Isis. The power was almost uncontainable. Her wings enveloped me. I spoke for Her. The mediation was not long but I know that Her presence filled the room. I know that many people were in tears. The mediation closed. I prostrated myself before Lord Osiris. I stood up and then to reassure people, I said, simply, *"It's me now."* But someone close to me began to invoke Isis again. My body began to shake as if the current was beginning to respond again but then with a gesture I shall never forget, instinctively and unconsciously, my hands with palms locked together shot into the space of my

THE GARMENTS OF ISIS

crown chakra, the current was immediately closed and finalised with the words, "*I have already spoken.*" I do not remember all of the event or all of the words spoken by the participants. When it was time to close, Lady Olivia asked me to bestow a blessing. Her wings enfolded me with authority, Her blessings was bestowed.

I have often thought of this event as a Pentecost, a description not welcomed by either pagans or Christians to be sure. Yet I shall be forever reminded of the biblical story when tongues of fire descended to bless, empower, inspire and authorise bringing the gifts of the spirit. Speaking personally, I find no difference between phenomena related to the Holy Spirit beloved of Christianity and phenomena related to Kundalini Rising. My contentious view has annoyed almost everyone but Jung too noted the similarities between the two experiences. The local TV station had followed the Parliament with interest and Lady Olivia was about to be interviewed. She insisted that I join her and suggested I wear, 'the lovely crown' that I had worn as the oracle, I did not wear any crown at all.

NOTES

1. Christine Campbell Thompson: author, esoteric practitioner. Christine worked as a secretary in a literary agency where she met John William Brodie-Innes, a member the Golden Dawn and later she met Dion Fortune. She joined The Society of the Inner Light where she met Charles Seymour and formed a partnership which lasted until his death. Their joint story is told in *Dancers to the Gods* by Alan Richardson.

2. Rosemary Clark: scholar, writer and exponent of Ancient Egyptian Sacred Science. Her books *The Sacred Magic of Ancient Egypt*: and *The Sacred Tradition* in Ancient Egypt provide a storehouse of information and inspiration into the practice behind the Kemetic Wisdom. In 1975 Rosemary founded Temple Harakhte, a non-profit education forum dedicated to the dissemination of ancient Egyptian spirituality and the practice of Sacred Science.

CHAPTER SIX

THE BREATH OF ISIS

I see now that I have been inspired by Isis all my life and especially since 1977 but my story is no more than template for the unfolding of your own story. The re-telling of my story shows me the many ways in which Her inspiration has come to me. The word inspire is derived from inspirare meaning, 'to breathe into.' To be inspired means to be infused with a rare quality of enthusiasm. Inspiration and enthusiasm go hand in hand, genuine inspiration produces visible enthusiasm. Enthusiasm, too carries a mystical weight since the word comes from the ancient Greek word *eufousiasmz* meaning, to be, inspired by or possessed by God or Goddess, this has been my experience. Inspiration is a uniquely human quality, invisible as breath it is nevertheless at the heart of our power to manifest, to create, to solve a problem, to envision the future and fulfil the many powers that define our humanity. In the past, the voice of inspiration was imbued with an almost mystical power. When creation was viewed as an act of divine intent, human creativity was also seen to be gifted by divine approval. Inspiration was a gift of the spirit, invisibly conceived and divinely bestowed through pneuma meaning breath and also spirit or soul. Inspiration must result in action if it is to have any value, otherwise it remains an ungrounded vision and unsubstantiated by verifiable fact.

My inspiration has led my life in a very particular direction. At times, the clues, camouflaged against the backdrop of ordinary life

THE BREATH OF ISIS

have been difficult to discern. At other times, the usually invisible signals stand out like neon signs rendered visible by some temporary disclosing fluid. But these moments are rare and far-flung. If we choose to follow the path towards eternity, we must also learn to recognize the sign-posts. Like Hansel and Gretel looking for the way home, we need to pay great attention to the road at our feet. I think I have spent most of my adult life trying to read such signs. Hindsight suggests that my first act of dedication was a profound turning point. A seed had been planted. My awakening to all things Egyptian opened the floodgates of my intellectual mind. I was eager to learn about Egypt. I read everything I could. In this initial phase I also read a great deal about magic both theoretical and practical. Everything was new to me, but of course not everything written is serviceable. My approach to metaphysical reading has always been the same. I read at first without judgement, ploughing through recommended volumes like a good student. If a book makes a deep impression, I return to sections of it over and over again, often taking out snippets or sections for meditation. If a book proposes ideas that I do not understand, I simply move the book and its contents into a neutral space in my mind. This means that I have noted its contents, but its meaning eludes me. Such books await a further categorisation, some will be embraced when I have grown enough to see their worth, some will be discarded when I have grown enough to see their lack of worth. I never believe everything I read. Some books grab my attention from the first page and remain my companions for years as I slowly attempt to become aligned to the gnosis hidden in the words. This remains true for the two books, *The Sacred Magic of Ancient Egypt* and *The Sacred Tradition in Ancient Egypt* by Rosemary Clark. I have returned to these texts over and over again, sometimes reading aloud for myself alone, sometimes performing solitary rituals, sometimes incorporating words into group performance. Rosemary's great insight has never failed me and I remain indebted to her tremendous scholarship.

THE BREATH OF ISIS

My first approach to Isis and Her Mysteries was therefore purely intellectual. This filled my mind with images and information which created a rich internal reservoir. It is hard to say when my focus shifted from the intellectual to the intuitive mode. The time spent reading lessened, the time spent in reflection or meditation increased. When my mind was quiet, I would hear words gently dropped into it like pebbles into a pool. I never committed these words to paper, almost as soon as I returned my mind to ordinary waking consciousness, the words had completely faded from view. I realised that I needed to learn how to bring the memory of these conversations back into waking consciousness. It was my daily practice to make a space where I might hear this other voice. Even at a time when channelling was becoming a talked about phenomena, I discussed my internal dialogue with no-one and refused to give it any special significance. I instinctively recognised the pitfalls of such self-deception. So, I carried on listening to this inner voice and all the while attempting to improve my ability to recall its message. I treated it rather like the reading that outstripped me, to be either kept or discarded in the light of other future evidence. At first my mind was only able pick up only general impressions. In fact, I had no sense that I was being asked to take small and easy steps towards Her, rather like a child learning to walk. Sometimes the impressions were strongly emotional, an overwhelming need to go somewhere, meet someone or do something. Looking back, I see that I also instinctively incorporated energy work into my periods of meditation. I did this for several years without any apparent result. Hindsight now tells me that such exercises were not wasted but an essential stage in building the *antakarana*, the rainbow bridge or inner vehicle. Curiously I kept no records of this period, there seemed so little to report.

Intellectual learning has its place in life but engagement in The Mysteries exceeds book learning and brings an engagement of spirit. I passed from wondering towards gnosis only slowly and by small

THE BREATH OF ISIS

degrees following the small signs placed in my path and the small words placed in my mind. Though I could not see ahead, the breath of inspiration gradually filling my life was to take me into writing, teaching and the transmission of sacred teachings. Learning to recognize signs and hear inner direction is part of a much broader picture. It is however a process fraught with the difficulties of discernment: distortion, delusion and self-deception lie in wait. I have succumbed to them all, they are I think unavoidable.

I am only able to see the inspiration at the heart of my life through the tangible results that have flowed from it. Inspiration is as fragile as a word whispered in the ear on waking, a puzzling dream that demands resolution or a powerfully impressed feeling. Such brief moments belong to gnosis, the knowing revelation which is the instruction of the soul. I have sat quietly on a deserted beach and been told it was time to honour Hathor. I have received the title for a ritual yet to be written. I have been gripped by a flow of words which does not cease until it is done. Inspiration, the possessing breath of the divinity may be as invisible as the air but its power fills the mind with vision and its strength generates the energy necessary to bring an idea into manifestation. There is something so remarkable about human creativity that it has often been seen as a mirrored image of divine creation. It is after all the power to bring something into manifest reality, to translate a visionary seed idea into a three-dimensional physical form. Moreover, inspiration seizes the mind with such vitality that it becomes a driving force and provides the reservoir of personal energy needed to carry the idea into manifestation. The journey from inspired idea to physical reality is invariably fraught with obstacles, new ideas are not always welcomed or even understood and great determination is usually required to carry an idea to its physical birth. Yet the story of creative vision is the story of humanity from our tool making ancestors to our technological contemporaries. Inspiration stands behind all creative acts whether artistic, social or humanitarian. At

THE BREATH OF ISIS

this time in our shared history, the world needs people of inspired vision. Genuine inspiration is the prime mover behind every field of human endeavour. In contrast to personal desire, inspiration is most often transpersonal since it provides a solution to or is an expression of a shared need and even at its most basic an inspired project will draw people towards it like a magnet. The inception of a visionary idea can even feel like a moment of mysterious revelation, a shared breath with the forces of creation from the universal and unbounded realm of spirit and the sustaining power of visionary inspiration is often inspirational to those who hear of its passage from inception to birth. Creativity and inspiration walk hand in hand like twins borne of the same mother. Yet so often the humdrum demands of life conspire to close the door on inspiration preferring instead to welcome utility and mediocrity. It is in part the long passage into the socialised, educated and workaday world that slowly robs us of the very qualities that pave the way for the inspired thought. Innocence of heart, spontaneity of spirit, curiosity of mind and openness to experience magnetise inspired revelation. These qualities share much in common with the enlightened state of mind. By contrast the ordinary adult mind is ever-full: preconceptions, egoic embellishments, personal projections and preoccupations crowd mental space leaving no room for creativity or inspiration. Engagement in The Mysteries preserves a space for spontaneous realisation, imaginative engagement and creative involvement. In this way the mind is made fertile for inspiration. The Mystery Tradition makes much use of the trained imagination which is the image making facility of the mind. It is the mage who manipulates images. Magic, which is transformation arises through the creative imagination. The imago represents the state of positive becoming. If inspiration provides the necessary energy and impetus required to act in the world, then the imagination provides the bridge between the idea in its pure form and its manifest reality. Creativity and inspiration need the company of the imagination.

THE BREATH OF ISIS

The gift of creative inspiration belongs to everyone. This divine possession brings passion to experience and a sense of mission and purpose to action. It is the special enzyme of human experience which makes us the co-creators of our own existence. This is the elixir of life, drink deeply of it whenever you can. Inspiration may take a thousand forms but it will always bear the hallmark of loving service in some way and it will be never be given to be used a trademark, a logo, a calling card or any other purely commercial enterprise detached from service. If you are open to inspiration, it will come to you through your own unique identity. For me this has taken shape through the inspired word, books, rituals and the transmission of sacred teachings. When I begin to write I usually hear a title in my mind. I have no idea how this theme is to be fleshed out. If I am to write a celebratory or initiatory ritual, I just start to write, all the while listening to a voice in my mind. If I am preparing a magical ritual based on a specific series of texts, I will have the texts open in front of me, but I instinctively know how to shape the speeches into a new pattern. I rarely stop to reflect on what I have written until the task is complete. I hear a voice in my head like an internal dictation.

In 2011, I was inspired to write under peculiar circumstances. I was planning to give a course to a small group but a few days prior to leaving, I came down with a high temperature and was confined to bed. Once the temperature was over, I still felt too unwell to resume normal life so I stayed in bed and was inspired to read *The Hermetica* which was to have been the theme of my seminar. As soon as I began to read, I felt the desire the write and the internal dictation began which lasted for about two weeks and did not cease until I had written 15 Commentaries. I started to write at about seven o clock in the morning and continued until the close of day. I have watched the creative process come to birth in others. One of our members was a professional artist. However, after his ordination in the service of Thoth, Lord of the Medu-

THE BREATH OF ISIS

Neter, he surprised himself by finding the inspiration to write a ceremony. Once the seed had been planted, he did not look back. He wrote beautiful stately rituals which combined traditional elements in new ritual forms. He made a wonderful contribution to the temple and for a while took responsibility for the archive. I too have been blessed by Lord Thoth. Many years ago not long after I had encountered the Kemetic tradition, a vision of Lord Thoth appeared quite spontaneously. I found myself in a typical Egyptian temple courtyard where a group of shaven headed priests were assembled as if for a meeting. As I walked forward, so the group opened up to welcome me and then I saw at once that a figure I knew to be Thoth was seated here. He called me forward and presented me with the scribal palette, ink jar and brush and told me that I would write, 'hundreds of thousands of words' in his name. At the time I not written a word, I was working as a school teacher. The relationship between the divinity and the devotee is of great interest to me. Over the years, I have observed how the qualities assigned to the divinity, slowly begin to manifest in the life of the devotee. This conforms to the ancient Kemetic template whereby each priesthood unfolded the skills and qualities indwelling within its patron divinity. The priestesses of Hathor like Hathor herself were musicians, dancers, sacred singers. The priesthood of Ma'at, the embodiment of Truth, became the law givers. The priesthood of Selket, the scorpion goddess became specialists in poison and bites. The priesthood of Sekhmet were vets and overseers at the slaughter-house. The priests of Anubis were the embalmers. This template remains serviceable today. The relationship with the deity begins with when the individual responds to the calling of the heart and enters the service of a chosen deity. This transpersonal relationship brings its own teaching and guidance through the inspiration bestowed by the divinity. As the relationship deepens the qualities and attributes of the deity come to birth within the individual.

At the dawn of the twenty-first century, such a holistic model has

THE BREATH OF ISIS

much to offer. Materialism, secularism and the decline of orthodox religious values has left a vacuum, a gaping whole has opened up in the western psyche. The results of this are apparent everywhere yet we live at a time of spiritual resurgence, there can be no doubt of this. In this new renaissance there is surely room for many paths. I have served in the temple both literally and metaphorically. Isis has made it very clear to me through spontaneous vision that the next phase of my work will take me beyond the confines that I am used to. I too must continue to be open to the breath of inspiration. It seems timely to me that the Isian current has flared most strongly into life for during my attendance at two World Parliaments, firstly in Chicago in 1993 and later in Melbourne in 2009. I bring you words of inspiration and hope from the 1993 assembly delivered by Dr. David Ramage, Jr.

> *We come to commemorate that glorious ground-breaking event of 1893 and we come to better prepare ourselves to meet the challenges of the present and the future. We ask that you delve deeply into the offerings of this event. They are rich and varied. But mostly we ask that you come to share, to learn, to enter into dialogue with others and to seek with others, ways to overcome conflict and ways to nurture and heal our world and its people. Most of us share the precept that it is good that we respect others even as we wish to be respected ourselves. May that be a watchword of this great and challenging opportunity.*
>
> *I try to be a person of hope. I ask you to join me in the hope that from this gathering great good may come. Thank you for coming, for your faith, and for your hope. Welcome to an occasion which might send out beacons of hope to a troubled and broken world. Let us laugh with joy, cry with sympathy and commit our efforts, both spiritual and temporal, to a future of peace.*

The words of The Oracle delivered in the arena of the world stage calls for a new dimension of engagement. Her message speaks with great clarity and forcefulness to those in her service. If you would truly serve the deity of your heart, look to the bigger picture. What is really happening to the world today? When you are touched by this reality, you will translate your feelings into action, and you will surely seek guidance and listen for the voice of inspiration. The oracle laid out a shared task, namely to, 'begin the work of reconciliation,' in recognition of the karmic consequences created by our collected group minds. This task can be set in motion in various ways; insight and intuition may be your best guides in such work. When I attended the plenary session at the 1993 parliament, Dr. Gerald Barney of the Millennium Institute, offered his deep apologies for the many mistakes and Christian errors of the past. Now it is possible to argue that he had neither the right nor the authority to say such a thing. It is also possible to argue that his blanket apology was simply irrelevant. In my heightened state of awareness and in that moment, it seemed to me that his personal intent had by its utter honesty and sincerity burned up some little portion of karma accumulated and accrued over time. As he spoke it felt to me that his words had great impact and meaning, almost as if something had shifted at some deeply held level. The power of sincere apology between people is evident, it releases the power of forgiveness without which no true healing can take place. This theme of karmic weight between the various faith traditions continued to run unbidden in my mind throughout the week. Curiously en route to the 2009 parliament, the same theme appeared when I found myself in conversation with a Christian priest whose parish had included the place of the twin towers. He was coming to the parliament to give a presentation of his work establishing The Gardens of Forgiveness around the world. His work was now about bringing reconciliation between former enemies. My conversation reminded me of the words I had been inspired to write in 1993 about releasing planetary karma.

THE BREATH OF ISIS

You, who are already awakened to spiritual realities, understand the many needs of our times. This is truly a time of great transition and transformation at every level of experience. The many manifestations of change are all expressions of a vast shift in human consciousness. Yet we should not glibly assume that all will be plain sailing into some glorious pre-ordained golden age. Humanity is being asked to redefine itself, to undertake an evolutionary quantum leap. We cannot do this without first releasing the past to which we are all bound through history and the pattern of incarnation.

Make no mistake the past still binds the present and the future. Simply look at the racial conflicts around the world. Touch the simmering hatreds of the centuries and you will know just how powerful these long established group minds can be. If we are to realise global consciousness and the essential brotherhood of the human family, the two key Aquarian concepts, we will have to transcend the very nationalism which has formed the past. This does not mean that the future holds no national definitions for us. However, we have to first release the accumulated shadows which so enmesh a land and its peoples.

A small group with focussed intent can have a huge impact on history. In fact all religious movements have begun in the hands of the few. The Way of The Mysteries is ultimately a way of engaging with the world through the application of an exalted consciousness and a compassionate heart. Such words must appear nonsensical to the rational mind. The long and arduous processes of realignment are the necessary stages in a long apprenticeship. Acts of magic aimed at restoring balance of many kinds to the greater group-mind share nothing in common with the small acts of magic designed to improve life or swing good fortune in your favour. If you are inclined to put your energies at the disposal of the greater good, perhaps begin by contemplating the collective mess we have created. Your

THE BREATH OF ISIS

access route to the shared mind of humanity is through your family tree which will provide a blueprint of the groups to which you have ancestral affiliations. It may throw up some curious situations whereby you individually represent historical enemies. Speaking personally, I find that my family tree puts me in touch with an extraordinary cultural mix including both the Russian and Chinese.

Spend time meditating upon the karmic bond created through the actions of one group mind upon the other. This is an exceptionally challenging task, namely to releasing deeds which are not personally yours but which you willingly represent on behalf of the group mind. Such acts of personal mediation should be aligned through a higher transpersonal spiritual power. Call upon Isis, it is her wish to bring together that which has been broken. Do not under any circumstances attempt this work without the certain aid of a transforming spiritual power. This work may be effected through meditation or through a ceremonial setting which is in essence a three dimensional meditation. This work will also have its effect upon the land. Writing now in in the spring of 2013, I note that recently the Prime Minister of Australia delivered a powerful and highly publicised speech in which she gave a full and heartfelt apology for the wrongs committed against the Aboriginal peoples. Accordingly, she addressed her words directly to the Aboriginal community on behalf of the Australian government with the following words.

> *I move, that today we honour the Indigenous peoples of this land, the oldest continuing cultures in human history. We reflect on their past mistreatment. We reflect in particular on the mistreatment of those who were Stolen Generations - this blemished chapter in our nation's history. The time has now come for the nation to turn a new page in Australia's history by righting the wrongs of the past and so moving forward with confidence to the future. We apologise for the laws and policies of successive Parliaments*

THE BREATH OF ISIS

and governments that have inflicted profound grief, suffering and loss on these our fellow Australians. We apologise especially for the removal of Aboriginal and Torres Strait Islander children from their families, their communities and their country. For the pain, suffering and hurt of these Stolen Generations, their descendants and for their families left behind, we say sorry. To the mothers and the fathers, the brothers and the sisters, for the breaking up of families and communities, we say sorry. And for the indignity and degradation thus inflicted on a proud people and a proud culture, we say sorry. We the Parliament of Australia respectfully request that this apology be received in the spirit in which it is offered as part of the healing of the nation. For the future we take heart; resolving that this new page in the history of our great continent can now be written. We today take this first step by acknowledging the past and laying claim to a future that embraces all Australians, a future where this Parliament resolves that the injustices of the past must never, never happen again – A future where we harness the determination of all Australians, Indigenous and non-Indigenous, to close the gap that lies between us in life expectancy, educational achievement and economic opportunity – A future where we embrace the possibility of new solutions to enduring problems where old approaches have failed - A future based on mutual respect, mutual resolve and mutual responsibility - A future where all Australians, whatever their origins, are truly equal partners, with equal opportunities and with an equal stake in shaping the next chapter in the history of this great country.

This statement of intent is clearly a powerful political move which must be supported in the future with appropriate social and cultural policies. However, beneath the obvious present and future ramifications, such words have the power to release blockages dammed up in collective consciousness. This is exactly the kind of

THE BREATH OF ISIS

healing indicated by the Oracle of Isis delivered at the Parliament. Reconciliation can only follow upon the recognition of a wrong committed, it is not a question of laying blame but of moving forwards from values and norms which have become obsolete. So, if you seek to be inspired by the breath of the Isis put yourself at the service of the world. Genuine inspiration is the prime mover behind every field of human endeavour. In contrast to personal desire, inspiration is most often transpersonal since it provides a solution to or is expression of a shared need. A truly inspired project will draw people towards it like a magnet. If you are in relationship with Her, open yourself to inspiration. She will breathe life into your life and take you on a journey into soul-service. Her love for all planetary life is unbounded, let Her love become yours too. My inspiration has now become grounded into the fabric of my being. The Breath of Isis has truly inspired my life. Come in the right spirit and Isis will inspire your life blessing you with creativity of vision and the enthusiastic power to manifest Her wishes. Hear Her words and be inspired. These words became part of the book, *The Garments of Isis* begun in 2009, completed in 2019 and published in 2022.

> *As a light is a great comfort to a traveller on a dark night, as a light is a great comfort to a ship approaching a new coastline, as a flare is a great comfort to the distressed, as a beacon is a great comfort to a besieged people, so I am a light for the soul. Only when your soul powers have begun to stir, will you seek me out. Until then you will be content with the world of appearances, you will not seek my light. As a light provides a guide in dark places, so my light shines without ceasing. As one flame may light another so I will ignite your soul powers so that you may come into the fullness of your own divine light. But releasing the illumination of the soul is more than the work of a lifetime, so I open the door of remembering which that you may walk in my footsteps following my light to where it leads. I have been*

THE BREATH OF ISIS

a light upon the earth, and it is my wish that my light shall burn brightly again. For where I am remembered upon the altar through the lighting of lights, so I am also as a light in your heart. This is where our relationship begins and where our lights may meet, the greater holding the lesser in its brilliance. Once we have embraced soul light to soul light, we are linked by the love in our hearts. For do not doubt my love for all that lives upon earth.

As our lights merge one into the other more and more, so your love for all that lives will increase without limit and my service will sit lightly upon your shoulders. My light in the world has become dim with forgetting and with the passage of time. The minds of peoples have become dull without the light of the sacred fire. The soul powers slumber and so you live in the darkness of your own making. But now is the time to awaken and live, for your world weeps. Do you not hear your own earth mother calling out to you?

Greetings to those who say my name, for then I know my light lives and the sacred covenant between us is unbroken. Do not doubt that if you love me now, you have loved me before and our alliance is deeply imprinted into your soul. Do not doubt that if you seek to serve me now, you have served me before and the gift of your service is deeply imprinted in your soul. So now I call you again with joy and in the light of my mysteries. I send out my name, pushing it from me like a newly birthed child to arise in your heart as the seed of your own becoming. I cannot find a resting place unless you embrace my name in love and honour. Hold my name dear and I will awaken within you, take my name in vain and my essence in you will wither in the instant. As the soul-seed shines gathering more light to itself, so I will breathe new life into your form and you will share in the knowing of my heart.

THE BREATH OF ISIS

My voice will be heard whispering in your inward ear. I may visit you in dream and plant the seeds of a special task directly into your mind. If you seek my service, I will entrust you with my service. In no other way can I assist the world except through you. You shall be my garments, my appearance in the world. As a garment dresses its owner, so your form will clothe my presence within you. You shall see with my eyes, hear with my ears, speak with my mouth, feel with my heart. My light will indwell within you, breath to breath, heartbeat to heartbeat. This is the Way of the Mysteries, that which is human makes way for that which is divine, the greater light encompasses the lesser light.

My service will bring you into joy even though my service is born in the face of sorrow. For without sorrow there can be no awakening and the heart will keep its slumber. It is sorrow which breaks open the shell case of the heart to reveal the soul-seed within. As I have grieved, so you will grieve too. Forget the romance and whimsy attached to my name, do not seek to hide yourself in display, there can be no hiding in my service. For my compassion, the weeping of the heart arises without ceasing. The sorrowful heart comes to life and sees what the heart must bear. I was not spared, I too have walked the path of grief and despair. I walk with you in your sorrow and share your tears. I am the lady of sorrows and you have asked to become my garment. Even sorrow shall be dispelled for all things move towards their own end and sorrow will not endure without end. I am called your divine mother and I know each of my beloved family by a secret name known only to me. And it is this that I whisper when I hope to awaken you once more. For when you are dressed in the body of flesh and earthly desires, so your forgetting is great, and the voice of remembering is but faint. And so I call your name often and surrounding it with the passion of my heart, I send it forth like a bird in flight seeking its rightful owner. And

THE BREATH OF ISIS

it happens that when you sound my name in secret hope, I will hear it returning to me like a bird finding its owner.

Call me, call me often and in the certainty that you will be heard. Life is not what the senses alone may reveal, and if you depend only upon your physical teachers, you will be easily deceived. For there is a greater life and a lesser life, your body is equipped through the teaching capacities of your senses. But your soul is equipped by the teacher in the heart, who speaks for the master of wisdom. You shall silence the lesser teachers and instead raise up the greater so that this voice alone may be heard by you in sweet silence. So, seek out the voice that speaks with the truth of the heart's knowing and accord your lesser teachers only a lesser place. Sit in silence often and turn the eye of the mind inwards upon itself so that you begin to see who you are not what you have come to own. Turn the eye of the mind inwards to the regions of being and becoming where it will swoop and soar on its flight as it looks for the seeds of light within you. And the eye of the mind must make a million journeys into the caverns that you have formed without intent. The soul bird will fly seeking its twin which rests in dreamless sleep and where the two meet and fuse as one, so the seed of light planted long ago and in another place shall merge and flash with a secret light preparing the way for the voice of wisdom and the fire of the heart. Let this be your first journey.

I cannot arise in your heart unless you clear a space for me for I do not come as an intruder but only as an invited guest. If you would hear my voice, then you must come to hear with your inner ear. If you would see my face, then you must come to see with the inner eye. If you would come to know me, prepare a place for me where light may dwell without shadow. To those who would know me I say awaken and throw open the doors

THE BREATH OF ISIS

of the heart so that the world and all that it is may be reflected there. When you watch the play of the world from within the heart, so your soul-service will arise as easily as waking from sleep. A thousand possibilities will show themselves to you and I will dwell within every one of them. Where you rejoice, so I rejoice, where you are sorrowful, I am sorrowful too. I place no burdens upon you that cannot be shouldered by the strong soul. I ask nothing that the soul does not already desire to give. I demand nothing that cannot be given by the loving heart. I wish for nothing that cannot come to pass. I call you towards your own illumination as you walk the path of becoming. These are my words. Do you hear my voice? Do you rise upon a new path? Do you desire to be among my service with all the powers of your heart? Do you turn to me with outstretched hands as a child reaches out to a mother? Do you yearn to know the love of my heart? Then come, I am not distant but nearby. I am not locked in the past but ever-present. I am as close as your next breath.

CHAPTER SEVEN

THE LIGHT OF ISIS

I was invited to appear at a conference called The Way of the Priestess. It was to be held at one of the halls in London University. The programme included a number of women from various traditions. I thought the topic interesting enough to tempt me travel to London. I have watched the reappearance of the priestess with great interest. My book, *Daughters of the Goddess* represents my personal effort to understand the meaning assigned to this role in various civilizations. The book took two years to research and as I read increasingly deeply and widely, I began see an increasing mismatch between historical fact and the current ideas in wide circulation. This first great realisation was a tremendous shock to me, it literally stopped me in my tracks. Up to that point and like so many other women I had derived my ideas from the books available at the time. But prime sources painted a different picture. I am by nature and training a scholar. I believe that questions produce answers, inadequate questions produce inadequate answers. I am wary of generalisations, suspicious of sloppy scholarship and immune to romanticised projections; a half-truth is at best misleading and at worst dangerous, it is just another question to be answered not an excuse for intellectual complacency. The figure of the priestess has become a magnet for so many women on the road to conscious empowerment and I applaud and support this development wholeheartedly. However any attempt to

THE BREATH OF ISIS

recast the present in the light of the past is open to problems, most especially if the past is distorted, consciously or unconsciously, to create a better mirror for the present.

In our eagerness to find a lost wisdom, there is a regrettable tendency to romanticise the past as a repository for our own projections. This preoccupation undermines our ability to create authentic choices based on present needs and distorts what has already served its purpose. This is not to deny that there is much wisdom to be gained by looking at the world in a different way but don't be beguiled by the gloss of romance. The figure of the priestess is one highly charged with magic and mystique, the past has its own story to tell. Even though sacred women played a definite and particular role in many varied societies, does the past have the capacity to teach the present? The movement for women's empowerment whether political, economic or spiritual is self-justifying, it requires no historical justification. There is no need to prove an authentic present need by recourse to historical record; women now wish to define themselves as sacred power-holders, that is sufficient justification.

A simple questions beckons – what did priestesses do? As we set out to search for the priestesses of the past, we are brought face to face with the difficulty of the task. It is too easily assumed that the current usage of the word is identical with past meaning. The shamanic priestess, psychic medium, and oracular mediator are not identical in psychic function. The initiator into women's blood mysteries and the initiator into the transcendent mysteries are not identical either in function or intention. Yet all fulfil sacred functions. We have to be prepared to look further than simple labelling if we are to understand what these women meant within their cultures. Priestesses were prominent in the vanished civilisations of Sumer, Babylon, Egypt, Crete, Greece, and Rome. Even this incomplete list indicates the breadth of any meaningful study. But what might a Cretan priestess have in common with a priestess of Hathor, the

THE LIGHT OF ISIS

prestigious Greek priestess of Demeter or even a priestess to the god Thoth! It is too easy to be deceived by glib answers. Who were the women who became priestesses? What function did they fulfil? By what authority did they take decisions or hold office? What was the nature of their service? What kind of daily lives did these women lead? Such simple question might not have simple answers.

In common with many women, I too have been swept away on a euphoric current of rediscovered Her-story. I was intrigued by the economic freedom of the naditu, awed by the significance of the first recorded priestess, Enheduanna, mesmerised by the bare breasted priestesses of Crete and empowered by the ritual of the sacred marriage. But deeper questions can bring unexpected answers. The *naditu*, were not the Sumerian entrepreneurs that I had expected but celibate and perpetually betrothed virgins. Living together in the gagum, the locked house, the naditu were betrothed to the god Samas and fulfilled the role of symbolic daughter-in-laws to his father, the moongod Sin. Constant attendance upon the god included twice daily offerings, special monthly offerings and seasonal festivals. Since all offerings were supplied from individual estates, their renowned economic activity was absolutely necessary and naditu women were most often the daughters of wealthy or royal families. There is more than a little in common with the institution of the convent: seclusion, betrothal and celibacy.

The life of Enheduanna, the first recorded priestess also yielded some surprises. It is unlikely that *Enheduanna* was a personal name but an official title constructed from the priestly title *En* denoting rulership combined with *Heduanna*, a name representing a manifestation of the moongod Sin. Her rise to political and spiritual authority was bound to the aspirations of her father the Akkadian king Sargon who as a military conqueror needed to consolidate his position and gain the acceptance of the gods. In a time-honoured tradition, he gave his daughter as bride to the God Nanna at Ur. Enheduanna clearly identified herself with Inanna but also with

THE BREATH OF ISIS

Ningal, the mother of Inanna who was also mythically married to the moon god Nanna. So Enheduanna, princess, priestess, poetess, was also the wife of the god. Enheduanna was installed into high office by her father, king Sargon who wanted to establish a Sumerian-Akkadian empire. The Akkadian goddess Ishtar was in reality also the Sumerian goddess Inanna. Enheduanna represented both the line of Inanna and her goddess mother Ningal who were together considered to be the patron deities of the family. As the family gained a foothold on political power, so the cult dedicated to Inanna was simultaneously exalted in the eyes of the people. The installation of a royal priestess-princess was a deliberate act of legitimisation in a political power game. So successful was this arrangement that succeeding kings followed the pattern established by Sargon. For some five centuries, the king's daughter became the reigning High Priestess and wife of the god.

There were many priestesses in Greece but none served any independent function, all were in the service of the state. The Priestess of Demeter enjoyed a high status and she was accorded a special place at the Olympic Games sitting upon a raised dais but her role was that of a civic dignitary. The Roman vestal virgins were in effect married to the state and their privileges were matched by loss of personal freedom and statutory punishment, indeed lethal consequences followed upon love in the real world; adultery to the state demanded the death penalty. Priestesses in shamanic guise were important throughout oriental history and were significantly found in Celtic lands and in the culture of Old Europe. But what did role did they serve? Moving beyond Europe, what did Cretan priestesses do? Women were undoubtedly power-holders here. But how was this power exercised? In the populist feminising imagination Crete has assumed a place of special significance as a matriarchal idyll apparently without a king, yet uniquely this island culture is dominated by the bull epiphany; kingship can take many forms.

Societies whether great or small, invariably derive institutions

THE LIGHT OF ISIS

and cultural forms from its prime story. Crete's mythos is bound with Minos one of the three sons of Zeus, and Pasiphae, the daughter of Helios and the Oceanid Perse. Together they have the offspring Ariadne, Androgeus, Claucos, Deucalion, Pheadra, Catreus and the ill-fated minotaur, born at the curse of Poseidon. Now the son of Minos, Androgeous won the Panathenaeic Games and was sent by the king, Aegeus of Athens, to fight a bull at Marathon but this time he was vanquished and died; the elements of Crete's unique myth are in place: bulls and bull games, death and revenge, an angry god and a curse. Minos set out to Athens to avenge his son, and after defeating king Nisus with the help of the royal daughter, he asked Zeus to punish the city. Zeus obliged with plague and hunger and finally to extract a protracted revenge Minos demanded a living sacrifice every nine years. The subsequent mythological episode of Theseus and Ariadne is known well enough not to need repeating. These insistent Cretan themes, bulls, kings and gods are all set in place in the mythological antecedents to Minos. Minos is fathered either by Asterius, a king whose name means the ruler of the stars or by Zeus who, in the form of a white bull abducts Europa, mother to Minos. However, this double fathership may have roots in a form of divine kingship for according to the Odyssey Asterius spoke with Zeus every nine years and received his laws straight from Zeus himself. The reappearance of the number nine is not coincidental. Homer refers to the Cretan nine-year king, retributive sacrifices were paid every nine years and Asterius the star-king speaks with Zeus the law-giver every nine years. It is even likely that every ninth year the bull games took on a particular importance since Crete resolved the age-old problem of the mismatch between the lunar and solar cycles by the addition of an intercalary thirteenth month in three years out of every eight making the ninth year, the ennaeteris the beginning of a new cycle. When he died, Asterius gave his kingdom to Minos, who promptly banished his brothers making himself the sole king. Curiously the offspring of Pasiphae

THE BREATH OF ISIS

and her cursed bull-lust is called Asterion. When Minos refused to sacrifice the best white bull to Poseidon, preferring to choose another kind of bull instead, he courted the wrath of the god who being denied his chosen epiphany, claimed his own revenge. This mythos does not have the making of a matriarchal paradise but it does present a fascinating line of research. What happened to the nine-year king at the end his limited reign? What was the purpose of the bull games? Finally, what did Cretan priestesses do? The answer will not be simple. Perhaps it is already apparent that, we need to ask more questions, to remain insatiably curious about the past, and to be mindful of the grave error of projecting a modern mind-set where it does not belong. So, as you can see, I was more than happy to speak on the subject of the priestess. However, I have always felt that an intellectual atmosphere is an inadequate, even irrelevant vehicle for such occasions. The Mysteries function only through engagement and participation, hearing yet another talk provides no insight into the living dynamics inherent in such psycho-spiritual processes. So, I planned to offer not a lecture but an experience. I invited four priestesses to share the platform with me. Unusually we were to stand on stage in a huge auditorium. The audience were seated in the hall and all presentations were delivered from the stage. I spoke from a position in front of the blue velvet curtains. Behind the curtains and unseen by the audience there were four shrines each attended by a priestess.

I delivered my talk which was in effect a brief biography. My role culminated in an oracle and then the curtains behind me opened to reveal five shrines. Four priestesses stood each behind their own shrine and in turn invoked one of the Egyptian ntr, Hathor, Nuit, Sekhmet-Bast and Nephthys. Each priestess had created a personal shrine. My own shrine was of course to Isis. I next invited anyone in the audience to come to the stage and receive a blessing or personal oracle. When I had planned the event in my mind, I thought that a few brave souls might break rank and ignore the public gaze to go

THE LIGHT OF ISIS

to one of the priestesses for oracular words. However, to my utter amazement the first row of the audience stood up without a second thought and were then followed by most of the audience who formed a silent line at the side of the stage. Where I had imagined that a few individuals might seek the shrine of their choice, instead the entire company began at the shrine nearest to the side of the stage and presented themselves to each priestess in turn. I recognized some of the participants, a few were friends, others were familiar faces but for the most part these people were unknown to me. I stood at the centre of the stage attending to my own altar and when the first member of the audience reached me, he simply fell to his knees, this was most unexpected then others did the same too.

Where do I begin to explain the dynamics of all this? When the priestess is wrapped in the embrace of the goddess, the two identities merge into one. It is not an intellectual pretence, not a trick of the light, not a flight of fancy but an epiphany usually reserved for sacred precincts. I had not expected this in a public place and I was as surprised as anyone. Once again, I find myself lost for words. The memory of the occasion is bright in my mind, but words will not convey the intensity of the experience to a reader. I can only speak for myself in my capacity as a Priestess of Isis. As each person stood before me, words flowed like water: eloquent and simple, immediate and pertinent. On reflection, perhaps a hundred people crossed the stage receiving the blessings. It may have been more, it may have been less, I have no way of knowing. As the time passed, I became aware chanting from the back of the hall, it did not impinge on my consciousness at that time. Finally, the last person crossed the stage and the curtains closed, I practically collapsed, I could hardly stand now that the power was withdrawn from me. I went home exhausted and amazed little knowing that I had stirred up a hornet's nest. I discovered later that the chanting at the back of the hall was a deliberate protest, it included certain people who really should have known better!

THE BREATH OF ISIS

Over the next few days, I received an interesting postbag. Every letter, with one exception, contained words of joy and thankfulness. A single correspondent pointed out the error of my ways, it was unthinkable that anyone should drop to their knees before another, even worse because men had been seen to drop to their knees before women, such political incorrectness was intolerable! Indeed, had my plans really been known before hand, I would have been advised instead to create a circle and chant the praises of the goddess in a non-hierarchical inclusive way! Moreover, our priestesses, 'were too beautiful to be role models for ordinary women.' I learned my lesson, I never took Mystery School dynamics into a public arena again.

Time passed, I licked my wounds and retreated back into my group, but nothing ever stands still. I received an invitation to go to America and give a seminar at a centre in Denver. The way was opened for me, I would stay with a friend in Boulder. My life was in turmoil once again. The opposition between serving divinity and serving my husband was a palpable reality. Even as I write the words, I am struck by the stupidity inherent in them. My husband, once a wiling traveller in magical worlds had reached a dead end, visible to no-one but himself. He was transfixed, pinned down by the weight of his own unrecognized and unresolved personal issues. The emotional and psychological baggage from his early life oppressed him like a ball and chain dragging at his every step. It oppressed us all too. Instead of laying down his early conditioning like an unwanted set of clothes belonging to someone else, he persisted in his attempt to impose dark, catholic, punitive values on us all.

The details of our domestic conflict are unseemly but instructive. The inner processes of magic will strip away everything unwanted for soul-service. In this on-going process of realignment, there is only continuous dying to the old and re-birthing of the new. Resistance brings its own pain. Israel Regardie and Dion Fortune both stressed the importance of psychotherapy as a necessary companion for magical practitioners. In the structured confines

THE LIGHT OF ISIS

of a Mystery School, it is easier to inculcate such teaching. Today when magic is worn like a fashion accessory and picked up from books written by people without lineage, the flotsam and jetsam of magical vocabulary is gathered as if it were treasure. But the treasure rests on the sea-bed far below out of reach and out of sight. Will you equip yourself to dive deep into waters unseen and unknown or will you be content to play upon the surface? Without the gift of psychological insight and spiritual depth, the recitation of magical words is no more than meaningless mumbo-jumbo. My husband in whom I had placed such hope developed neither insight nor depth and for him the words became meaningless mumbo-jumbo. He wanted only an orderly house and a safe career path, this was his refuge. I needed to walk The Path of The Mysteries, there could be no refuge for me other than the path itself. The conflict at the heart of my life never left me for a moment, neither by day or night. I was often ill and always stressed. I was a bore to my friends to whom I turned for support. I tried always to mend what was broken; I did not want to see that it could not be mended. The trip to the States was a welcome relief in the unremitting battle-zone of my domestic life.

I had expected to give a workshop, spend some time being a tourist, have a break and return home. Expectations are rarely met. The trip took on a life of its own which bore no resemblance to my preconceived notions. I arrived in Boulder to discover that my workshop was about to be cancelled, the bookings had been poor. I was not unduly disappointed, I could relax and just be a tourist, or so I thought. My friend Bonnie took me shopping in Bolder. Its main street, Pearl Street was like an extended emporium of spiritual wares. It was another Glastonbury set far away. It was all a pleasing delight to me. We popped in and out of book shops, strolled into shops selling beautiful Tibetan artefacts, and talking all the way exchanged news views and simple girlie chatter. It was all a welcome break. We stopped to gaze in at the window of a crystal

THE BREATH OF ISIS

shop and like any other shopper went inside. But as we crossed the threshold, I experienced something close to a mild electrical shock, not painful but strong enough to make me pay attention. The store was packed with huge crystals. As we wandered around, I could not help but notice a framed papyrus picture of Sekhmet on the wall behind the counter. Then I saw a bookcase packed with books on Egypt. The titles replicated my own almost perfectly, *Hathor Rising* was there and numerous books by both Isha and R.A. Schwaller de Lubicz. My curiosity was aroused so I spoke to the sales assistant. I discovered that owner was out for the day, and I was encouraged to return the next day. I already felt a sense of connection with the woman whose interests were so close to my own. So, in readiness for the next day, I decided to take her a small personal gift. I had a few copies of *The Veil of Isis* with me. Our magazine was produced for group members and extra copies were distributed to friends. Although it was produced without commercial expectations, the quality of the work was extremely high. I thought it would make a fitting gift for a new friend, so the next day Bonnie and I set out for the shop. We met in the shop and introductions over we set out for lunch. I instinctively felt an instant kinship with my new friend. Lorraine too was a writer currently engaged on a novel which was to emerge some years later. The three of us had lots to talk about so at a suitably quiet moment I reached into my bag and drew out my gift, placing the magazine on the table. Lorraine looked at it and said in a tone that I still remember, "*I have that.*" I was literally dumbstruck. How could this be? I was in another continent, I was in the company of a woman who until that moment was unknown to me, yet she already had one of the few copies of a magazine produced by our small group in the suburbs in the UK. It turned out that she had received her copy from a stateside friend who had received her copy from an English friend who had received her copy from one of our group members. The one copy had changed hands making its way right across the Atlantic. Isis has a way of knitting

THE LIGHT OF ISIS

together that which She wishes to be joined. This synchronicity alone was enough to lighten my heart and justify my trip. My dear friend Bonnie spent much time talking with me. She was wise and patient. My visit slotted easily into the timetable of their lives, we shopped, ate out and one evening I went to The Sunshine Ranch a community where both Bonnie and her husband were involved. On this particular day Bonnie had been working in the kitchens so I went to help by clearing up in the dining hall at the end of the evening meal. When I arrive on site, I read a notice in the lobby stating that Jean Houston's Mystery School was in week-long residence. Now this was an astonishing coincidence as I was already familiar with Jean's wonderful books, and we had used *The Passion of Isis and Osiris* as a text-book in the group.

The evening meal was in full swing and the dinner hall was packed and filled with noisy conversation. What excitement. I remember that I was introduced to Jean. My introduction which I think Bonnie organised, felt a little intrusive as Jean sat at dinner among her students. Nevertheless, I was thrilled. When the dinner hall began to empty, I began my task and began to clear away the tables. Finally, the hall was practically empty except for one table with a few last stragglers. I could not help but engage them in conversation. They were genuinely interested to hear that I also worked in Mystery School tradition. One of the women suggested that I might enquire about joining the group however briefly. Now I knew that this is not a sensible request yet even as she spoke the words, I palpably felt a dynamic power well up from nowhere and envelop me. One woman was so determined that I should stay that she volunteered to speak on my behalf. However, conversation at the table was not united and a third woman made her objections clear, quite rightly too. I knew I was flying the face of all accepted protocol. My willing sponsor disappeared on her self-appointed errand and returned shortly to tell me that she had spoken with Jean's second-in-command. I continued to clear away the dinner

THE BREATH OF ISIS

things but as I did so I became increasingly aware of a pressure mounting within myself: that same feeling once more, always reserved moments of magical intensity, always unbidden, always insistent. I finished clearing away in the dining hall. I was fully aware of the irregularity of my request, seeking permission to join a Mystery School in full session breaks every unwritten rule. But the feelings were overwhelming. Someone came to fetch me and I found myself speaking with Diana. I have no memory of what I said but my outrageous request was not turned down but passed directly to Jean. I remember being told later that in considering her response, Jean had said, *"there is no such thing as an accident,"* so despite my irregular request, I was to be allowed to join the first session with the proviso that I could be asked to leave before the second more intense part of the evening commenced. I readily agreed. Arrangements were hastily made with the organisers; I did not need a room for the night as this was to be a night of shared temple sleep. A blanket and pillow were provided. I was allowed briefly into the ceremonial hall to place my bedding on the floor among the others. It is difficult to convey the pace at which this all this unfolded. I had arrived to clear tables, less than an hour later, I found myself standing in a throng of students waiting for the ritual events to commence. Everything had happened so quickly, I had no special clothes to change into, I did not even have a toothbrush, though Bonnie drove, home and returned later with fresh clothes for the next day. I stood amongst Jean's students, a stranger in an established group-mind. Those standing close-by smiled, some spoke and enquired curiously about me. We all waited together in a lobby which served as an antechamber. When Jean, Diana and Peggy were ready, the doors to the main hall were opened and at the threshold we each crossed from the mundane to the sacred. At the doorway, a woman stood holding a bowl of water waiting to offer ceremonial purification as we each passed through. She was the woman who had voiced her opposition to my joining earlier

THE LIGHT OF ISIS

that evening. When I stood before her, she splashed water into my face making her personal view crystal clear. She regarded me as an intruder, I understood her position completely, I didn't know what I was doing there either! The group passed through the glass doors at the far end of the hall out into the gardens beyond. It was a beautiful warm summer evening. Once outside, we gathered around the small lake in the grounds. Each person briefly spoke, offering up a clear motive and aspiration and then when we had all spoken, we moved back into the hall and the next part of the evening began. It was quite unlike the Mystery School atmosphere I was used to, here was an entirely different environment. Jean's participants had come together for an intensive week, most were strangers to one another. It was a large group, I think in excess of fifty participants. By contrast I was used to working in small groups with familiar faces. The first part of the evening was noisy and full of laughter. There were dynamic group games intended to encourage spontaneous interaction, release inhibitions and free the emotions. I remember a small group dressed in amusing costumes which had clearly evolved from activities earlier in the week. They clowned around and all this good humoured fun made me think of ancient festivals where loosening the tight corsets of everyday life preceded solemnities. As this part of the evening drew to its close, I wondered what my fate might be. I had agreed to leave at the close of the first session if asked. When I was told that I might stay the night with the group, I was overjoyed.

The atmosphere changed, the festivities were over. An altar had been established at its centre of the hall, decorated with offerings from each individual, it expressed the hopes and intentions of the group mind. Encircling the altar and spiralling out to fill the room, everyone's bedding was laid side by side. Another part of the hall had been separated off, marked out by a wall of plants to create a small enclosed area. I was told that this small space was to be held by dance, performed with the specific intention of generating

THE BREATH OF ISIS

energy which Jean might draw upon as the night progressed. This too was something new to me. I was asked if I willing to share in the rota and my name was placed on the last shift between 1 – 2am in the early morning. As the second session opened the atmosphere shifted again to one of shared focus and individual awareness. I recall that a young woman invited me to share in energy work with her. She briefly explained that she had developed her own approach, I just needed to visualise the images that she would describe. This is a pretty standard approach, and I am used to working with the energies which surround and interpenetrate the body. However, I rarely choose to open my energies to others, even if asked. On several occasions my equilibrium has been quite destabilised by well-meaning but incompetent invasions of self-professed experts, so it was with some resistance that I agreed to participate. But as soon as she began to work, I knew that my fears were groundless. She began to call up beautiful images in quick succession, "*a snowdrop breaking through, a white horse running, a blue jewel, sun on the horizon.*" With each image she just placed her hands within my energy field moving swiftly and with deliberation as if she were fixing these fragments of beauty invisible to me. The effect was just exquisite, I can add no more but to thank her and hope that others have benefited from her unique approach too.

Several places of particular focus were established around the perimeter of the hall, each marked by its name written on paper. I do not remember all the names. I know that I passed some time at a station set up to share Tarot. As the time passed, I found myself entering a deep and private state, I had much on my mind, my domestic life was in a prolonged crisis. I circumnambulated the hall, creating my own personal ritual, passing others in small groups scattered around the hall. A station had been set up: *The Dark Night of the Soul*. I sat there a long while in silent contemplation. Meanwhile Jean had established herself in a small side room. Everyone would have the opportunity to speak privately with her.

THE LIGHT OF ISIS

I believe she called this the gifting time. I put my name on the list and meanwhile passed the time in private contemplation. When my time came, I was ushered into the room by Diana. Immediately I found myself sitting opposite to Jean. She asked at once why I had come. In a sentence I told her of my domestic agony, and she asked if anyone else was involved, I replied truthfully, 'No.' She closed her eyes and in her unforgettable voice said, "*I see you moving deeper into mystery.*" The floodgates opened I began to burble, trying to express so much in so short a time. I spoke about my work in The Mysteries and even about the magazine *The Veil of Isis* and she remembered when my dear friend Vivienne had approached her husband Robert Masters with a request to write for us. Then suddenly there were no more words, she held up her hands, palms opened and I did the same matching mine with hers. It was as if the space between our hands was filled by Isian energy. It was a moment of instant, seemingly effortless but sublime contact. Earlier in the evening, Jean had reminded us that in this gifting time, she sat in quite another state of consciousness. I knew it was true. She brought salve, it seemed, from another dimension. This was not a consultation but an encounter with spiritual presence in shared silence. When the bridge between us dissolved, it was time to leave. Like many others, what I had voiced came to pass in the fullness of time. Jean sat hour after hour without tiring, women danced to feed the energy of the sacred place. After my gifting time, I needed to rest without sleeping since my time for dance had not yet arrived. I found my sleeping place and made myself comfortable, and realised I had unknowingly placed my bedding beside the woman who had served as doorkeeper at the start of the evening. I kept myself awake despite wanting to drift into sleep. I had much on my mind but wanted to use the time more profitably, I had no idea of the next nodal point needed in my own group. So, I put my mind into a receptive state and actively rested.

My dance-watch finally arrived, and I got up. The dancing area

THE BREATH OF ISIS

was a small space set within a row of tall plants lined up to make an enclosure. A beautiful young woman was still dancing. I think we were supposed to follow one another sharing the time between us but her dancing was so exquisite and delicate that I could not help but enter the space to dance with and not after her. She in turn was clearly happy to dance with me. This memory of our shared dancing remains sweet in my mind after all these years. I experienced something quite unique. Whether the space was literally replete with the living energy so generously donated by the dancing of others, or whether we created a unique energy of our own, I cannot say, but as we danced streamers of light almost took visible form. As we reached up, hands upraised in complete harmony and rhythm, we gathered up ribbons of energy sharing them between us like bright garlands. In our shared silence, we delighted equally in the experience, scooping up this living light, showering the space with its bright particles, bathing ourselves in its radiance. At the closing, our mutual bows, were both to each other but also to the unique experience of the space. I have never touched this graciousness since. This profound experience with dance reminded me of the priestesses of Hathor who danced not for themselves but in the name of the divine. Today dance is a secular even a sexualised statement of self-expression. Without detracting one iota from the many pleasures and delights of dance, it is rare to glimpse into another dimension of the interface between movement and living energy. Though we have become familiar with ideas about the energy field which surrounds the body, these have been developed into mainly therapeutic uses. Movement and energy have been combined in Tai Chi and Chi-Gung but dance has become separated from its etheric-energetic-spiritual framework. Sacred dance is neither performance, nor pleasure, neither artistic nor personal, yet it is all of these placed in the service of Life itself in its fullest interpretation as the great encompassing vessel that holds and embraces all. The contemporary dancer Suraya Hilal,

THE LIGHT OF ISIS

has instinctively, even perhaps unconsciously made her way back to the temple tradition. She synthesises many traditions including yogic movement and Tai Chi energy work with dance to create a unique experience of sacred beauty in motion. It seems to me that she has restored a forgotten connection between dance and life-force thereby creation, returning dance to its sacred function. It has always been my belief that the priestesses of Hathor danced to extend, enliven and exalt through a sacred understanding of movement as the conductor of sublime and ecstatic energies. The experience at Sunshine Ranch and my encounter with the work of Suraya Hilal much later in 2013 tells me that this is still possible. After my dancing was done, it was late. The hall was filled with sleeping forms. It was time for everyone to sleep. Jean emerged from her own space where she had finally completed her personal gifting sessions. With a single gesture, Jean blessed the silent room in the name of Aesculapius and the night was opened to temple sleep. I too hoped to incubate a dream.

The morning began as most mornings do with the necessary domestic rituals of the day. After breakfast we gathered once more in the hall, bedding had been replaced by chairs and the session opened with Jean asking for any dreams from the night. About a dozen people had dreams to share and Jean called them to sit at the font of the hall. I am familiar with dream work, but Jean's insight and analysis was piercing. As the session proceeded, most dreams yielded their meaning, but one dream was insistent, the dreamer was my sleeping neighbour, the same woman who had so generously splashed water in my face the evening before. She had dreamed about something being stuck in her throat. The dream gave up its purpose soon enough, things that stuck in the throat, words unspoken, emotions transfixed. Under Jean's insightful questions, the nature of this obstruction became clearer, much was tied up with negative conditioning at the hands of a male dominated culture, and even perhaps at the hands of individual men. It is impossible to describe

THE BREATH OF ISIS

the intense atmosphere as a genuine catharsis unfolds following its own interior momentum. Like a house of cards cascading, honesty and truthfulness dissolve long held blocks as water breaks over a dam. Jean pursued her quarry, the dream's full meaning, with the skill of a surgeon peeling back further layers, gently but deliberately. The group had but one man in it, Jean asked if he was willing to stand as a surrogate for all that had passed at the hands of men while also asking if our dreamer was willing to embrace him in the same spirit. This description may sound trite, even perhaps false to those unused to the dynamics of the psyche unleashed at full pelt. It is impossible to describe the impact of their shared embrace, but we all knew that some deep hidden inaccessible block had been lifted. The encounter begun so innocently in dream, now seemed complete. But Jean checked again, asking the woman was the obstruction gone and to everyone's surprise, she replied, "No." Asked to describe what remained, the woman thought with some amazement on her own face, and replied that it felt like a crucifix rammed deep in her throat. To gain further insight, Jean asked the woman to stand against a nearby pillar with arms outstretched in the crucifix position. The woman's distress was intense and painfully obvious as her whole being searched itself for answers. It was at this point that something very strange began to happen to me. Quite involuntarily my body began to shake and rock, I tried to control myself, but it was not possible. My breathing shifted becoming more rapid. I had no idea what was happening to me. Jean who was some few rows ahead of me clearly spotted everything and asked me to step forwards. She speedily introduced me to the group as a priestess of Isis from England and then without warning just asked me to take over. I have no idea what I thought because at times like this, there are no thoughts whatsoever but, 'something' else kicks in. Jean led me towards the woman, standing outstretched going through her own crucifixion. Immediately the Isis in me flared into life and I found myself circling the woman, almost dancing around

THE LIGHT OF ISIS

her, spontaneously weaving her life force in my hands unknotting it, reconnecting, restructuring it. Jean just quietly spoke offering almost a commentary to the group, *"the weaving of Isis,"* she said, I have no idea if I spoke though I think not. I do remember that earlier in the week I had fallen off a bike and badly grazed both my palms. As I opened my palms to mirror her outstretched hands, my grazes took on a symbolic significance now so appropriate. I have no idea how long the incident lasted, probably not more than several minutes. At its close I crossed my hands over my breast, it is something I have always done instinctively. On reflection, the gesture probably closes the aura. I returned to my seat, Jean resumed control and turning to the woman still standing in front of the pillar, she asked her previous question once again. By her admission, the blockage was now dissolved. Tears flowed and the sense of release was palpable. Jean gave the group a much needed break and my neighbour, earlier so opposed to my presence, came to me and we hugged and laughed and rejoiced. I too had gained what I needed, my own dreaming had produced the gentle realisation that I might usefully investigate The Muses. Now this was not a Mystery Stream I had ever dipped into and at the time, I knew almost nothing about these figures. My present reflections however tell me that it is a rich and deep source for inspiration and transformation. Indeed, the Nine Muses offer a full curriculum to anyone with the eyes to see it. My work has always centred upon the Egyptian tradition and it has left me little time to explore other equally valid systems. Nevertheless, I can recognize the hallmarks of esotericism in the Greek Muses. I see the universal signposts that unite seemingly different traditions. In a fascinating footnote to history, Diodoris states in Book I.18 that Osiris first recruited the nine Muses, along with the Satyrsor, the male dancers, while passing through Ethiopia, before embarking on a tour of all Asia and Europe, teaching the arts of cultivation wherever he went. This comment links both these great civilizations and their inherent

THE BREATH OF ISIS

Mystery traditions which provided the seeds of culture, learning and all the civilizing arts. Pausanias records a tradition giving the Muses two ancestral generations. Commonly the Muses are considered to be the offspring of Zeus and Mnemosyne but they are also considered to be the first being daughters of Uranus and Gaia, the heavenly father in union with the earth mother Gaia. The earth mother was worshipped at Delphi from prehistoric times, but it was later rededicated to Apollo who among his many names was called Apollon Mousagetés, Apollo Muse-leader. This role was later shared by Hermes a Hellenised form of Thoth, the lord of learning and wisdom. The Muses are, Calliope, Clio, Euterpe, Thalia, Melpomene, Terpsichore, Erato, Polyhymnia, and Urania. Each is designated to an area of learning and creativity symbolised by an emblem. Calliope (epic poetry) carries a writing tablet, Clio (history) carries a scroll and books, Erato (love/erotic poetry) carries a lyre and a crown of roses, Euterpe (lyric poetry) carries a flute, Melpomene (tragedy) wears a tragic mask, Polyhymnia (sacred poetry) wears a veil, Terpsichore (choral dance and song) carries a lyre, Thalia (comedy) wears a comic mask and Urania (astronomy) carries a pair of compasses and a celestial globe. As the embodiments of metrical speech, mousike, the nine Muses together informed the shape of learning itself. The first Greek book on astronomy by Thales was written in dactylic hexameters as were many of the works by the pre-Socratic philosophers. The spoken word shaped the formation of information, mousike, the gift of the Muses and the child of memory is parent to other disciplines. Both Plato and the Pythagoreans saw philosophy for example as a descendent of mousike, the spoken word. *The Histories of Herodotus* were divided by later Alexandrian editors into nine books, named after the Muses. When Pythagoras arrived in Croton, his first advice was to build a shrine to the Muses at the centre of the city, to promote civic harmony and learning. Pythagoras had already spent over twenty years in the Egyptian temple tradition and he was without a doubt both an initiate of a Kemetic Mystery school and the founder of a Graeco-Egyptian school of metaphysics.

The word mousa means art or poetry but also includes the feminised sources of inspiration personified as the divine goddesses, the Muses. In classical times, 'to carry a mousa', meant to excel in the arts. The concept has remained for the artist is ever searching for his muse, either a source of inspiration or through the inspired presence of a real woman, often with unhappy even tragic outcomes. The word has crept into our language almost unobserved. A museum is derived from a mousaion, a shrine to the Muses, a cult place of the Muses, and a place for the public display of knowledge. Even the word music is derived from mousika the original word for inspired metrical speech. To, 'muse upon' something is to think deeply while waiting on inspiration. We have managed to relegate the esoteric to the backwaters or to the realm of the eccentric. So deeply are we ingrained in monotheism that we cannot find the divine in anything but a single mirror, this is our collective and individual loss. Solon the great Athenian law giver, who incidentally was among those who travelled to Egypt in search of its wisdom, described the Muses as, 'the key to the good life.' He arranged for poetry and the invocation of the Muses to accompany the introduction of political reform and like his contemporaries he believed that the Muses would inspire people to do their best. To live without a muse, to be eu a-mousoi. Amusement carries the meaning of a mindless distraction, utterly pleasant but also without intrinsic meaning. To be amused is to find satisfaction in the superficial, in the witty banter of the mentally dextrous or the clever contrivance of the moment. According to Socrates to live eu a-mousoi is to live without divine inspiration and the higher insights that accompany it. The difference in life experienced described by Socrates is perhaps that expressed by J.K Rowling as the difference between the magician and the muggle. Invocation, a magical use of speech has been lost to the mainstream where all the norms reign, yet many famed authors have invoked the help of the Muses when writing poetry, hymns, or epic history. This is nothing more or less than a call for help, a request for divine assistance, an invitation to work in partnership with inspiration itself. Robert Graves reinvigorated the idea of the Goddess-Muse as the *White Goddess* by drawing upon native traditions of inspired poetry. The revelatory significance of the Greek Muses was not lost upon later generations with the eye to see. Some enlightenment figures sought to re-establish a 'Cult of the Muses' in the 18th century and a French Masonic lodge took the title the nine sisters, Les Neuf Soeurs. Now this fragment of a wider Greek esoterism is highly instructive, the goddesss-figures are not objects of worship but nodal images for personal processes of internalisation and assimilation. The Muses are the daughters of Zeus, the royal impregnator. Without the fertilisation of memory, learning is impossible. In an age of public speaking, oratory and oral memory, the spoken word assumed a social even a political significance. This classical requirement was translated into the renaissance Ars Memoria, the Art of Memory. As the deeper meaning expressed through the nine muses becomes clearer, so it is easy to recognise that this too is another technology of consciousness, a sacred psychology, an esoteric system of holistic development which is always a sanctified journey. The event that grew from the seed planted in my mind during temple sleep of the Aesculapeum manifested as a group weekend. Among other things, an altar displaying the relevant emblems was created to each of the Muses and the altars were arranged in a large circle. I took the role of Mnemosyne, the Mother of the Mysteries and wore a dress with long sashes of coloured cloths. In an orchestrated dance, each of the nine various priests and priestesses to the Muses took hold of a length of cloth so that when I turned at the centre, all the colours of learning were unfolded and revealed. It was a very creative weekend. For me it did not pack the punch of the Kemetic tradition which is sharp and clear like a laser but this later modus operandi was

THE LIGHT OF ISIS

perfectly workable. This new tradition seized three of our group with such force that they became infused with its inherent creativity and formed their own group, The Order of Minerva in the West which I believe may still be in existence today.

I count myself so fortunate to have been blessed by this fortuitous meeting with Jean and the truly magical transformations she facilitates. I stayed with the group until the afternoon tea break and then took my leave certain in the knowledge that whatever had led me there, by whatever curious means had been fulfilled. I remain thankful for this brief encounter with Jean's extraordinary and unique work. I cannot begin to fathom the mysteries of a universe which sometimes seems to rejoice in the creation of astounding coincidence, the knitting together of everyday experience, the impossible and the improbable drawn together like the magnetically charged particles of a secret jigsaw, arranged to amaze and delight as if to personal request.

NOTES

1. Israel Regardie: writer, occultist, mage, therapist. He was born in London to a Russian immigrant Jewish family. He began a correspondence with Aleister Crowley and became his secretary. He wrote *The Tree of Life, a Guide to Magick, A Garden of Pomegranates* and a biography of Crowley, *The Eye in the Triangle*. He also published the rituals of The Hermetic Order of The Golden Dawn. His relationship with Crowley led him to regard psychotherapy as an essential component of esoteric training.

2. Jean Houston: scholar, lecturer, author, philosopher and teacher. Together with her husband Robert Masters, Jean co-founded The Foundation for Mind Research. She has advised political leaders, Unicef and since 2003 she has worked with the United Nations Development Group training leaders in the new field of Social Artistry. Over a long career, Jean has worked closely with many other cultural luminaries including her teacher Margaret Mead and the mythographer Joseph Campbell.

3. Robert Masters: pioneering thinker, teacher, writer, academic and researcher. Masters is recognized as a leading pioneer in consciousness research and human potential. John Lennon's song *Mind Games* is based on the book of the same name written by Jean and Robert together. His book *Sekhmet –Psycho-Spiritual exercises of the Fifth Way* grew from his exploration of ancient Egyptian psycho-spiritual practices.

CHAPTER EIGHT

THE MYSTERIES OF ISIS

There is no comparison between contemporary religion and the ancient Mystery religions. Your experience of church, if any, even your conceptions of God will not assist you in grasping the essence of the Mystery Tradition. It is not easy to make a bridge from the present to the ancient past by drawing upon the religious understanding that you have imbibed, it is best abandoned so that you meet the ancient Mysteries as a tabula rasa, a blank page. The word Mystery is derived from the Greek word myein meaning, 'to close' or, 'to shut,' usually with reference to the eyes or mouth. This provides the first clue. Typically it has a multi-levelled meaning. The obvious and literal meaning is that of shutting the mouth, in other words of keeping silent. This is turn has certain implications and is open to misunderstanding. Keeping a silence is most often interpreted to mean keeping a secret and the very idea of secrecy give rise to all sorts of confabulations. However, the gesture of silence conveyed in the image of the child Harpocrates with a finger raised to the lips is not one of conspiratorial secrecy but one of mystical silence. The difference is profound. The meaning of silence is best conveyed through simple allegory; can you convey the sound of a wonderful symphony to a person who is deaf? Can you share the image of an unfolding flower with a person who is blind? Can you describe the scent of a rose to a child? In these instances, it is impossible to convey the quality of experience to someone not

THE MYSTERIES OF ISIS

equipped to grasp the experience. Words alone cannot describe what cannot be described or convey what cannot be heard. There is no secret, there is no conspiracy of silence merely an unbridgeable chasm in experience and receptivity. The deaf cannot hear, the blind cannot see, the immature cannot understand. The phrase, 'for those with the eyes to see,' is commonly used in the vocabulary of the Mysteries, the meaning should now be apparent. The ancient gesture of silence remains at the heart of the Mystery Tradition, its significance is preserved in the modern injunction – To Dare, to Know, to Will and to Be Silent. There is nothing in contemporary exoteric religion that calls for such silence where all is a matter of shared and external experience, passively hearing sermons plays no part in ancient esoteric Mystery religion.

The modus operandi of the Mysteries, both ancient and modern is that of identification or more precisely, a re-identification through a dramatised connection with a transcendent archetype expressed through the divine personage of a deity. In this way, the localised self, contained and expressed through the personality may make contact with universal and transcendent forces of life. In time and through sufficient process, the life force within the personality become aligned, opened and finally infused with the greater, richer, deeper and universalised life forces expressed through the divinised centre of consciousness. This is the Way of the Mysteries. It should be increasingly clear that this esoteric perspective is closer to depth psychology than contemporary religion. Exoteric forms of religion are ostensibly external, comfortably social, inherently conformist and invariably conservative. As templates for social and even political cohesion, religious belief achieves the goal of creating moral and ethical standards of behaviour which bind and blend diverse human beings into recognisable groupings. The process of re-identification here is that of joining the group and becoming a recognisable part of an established identity easily recognized by its norms, beliefs, values, even clothes and diet. Exoteric faith seeks

THE BREATH OF ISIS

to answer fundamental questions of life and especially death with promises of salvation and reward in the life-to-come. There is no doubt that this is a powerful appeal in the equation laid out in the name of exoteric religion, namely that faith equals salvation. This is not the Way of the Mysteries.

By contrast, the esoteric perspective shares recognizable territory with that shared by depth psychology, but esotericism is not psychological method, it rests on a different philosophical basis. It might however be appropriate to speak of esotericism as a marriage between depth psychology and the personal quest to attain wisdom since the word, 'philosophy' means the love of wisdom. This equation is so different from that proffered by exoteric religion that it should be perfectly apparent that there is no commonality, other than the fact that it is possible to move from an exoteric perspective into an esoteric perspective. It is however not viable to transit from the esoteric to the exoteric, the greater cannot be confined to the lesser. Now that academia is taking a scholarly look at esoteric current in history and culture, the definition of esotericism proposed by Antoine Faivre has gained a working acceptance.

The differences between the esoteric and the exoteric paths only continues to diverge and deepen since each holds a distinct view of what it means to be fully human. Christianity, the faith of the West for some two thousand years offers a view of the fallen human, exiled from the Garden of Eden, contaminated by original sin and in absolute need of redemption through salvation. In this closed system faith must be placed outside the confines of the self which is, as defined by this belief structure inherently incapable of self-revelation despite being made in the image of god, a curious contradiction I have always thought. Christianity is a relative newcomer to the world, there were and are, other views of the human condition. Moreover, it is possible that Christianity might have been primed to become a new Mystery religion but

THE MYSTERIES OF ISIS

early on it was moulded by the hand of Paul and in fact became Pauline Christianity and was then set to become a state religion not an esoteric experience. Christianity functions perfectly well as a mystical apotheosis and for those who have truly birthed the Christ within, it serves both the demands of depth process and the attainment of wisdom. But this esoteric path of spiritual awakening is the path of the few not the many.

It is with these few thoughts in mind that it is possible to now return to the ancient Mysteries of Isis and Osiris. The story has already been told, but it must be lived before it can come to life. The ritual and formalised presentation of this story is the vehicle which carries the participant forward on the path of re-identification with its two different stages as the questing Isis and the resurrected Osiris. The Mysteries of Osiris have been described as plays or pageants but this is to miss the essential purpose of sacred drama which is to effect the essential re-identification of self. In Egypt, we find two parallel sets of rites, the public and the priestly, the exoteric and the esoteric, the arcane and the mundane, both took the form of enacted dramas. Herodotus clearly attended mystery plays which concerned the life, death and resurrection of Osiris. This theme was presented in wholly human terms for the populace at large who were invited to empathise with the life of the good god, to mourn his murder, to search for his body as Isis herself had done and finally to rejoice at his resurrection. The cycle of his life was celebrated throughout the year in exactly the same way that the Christian calendar revolves around the birth, death and resurrection of Christ. His festivals were universally celebrated through every nome (district) in the land. The month of Khoiakh was dedicated to him. All the symbolic enactments of the month displayed the theme of rebirth. A hollow effigy of Osiris was filled with barley and sand. It was watered and placed in the sun. The Osiris figure from the previous year was raised from its sepulchre and placed on sycamore twigs. The Djed column was raised representing the resurrection of

THE BREATH OF ISIS

Osiris. This level of enactment was simple and populist. At Abydos the public rites were full bloodied. We have a wonderful account of the proceedings from Ikhernofret an officer who took the key role of Horus and described the drama on a memorial stone. We need to imagine the intense activity as people arrived from all over the country prepared to take sides and physically fight for their own team. Eight acts took place over seven days. In the first act the jackal headed god Upwawet prepared the way for the appearance of Osiris. "*I celebrated the procession of Upwawet,*" says Ikhernofret. Osiris appeared in the second act in a sacred barque. However, the voyage was duly interrupted by the enemies of the god, dressed as Set and his cohorts; battle took place. "*I repulsed those who were hostile to the Neshmet barque, and I overthrew the enemies of Osiris,*" says Ikhernofret once more. Both Ikhernofret and Herodotus, who witnessed the same events some fifteen hundred years later are silent about the details of the death of Osiris which took place in the third act. In the fourth act, Thoth searched for the body. In the fifth act, the body was prepared for burial. As Horus, Ikhernofret procured the sacred barque, a ship shaped sledge built from sycamore and acacia decorated with gold, silver and lapis lazuli. Inside he installed the statue of the god. The burial procession made its way across the desert. "*I equipped the barque, Shining in Truth of the Lord of Abydos, with a chapel; I put on his beautiful regalia when he went forth to the district of Peker.*" The funeral way was again obstructed by the followers of Set. Finally in the sixth act, Osiris was placed in his tomb accompanied by the populace who marched out into the desert to watch the god being laid to rest. In the seventh act a final battle took place on a lake between the followers of Horus and the followers of Set. "*I championed Wennofer on That Day of the Great Battle, I overthrew all the enemies upon the shore of Nedyt,*" says Ikhernofret. The outcome was of course inevitable. Yet battle was joined with great gusto and men were injured. At last Osiris was restored to life amidst a triumphal procession. His

THE MYSTERIES OF ISIS

resurrection was seen to be complete. Thus were The Mysteries of Osiris celebrated at Abydos. This extraordinary mix of priesthood and populace created a seven day human drama which moved from one landscape to another using water, desert and mountains as a backdrop. Contending sides fought like a rugby scrum. The populace knew the story of Osiris, they had fought in his defence of for his enemies. Through this wild and intensely human involvement the populace came to know the stories of their gods. Through its inner form the priesthood came to know the gods.

The priested proceedings were of an altogether different nature. The drama of the death of Osiris was celebrated on the first of the month of Paschons. His resurrection was enacted on the 22nd of Thoth. In the intervals, the priesthood performed the interior ceremonies in private. By contrast to the great and often rowdy public festivities, these rites took place with solemn dignity. At Philae, the drama of the death and resurrection of Osiris was celebrated not in a week but in the space of one day. The story was described through twenty-four scenes, one for each hour of both day and night. Accordingly, the rite began on the first hour of the night at six o'clock and concluded at the same time the next day. Each hour contained its own drama. The drama moved from the death and attendant lamentations to the resurrection. The rite is depicted on the walls of the temple. Osiris is shown first in his mummy form enveloped in a funeral shroud upon a bier. The mummy is surrounded by ritual regalia, crowns, sceptres, vases containing myrrh and other fumigations. The presence of Shu, Geb, Horus, Anubis, Isis and Nephthys were represented by members of the priesthood. The drama unfolded as texts were recited in formal and solemn fashion and lamentations took place through the mediation of two priestesses. After the long lamentations the drama proceeded to its next phase. At the sixth hour a vase containing water from the Nile water was brought in. Osiris himself was often likened to Nile water. The process of resurrection began when the body of

THE BREATH OF ISIS

Osiris was sprinkled with this sacramental water. Osiris passed to heaven accompanied by his ka. The gods themselves reassembled the dismembered Osiris. First the skeleton was assembled followed next by his flesh. The soul was recalled through magnetic passes. The completed body was restored through holy water, oils and unguents. The drama proceeded. On the sixth hour of the day, the Djed pillar was raised. At midday when the sun was at its height Osiris was fully restored. The pharaoh himself brought offerings. At the twelfth hour the rite was finished, lamps were lit, the doors were opened; the god was resurrected. In 2010 I jointly facilitated a weekend seminar with my dear friend Caitlin Matthews. The weekend was based on The Mysteries of Isis and Osiris. The flyer for the course read thus:

> *This is a rare opportunity to participate in the shared enactment of The Mysteries of Isis and Osiris. These ancient Mysteries reliving the death and resurrection of Osiris stand at the source of the Western Mystery Tradition and will be of special interest to anyone working within the tradition. Embodying the great human themes of love and loss, this story speaks directly to the heart. The weekend will include group meditation, reflection and ritual as we enact the stages of loss and renewal in this classic initiatory drama. This ancient myth of triumph over death is as potent today as it was in the distant past.*
>
> *The weekend will be experiential and transformative; its gifts bring a sense of rebirth and the greening of the heart. The course opens up the fascinating world of the sacred traditions of Egypt at a time when the core of western society is being dismembered. As Osiris, the Good God, the green-faced God of death and renewal, was tricked by treachery, made vulnerable by trust, so likewise we have been betrayed by trust. The family of humanity now has unprecedented opportunity to recognise itself as never before and discover Isis, the winged Goddess of*

THE MYSTERIES OF ISIS

Ten Thousand Names, whose infinite compassion seeks out the dismembered beloved to preside over the Mysteries of Rebirth in the infinite cycle of being and becoming which makes the world new again.

The marketing had attracted some relative newcomers to the weekend, but its centre was stabilized by a core of long-standing initiates. Without such a core it is impossible to reach the depths required to seed transformation but our small assembly was blessed by good companions. It is hard to convey the difficulties of condensing so profound an experience into so short a space of time. The group does not assemble until Friday evening and it will dissolve after Sunday lunch. Yet in the space available it is necessary to effect some degree of identification with the mourning Isis, the dismembered god and finally with the triumphant newly birthed Horus – quite a tall order for a mere two days! So the shift to a different state of mind must commence in all swiftness. Meditation and invocation serve to re-orientate the inner compass away from the mundane concerns of the world and the limitations of the personality. These shared techniques also serve to create a group mind sufficient for its relatively temporary purpose. We drew upon the most accessible features of the tradition and everyone made a small clay figurine of Osiris. Sprinkled with fast growing mustards and cress seeds, a greening was visible even in the short time we were together. These represented personal hopes for renewal and new birth which everyone must find if life is not to become a stale repetition of the familiar. I too had come in search of renewal as the progress of my life had been completely stalled by circumstance.

The bond of love between two people as exemplified by Isis and Osiris was easily accessed in a beautiful session of movement and music. Without such love there will be no questing for the beloved and no endurance in the face of trial. In an extraordinary synchronicity one of our group was named Isis, it was indeed her birth name and she was recently bereaved. I was concerned that

THE BREATH OF ISIS

our focus would be too painful for her but in fact her burden of grief was lightened by the end of the weekend. The intention of the weekend was to move towards the enactment of the ritual which contained and expressed the themes we were incubating; loss, love, passing, triumph, renewal and resurrection. I had prepared a scripted ritual ahead of time based on the ancient sequences of the passage of the night drawing upon the majestic and powerful transliteration to be found in *Awakening Osiris* by Normandi Ellis. It was of course the perfect text to use, but preparing a ritual drama is far more complicated than merely copying and pasting suitable text. A ritual has its own sequencing which needs to be followed so that openings and closings are clear and serve as demarcating boundaries. The dramatis personae both physical and otherwise require to be introduced in an appropriate manner according to both the myth and the historical precedent. Then there is the delicate task of assigning roles as each person is allotted a particular part. When required heavyweight roles are assigned to more experienced participants as this is not a matter of acting out a role but of instant and meaningful re-identification plus of course the equally important role of dis-identifying with the source of transcendent consciousness when the personality must resume its conscious control. Additionally, the drama must be choreographed as necessary so that everyone understands and anticipates all cues, entrances, exits, any sequences requiring movement or particular actions. Like any other drama or play there must be a simple walk-through rehearsal so that all instructions are doubly clear. Such rehearsals are vital but need to be handled with a light touch. The scripted words are never delivered during the rehearsal as these words of power will open the gates to the numinous. It is merely a case of fixing the ritual structure in the mind. These preparations may seem absurdly theatrical when compared to the free-flowing ceremonies commonly found in other traditions. However, these are neither ceremonies of the season nor rituals of celebration but

THE MYSTERIES OF ISIS

carefully created containers to be filled by levels of living energy, both etheric and otherwise so that these increasingly subtle aspects of consciousness are blended and orchestrated in harmony with the unfolding story. Rehearsals are one thing, but the process of enactment is quite another. Words lift from the page laying bare an emotional content previously masked, the air becomes impregnated with meaning and significance as the drama unfolds, spaces left for oracular utterance become filled as the spirit of inspired speech and vision settles on various people, emotional responses arise spontaneously as words and meaning trigger memories, feelings and needs. Yet outwardly all is contained and will be held until the following and necessary debriefing session provides the chance to remember and release personal feelings, momentary insights and realisations. These are the personal seeds which will be carried forwards into possible fertilization and manifestation in real time. This is the Way of the Mysteries.

Even though the script has been prepared in advance and every eventuality seems covered, as the instigator of the proceedings, my mind is attuned to both higher hearing and seeing as the commencement draws near. In this instance I suddenly decided to incorporate particular visualized imagery as a means of moulding mental matter upon the ritual container as required. I was at the last moment instructed-inspired to use the group mind to create The Boat of Millions of Years above us and below us the Duat. This polarity of heaven and earth was connected via the axis mundi represented sequentially by the tamarisk tree wherein the chest containing the body of Osiris is found, the pillar of the palace where Isis first takes her bird form and finally by the descent of the living Horus from the above. So, our ritual drama followed the script while simultaneously extending our presence into unseen and invisible dimensions by reaching out to the company of the gods and to the potentiality of becoming. Our passage through the night of resurrection followed the time-honored sequence

THE BREATH OF ISIS

of reconstruction. At the nuptial meeting of Osiris and Isis the assembly tuned outwards while a rock crystal bowl was struck to produce a sound that hung on the air like a bird. I do remember that during this sequence, my body started to shake quite involuntarily and the person next to me kindly placed a supporting hand on my back. We had early experienced the visualized meditation *The Roses of Isis* where She opens Her wings rose petals descend to the earth bringing love and compassion. As the ritual proceeded the skies literally opened and the rains descended. Curiously in the debriefing the next morning, several participants had connected the descending rain with the shower of rose petals blessing us earlier. In the time allotted to us we had not dwelt upon the Lamentations of Isis and Nephthys yet this episode of mourning and lament is a vital part of the full story. In Egypt the rising Nile was described as the Tears of Isis and we duly received our due portion of rain-tears-roses, of course, the traditional blessing of Osiris was given with the words, *"Receive the cool waters of Osiris."* We were indeed blessed.

In case you should think such things to be no more than flights of the mind in fancy dress, subsequent personal reports are invaluable. There are often immediate flurries of synchronicities and coincidences but deeper seeds take more time to mature and require a larger time reference. It is a little over two years since these events. Speaking personally, my life has moved from an arid desert of constriction to the greened possibilities of creativity, enrichment and a return to stability. I too have been renewed and restored to my passion which is the Way of the Mysteries, called at the behest of Isis and Osiris jointly and together in blessed harmony.

THE MYSTERIES OF ISIS

NOTES

1. Antoine Faivre: scholar, academic. Antoine Faivre is an important figure in the academic study of esotericism. He has contributed to theory and method in the study of Western Esotericism and to the study of western historical currents: Hermetism, Christian Kabbalah, Alchemy, Paracelsianism, Theosophy, Rosicrucianism, Illuminism, Naturphilosophie, and Traditionalism. He is the Co-editor of *Aries, The Journal for the Study of Western Esotericism*.

2. Normandi Ellis: author, workshop facilitator, minister, astrologer, clairvoyant, expert in ancient Egypt. Normandi conducts guided Nile trips along with workshops on creative writing and ancient Egyptian spirituality. She is the author of the much acclaimed book, *Awakening Osiris*.

CHAPTER NINE

THE SORROW OF ISIS

I first experienced the meditation, *The Sorrows of Isis* at a public workshop meditation led by Dolores Ashcroft-Nowicki. I remember that I sat with three friends all together in a row. As the meditation proceeded, we took on the identity of the mourning Isis and took on her tears too. The story of Her loss, made real through the directed attention of a guided meditation, filled the mind and opened the heart to grief. We wept quietly, inwardly and without sound, the tale had found its mark. I did not know it then, but Her story was to become the myth of my life. It is a cliché to say that everyone lives through the ups and downs of life, relationships shift, careers change, circumstances unfold. Life is a dynamic movement of change, trials and tribulations are unavoidable. Yet challenge and change notwithstanding, when I observe the settled rhythms of other lives, I have to wonder at the rhythms that have unsettled my own life. I have no wish to write a personal autobiography. The details of my private life are mine alone to review. Yet I now see a compelling interplay between the life I have lived and the mythic identity which has encompassed me. This overlap is worthy of closer attention. I do not believe it is possible to serve Isis in the capacity of hm-ntr without also experiencing Her tears. Nowadays a great romance follows in the train of Isis. Her beauty is magnetic. Her magic is alluring. Her mystery is compelling, it seems that today She has become everyone's favourite goddess; pagans of all

THE SORROW OF ISIS

traditions, ceremonial magicians, wiccans, solitary witches and magical practitioners of every persuasion call on the name of Isis. Yet underneath Her beauty and despite Her winged majesty, Her story is one of suffering and grief. It is a story shared by so many, for every human being will come to know the grief of loss and the pain of separation. Death divides loved ones, one from the other. Isis too shares in the common fate of the human heart, but Her suffering is made even greater through the tragedy of deceit and betrayal. How many times in human history has a good man been brought down by the jealousy and envy of another? How many times has dawning of hope been crushed by the devastating use of ruthless power? The lure of power is a compelling aphrodisiac. This is the stuff of Shakespearian tragedy, Othello is destroyed by the machinations of Iago, the sleeping king Malcolm is murdered by the usurper to the throne Macbeth urged on by the ambitions of his conniving wife. Political assassinations fill the pages of history up to the present day. The murder of Osiris was also a political assassination. The throne of Egypt was a powerful enough lure to overcome any family loyalty. This theme has been played out upon the human stage so many times, there is no rivalry more devastating and cunning than that devised to steal the power to rule.

Queen Isis lost her beloved husband to the jealousy of their brother, Set. The throne was deprived of its rightful heir; the beautiful queen was reduced to the appearance of a beggar woman dressed in the rags of lamentation, she wandered the kingdom like a mad woman possessed by grief. This scenario touches upon all those made widows by war, all those robbed of a loved one by untimely death, all those plunged into grief by personal tragedy. Isis is The Lady of Sorrows, she knows the human condition. She is the mother of compassion, for like us She has wept in the face of death and I have done the same. My personal life has been marked by two close deaths, that of a child who did not emerge into life and that of an ex-husband who chose not to remain in life. The devastation

THE BREATH OF ISIS

created by the wake of such untimely passing is incalculable. Like a giant wave sweeping sanity off balance, it sucks stability down into a vortex of grief where everything becomes dark. Such terrible interludes mask hope with despair and place a dark veil upon every moment of life by day and night. Each day is filled with a torment of questions and a dialogue of self-examination which continues in the mind until this interrogation of the soul is finally quietened through an exhaustion of the spirit. The quest for answers and explanations is a ceaseless compulsion to find peace of mind. Along the way, there are tears, so many tears. Like Isis, the deity of my heart, I have been shaped by grief. Isis quested first to find the body of her beloved and next to collect the parts of his body broken and scattered across the land. My task was so much simpler. I quested for the fragments of a story which lay scattered in places unknown and in things unsaid. My journey into the madness of grief was to recollect pieces of experience and life narrative so that I might weave together the garment of my own becoming again. I know that in places twisted and broken by war, others like Isis have journeyed into the hell-world of human cruelty to literally collect the broken bodies of their beloveds. Massacre and mass graves deny human identity to the individual but the desire to find and honour the beloved is so strong that much human effort and energy is expended upon the recovery and naming of the lost so that they might be united in spirit if not in the flesh. The first quest undertaken by Isis recognizes this deep human need to make peace with tragedy and find resolution through bestowing appropriate honour and dignity upon the dead. As Abydos commemorated the place of Osiris and gave honour to his name so we too honour the war dead in rolls of honour, cenotaph and monument. Their names are carved in stone so that we the living shall not forget. Isis raised a shrine at every place where a part of Osiris was recovered. We do exactly the same today by marking the sites of battlefields, or naming places where a life of significance has passed away. The

THE SORROW OF ISIS

dead sanctify the land and remind the living of life's value. Her tears are not so different from our own. In the ancient tale, Isis is the heroine. She quests alone and even in her despair never gives up. She is eventually successful in finding the body of Osiris and in her endeavours to secure a rightful heir to the throne. We in our modern world prefer heroes not heroines. Women are rarely portrayed as exemplars. We still choose to award the laurels of victory to men. Even though the tide is slowly turning, the bitter reality of daily life in so many places is one of disempowerment for women. In today's world god is singular and called father, in the ancient world, divinity is plural and is called both mother and father. This divide in perception seems unbridgeable. Yet it is clear that monotheism has wrought a savage inheritance upon the world, for exclusivity can only breed heresy and heresy is always punishable.

Isis is a mother and a wife, western spirituality has traditionally placed women and mothers outside the temenos. Only virginal women may belong to God; wives and mothers belong to their husbands. The sacred and the sexual have become separated drawn out from a single amalgam and wound tightly upon different spools to prevent any possibility of merger or intermingling. This separation of life-giving powers brings a deep wound to the human psyche where both the sexual and the sacred represent the same drive to find union beyond the self. Western theology finds nothing sacred in sexuality, the tone is set in the Garden of Eden where sexuality, temptation and shame are sins laid upon the shoulders of Eve. The burden laid upon her is inherent in her female nature, it can never be lifted generation after generation. The burden picked up by Isis is that undertaken through love and choice, it is hers alone. The name of Eve has become synonymous with sin and human disobedience is responsible for the Fall, the prime separation between the divine and mundane worlds. This terrible burden of guilt has been laid upon mother and daughter ever since. Sexuality has become the poisoned chalice of the human condition, the act of love has been

THE BREATH OF ISIS

deformed into the carrier of original sin by theologians bent on separating the spirit from the body. How Isis, the beautiful goddess must weep for her daughters rendered prisoners by the tyranny and stupidity of the self-righteous.

The Virgin Mary has often been compared to Isis. As a Christian icon, she has been seen as a later form of The Lady of Sorrows. These two heavenly queens do appear to share much in common. Virginity carried no special sacred status in ancient Egypt and such a biological definition was certainly never linked to a template of womanly perfection and purity. When the Virgin Mary became the beloved female icon of the Christian church, she was offered up as a paragon of virtue, a model of humility and as the pious and perfect handmaid of the Lord. This impossible template served only to disempower, how can the ideal of virginity as a de-sexualised holiness serve a real woman? This slavish adherence created a particular view of womanhood both secular and sacred; obedience to the heavenly father and the earthly husband became a prime virtue.

Isis too was seen as a role model for women. Her cult was especially popular in the Graeco-Roman world where it over-spilled the confines of the temple to become a religion for the people. Women counted for the greatest number of her devotees. Her story carried a familiar ring at a time of unexpected death. Isis was seen as the good wife and loving mother not as the distant and virginal queen of heaven. Her appeal was immediate and present. Women knew what it meant to seek the bodies of the beloved slain upon the battlefield, to mourn the death of a life cut short and to hope in the depths of the heart for the possibility of a life to come. This was Her appeal for women. Men hoped to be an Osiris, not forgotten in death, not lost in memory, not left in the hands of the enemy but lovingly sought out, honoured and dignified. These understandable human concerns emerged as the tradition was lifted out of its temple setting and transplanted onto new soil. Once separated from

THE SORROW OF ISIS

the temple, The Mysteries took on the nature of religious worship and ceased to be part of a great and overarching metaphysical philosophy: the Sacred Science.

The Sorrows of Isis are known to every loving human heart. Her desire is to mend that which is broken, to heal that which is wounded, to reunite that which is scattered. She gathered the fragments of being and re-membered the parts that have been sundered through the many traumatic experiences of life. Soul loss is understood in shamanic traditions and though the name of Isis is rarely associated with shamanic practice, she has many names and many guises. The restoration of soul is among her many healing gifts. I have lived through much sorrow not only the tragedy of untimely death but also the death of two marriages and my own subsequent disintegration in response. There are many ways in which the fragmentation of being occurs. In fact, the divisions and fractures within the human psyche might even be described as the common fate, neuroses, depression and a whole host of common psychological disturbances are signs of fracture within the dimensions of the psyche. The task entrusted to the candidate of the Mysteries is that of self- reconstruction. Under the aegis of the charge, to Know Thyself, the candidate begins the work of self-realisation. This is ultimately a task of self-healing and rebirth. It is a long process, it is the quest to find and re-member all that has been broken, divided and scattered. Jung has called this the process of individuation, it is the lifelong task of becoming yourself. Without an internal, self-directed drive, the external values of society and peer group norms will create not an individual but a clone. At times, I have felt unequal to the task, overwhelmed by the magnitude of the broken landscape in front of me and beset by the forces of chaos tearing away at the fabric of my life once more. I know what it is to be incapacitated by fear and frozen by circumstance. Even worse through these periods of disintegration, I was haunted by my own sense of failure in the spiritual tradition I had espoused so loudly.

THE BREATH OF ISIS

My spiritual commitment had led me into a cul-de-sac. Far from bringing peace of mind, my chosen path brought a second crashed marriage, financial responsibilities I felt ill equipped to shoulder and a life stripped of all shared magical endeavours; daily life had swamped by inner life like an invading tsunami. The demands of the mundane world and the creativity of the divine world now pulled me in two opposing directions. The divine world had to wait, daily life had me in its grip and would not release me. I was forced to build a new life. Like the Tarot card of The Tower, the House of God, I had been shattered by a lightning bolt and was broken yet not destroyed. My despair was greatest when I reflected on my high ideals and spiritual aspirations: to Know and to Serve. It seemed to me I had learned nothing and through my service to the gods, life had reduced me to just another statistic, a single mother bringing up children. Magic did not save me, Magic had precipitated my headlong fall into the very unmagical world of struggle and strife. Real Magic, not the appearance of magic, is a path of soul making and this shall not be accomplished without much undoing. This is a path of continuous death and rebirth as layers of the psyche are peeled away and sloughed off like papered skins. All life experiences of dark and light must find equilibrium. This is the Great Work. It is an alchemical process which does not cease but bubbles and seethes beneath all outer appearances. Every ritual engagement, every spiritual act of intent is but another flame beneath the cauldron of becoming. This is the Way of the Mysteries, it is the path of transformation.

The common idea that the spiritual Path of Magic brings a protective overcoat to life, that spells may save or that the gods may sweep in to rescue their own is utterly false. The reality of magic is quite otherwise. Magical groups soon become hothouses where personality traits walk larger than life and inner plane dynamics wreak havoc. The early history of the Hermetic Order of the Golden Dawn shows the abrasive action of big personality meeting

THE SORROW OF ISIS

big personality. Ultimately the personality must become the servant not the master in the house of self but along the way the personality can become hugely inflated by the influx of spiritualised energy. The particular definition of magic understood in the Mystery tradition is one which brings an active partnership between the mortal and immortal realms. As this personal relationship is slowly forged so the inner mind must be finely tuned like a receiving station. Those who come to the Western Mystery Tradition in the expectation of an easy ride by courtesy of some inner plane kindness are quite deceived. Dion Fortune who also lost a marriage along the way, rhetorically asked the question, *"How do you know when your request to serve the Masters of Wisdom has been accepted?"* Her answer: *"When your life falls apart."*

My life has fallen apart more than once, the container of shared experience that I expected to be expansive and open-ended proved to be rigid and quite incapable of growing to incorporate a magical dimension. This shocking realisation dawned only slowly and by degrees as all my drives for magical experience were gradually thwarted, rebuffed or traded in the same way that all partnerships must include the art of negotiation. However, for me magic was non-negotiable, it was the bedrock of my life. Over time, all the magical life was squeezed out from my marriage like water from a sponge leaving only a dry husk behind. I had every reason to expect partnership rooted in magical connection, magic had brought us together but it also drove us apart. Never underestimate the strains created by bringing the overlay of magic into the domestic arena. Many tales might be told here, but telling my own is my single responsibility. I can document my own fall with savage detachment. My partnership was based not on a shared commitment to the Way of the Mysteries as I had believed but on a masquerade. As the path deepens so motives that were once shrouded become crystal clear. Secret desires for self-importance or self-aggrandisement appear as millstones to be ground down, inflated egos await only destruction,

THE BREATH OF ISIS

idle curiosity succumbs to boredom. These are the traps embedded in the path of self-realisation. I had expected a level of support and understanding from my domestic life which was promised but never delivered. In its absence I increasingly supported myself through my friendships and from within. But this self-consuming strategy proved costly to my health and general well-being. When I went for acupuncture, my first diagnosis showed that my yin energy was so depleted as to be almost exhausted. As the therapist said to me, *"This is the energy of self-protection and nurture and you are empty."* Her statement had the ring of a question. I replied that I had a lot of stress at home, inwardly I knew I been sleeping with the enemy. Escaping from domesticity did not bring instant relief and the strains I had internalised found their way to the surface and a complete breakdown into a paralysis of spirit. So great was the fall, that I required professional help to reconstruct myself. Whenever the therapist asked me to name my achievements, invariably I could name none. My psychological understanding made me a wary client yet I could not resist the process. Eventually I felt able to face the world again, I stopped sleeping cramped into an armchair and commenced the work of personal reconstruction once again. I watched my peers rise to positions of responsibility as teachers, writers and international workshop facilitators. My dreams of being a voice with something to say had vanished like a phantom on the air. Yet I did have something to say and my inner voices were rarely silent. In fact, had these inner promptings faded altogether, I might have accepted my lot with more equanimity. So, in the worst of circumstances, or perhaps the best of circumstances in heavy disguise, I managed to get a book commissioned. Living on state benefit, I set about the task of writing *The Aquarian Qabalah*. I wrote for a year and a quarter, all day, every day including weekends and evenings. I wrote until my eyes were sore and my head ached with obscure metaphysical concepts. When I eventually handed over the manuscript, I went home and slept for twenty-seven hours.

THE SORROW OF ISIS

Yet I am pleased that I put pen to paper, or mouse to keyboard if you prefer.

Shall I continue the tale of tedium? It is merely the story of death and rebirth couched in its many guises. It is merely my tale of becoming. But what had I become? Labels are rarely as useful as they might appear. I had become a single mother struggling with the everyday demands of life. I had become an author struggling to find the time to write. I had become an outsider struggling to find a place of identification even while I still desired to count myself among the builders of the Western Mystery tradition and to speak on its behalf. I had not yet fully become myself. Time passed, my exit from the world of magical engagement seemed complete. I could envisage no way back. This certainty made me miserable. I had several books to my name but neither the time nor the capacity to support my ideas with groups or workshops. I had finally returned to teaching and was able to support my life. But this was not the life I wanted. I had now joined the system and become a single cog in its vast mechanism. I worked among good teachers, some young and bright-eyed about the future, others looking towards retirement. Despite my competence in the job, I did not belong here either. I winced at the thought of years spent in the classroom.

I was in the process of applying for future work when my mother asked me to help her with my father. My father had suffered much ill health over many years including a stroke followed by the onset of Parkinson's. My mother had looked after him with both dedication and determination but now she was experiencing increasing problems with her own health. She asked me for some short-term help, a couple of months at most, I lived there for a year and a quarter. This episode proved to be another extremely testing time. My son was now at college but hardly an adult he could not be expected to run the house as well. So, I commuted between the house where my father was dying to the house where my son was partying. I drove between these two extremes bearing shopping and

THE BREATH OF ISIS

necessary supplies spending part of the week in each place. My mother's house ran like clockwork as it had to, in order to manage an illness like Parkinson's. Medication was given at precise intervals, meals were served on time. Every day had a pattern and it revolved entirely around my father's needs. From the first waking moment to the last, the household rhythm revolved around him. His bedtime was a long drawn-out ritual of its own, washing, changing and settling took on new dimensions as his mental state deteriorated and night-time hallucinations became frequent. My own home provided no comfort. Here chaos reigned. My son for the most part managed to attend college and keep up with his work, no more could be asked of him. Housework did not get done. I often arrived to find an assortment of scooters on the drive or as I left the party would be just starting. My mother who was always indefatigable in the face of adversity suggested that we might use the time well by organising the much needed improvements to my house. I chose a builder who had previously completed work for me. A trench was dug, the garage was reassigned to become a room and the builder disappeared with the deposit. The treachery by the builder made me physically ill, I could not get out of bed for two days. I had such pains in my back; life had to go on.

Over the next year and a quarter, I travelled between these two extremes. I spend as much time as I could with my son encouraging him to keep going. As he became more responsible the partying diminished and work on the house resumed with good effect. At my mother's house we were both becoming exhausted. My mother was burned out from years of caring and I had slipped back into depression triggered by the builder and the strains of being rootless and without rest. Yet beneath the obvious difficulties, this time offered riches I had not expected. I had entered into the marrow of their lives and was privy to moments of great poignance: music played in memory of happier times, unexpected emotion as they both realised in absolute synchronicity that this was the time to say

THE SORROW OF ISIS

goodbye and to make peace with life itself. My father had much to make peace with. Five years in prison camp has undermined his health and robbed him of his belief in the goodness of human nature. Jewish by birth, he had abandoned all faith as self-deception. Raised in the stultifying atmosphere of colonial luxury, his adult life in contrast had been one of financial struggle. Estranged from his cultural, spiritual and religious roots he had come to live the life of an exiled soul never quite at peace with the new motherland. The one unshakeable constant in his life was my mother and he knew with absolute certainty that he would be leaving her soon enough. Now there was time to knit up the threads of life, there was nothing else to do but live into death. His life came to a close unexpectedly, I had already booked a holiday for myself before I lived with my parents and it was agreed that I should go, the much needed recuperation would be good for me. Though I did not know it then, before I had even reached the airport, my father had made a decision. Over breakfast he announced that he would not be taking any further medication and discussed his funeral wishes. My mother did not want to destroy my holiday before I had even unpacked. Other members of the family stepped in at home. I don't remember quite when I took the phone call asking me to come home but I just could not mobilise myself. I had spent a day laying on a balcony in the sunshine. It sounds like idle sunbathing but it was more of a physical collapse. I had no strength left to pack and return. I was only due to be away until the weekend though my mother was insistent that he would not last until then. On the Tuesday night I had a dream in which my father spoke and simply said, "*Don't worry, I will wait.*" I was reassured, I was always guided by my dream and I began to turn my thoughts to home. I felt restored by the sunshine and travelled home a day early. On the way home, every thought in my mind shouted, "*Wait for me, I'm coming.*" I arrived and went to him. His eyes were closed but he squeezed my hand. I thanked him for everything he had given me

THE BREATH OF ISIS

for my life itself which carried his genes forward. I told him that I loved him and that I would look after mum. He knew I was present. We had said our goodbyes. I left him to rest and when I returned to the room he had passed into unconsciousness. He was now on a morphine drip and nursing staff attended by nursing staff. What a blessing for my mother who had done so much for others. Now his fate was quite out of her hands. Family members took it turn to sit with him, as much for their own comfort as to comfort him. I used to lay down beside him and take his hand much as I had done when I lived there. Previously, I was there to give him medication. Now I did my best to administer a different kind a medicine, that designed for the soul. I closed my eyes and entered into the familiar territory of a deepened state where I sought him out in my mind. In my mind's eye, I met him seated on a bench in a woodland clearing. We spoke and I suggested we walk together on a path which we did. I knew he was afraid, so we did not go far. Each time I sat with him, I travelled to find him and each time we travelled a little closer to a riverbank. I told him I could not cross with him. He needed only to sit quietly by the river and look to the far side. Each day physically he diminished. His breaths became slow sometimes I thought his breathing had ceased altogether but then he would inhale again. The family sat with him in turn speaking kindly to him. Nurses came and went. Everyone wondered how long he could last. He seemed to be hovering at the very border of life. When it was my turn to sit with him, I called upon Isis. I sensed her presence. In my mind's eye I saw her create an umbilicus from his sleeping form and in some manner fuse it into her own being. I have no explanation other than its symbolic significance. I said my final inner goodbye to my father. I had done everything I could to ease his passing. He finally passed on the Tuesday morning at about 3.15am. The night nurse called us and we were at his bedside in moments. I was not afraid to enter the room and look upon him. But almost immediately I was aware of a feeling in the room that was utterly new and unrecognisable. When

THE SORROW OF ISIS

I stepped out from the room the feeling was absent as soon as I stepped back into the room, I was aware of this new unrecognizable quality. Upon death there is much to do. Phone calls must be made, arrangements must be organised. There is no time for grief only for necessary activity. We waited altogether for the undertakers to arrive. Almost two hours had elapsed now and I was becoming aware of a curious sensation. It was as if my father's life force was gently dissipating throughout the house. It called to my attention so insistently that I could not keep my eyes open. I lay across the sofa inwardly watching but quite unable to speak with anyone. It seemed to me that each of the chakra centres in turn registered the presence of subtle energy like an internal radar system. My mother, the ever patient, momentarily ran out of patience and rebuked me. I seemed to have lapsed into sleep, but I was not asleep, I heard her voice and could not respond. The undertakers arrived and respectfully took my father's body away. At the instant his body was taken across the threshold, the etheric atmosphere was gone too, lifted suddenly and completely. I sat bolt upright, eyes open and wide awake. I took my father's funeral giving him the due dignity that I did not expect a stranger could deliver. In the days after his death and around his funeral, I wondered whether there might be some visit from him, a dream or a vision, but there was none. I never saw him, later on however my mother did.

My mother entered a period of deep grieving, she had lived as she said, inside his skin anticipating his every need. Now she needed to find herself again and rebuild her own life. She thought she would never recover but she did. I was quite exhausted by the events of the time and when an old friend invited me for a trip to Wales, I decided to go. It was a decision with far reaching consequences. My old friend from Wales was another walker on the treacherous Paths of Magic. We had not seen each other for about 25 years and we found much to talk about. We had been present at the same rituals and moved among the same circle of friends. I visited for almost 2 years and took up residence for a further year. On reflection it was a time of mutual healing, two souls battered by the path of becoming. It was here that I began to write again for the first time in years, doing nothing more than walking in nature, resting and taking photographs, it was a balm for my soul. However, we belonged to different traditions which would not meet happily except as it turned out through the aegis of Dion Fortune but that is another story. The little magical work that we did together bore strong fruit, but our individual paths lay elsewhere. At a time of life when most people are enjoying the company of grandchildren and the benefits of a career, I had neither to my name. I emerged from Wales on the boot of another ending. I had sold my house to procure an income and returned in my late fifties to commence another peripatetic life moving this time between my mother and my brother who made me equally welcome. I had accomplished yet another undoing by refusing to walk away from the Egyptian tradition and the voice still speaking in my mind.

My story is almost up to date. But at that time my life lay as a series of disconnected threads, separate chapters always ending in dissolution. Once again, I was forced to return to the task of building a life, soul-making was on hold. I began an M.A. in Western Esotericism at Exeter University but soon discovered that the circumstances of my life conspired to defeat my new self-appointed goals. I soon realised that I could not devote myself to study while living another peripatetic existence. Narrative records events but insight alone gives meaning to them; hindsight now shows me the folly of my own blindness. I needed nothing extra in my life, it contained all the elements required to reconstruct another life. But I was slow to see the giftedness within the appearance of emptiness. I did not have a relationship, I was not ready, I did not have a career, it would have been a burden, I did not have a house of my own, but I was invited into my brother's home where he and his wonderful wife generously provided me with a roof over my head, with food on

THE SORROW OF ISIS

the table and with the support of loving friendship. This period so recently minted in memory was sharply punctuated by the sudden death of my mother. She had emerged from the tunnel of mourning and spent the remaining years of her life in the gentle company of an old friend with the gift of making her laugh. She deserved her brief respite. I had sensed her forthcoming death in the dreams she shared with me. She several times dreamed of a beautiful place with sharp brilliant colours. I said nothing. She told me she has heard my father's voice speaking her name one morning as she woke up. I said nothing. She even phoned to say she has seen dad in the garden smiling at her. I merely asked if she had seen him with her physical eyes or her inner eyes. When she said she had seen him with her physical eyes, even I was a little surprised. I said nothing more, I did not have to. My mother was a remarkable woman with great sensitivity and understanding. Her passing was swift and merciful. She lived into her last day and went to bed that evening as usual. She had a stroke in the night from which she could not recover. The family reached her bedside on the Saturday afternoon. She passed at 7 o'clock on the Sunday morning. My sister-in-law and I stayed with her all the while watching the oxygen readings tell their inevitable story. As her passing approached I called silently upon Isis, my sister-in-law, who also has a sensitivity to things unseen, suddenly looked at me, "*Someone has just joined us, a being with wings.*" We returned to our silence. My mother gave a violent cough, almost sitting upright for a milli-second and then she fell back. She was gone. In due course I delivered her eulogy offering her the praise and love of family and friends which she rightly deserved. My mother's passing was a great blow to me. I had spent much time with her. Even when I saw no light in my future, she remained optimistic on my behalf. Quite soon after her passing I began to hear clear voice and common sense speaking in my mind. Her closeness continues to this present moment. What can the reader make of this tormented tale? A lifetime of commitment

THE BREATH OF ISIS

had led me exactly where! My doggedness and determination had seen off two marriages and a third relationship. I had managed to produce only a handful of books, lead small groups and facilitate small workshop – always close encounters of the Kemetic kind! Then everything changed again. In 2009 Isis reappeared in my life with an unmistakeable signature, Her voice clearer than ever before, *"Speak my Truth"* she said. In an utterly remarkable series of experience which took place in Melbourne Australia. It happened in this way. I had planned to attend the Parliament of World Religions taking place in Melbourne but as the time drew nearer, a family crisis erupted and in the end I decided that I could not leave. One week before the Parliament was due to open, I was overcome by the desire to travel. By now the crisis had settled and my presence was no longer needed at home. I made enquiries, I could get a plane ticket and I could get a ticket for the parliament but I could not find any accommodation, hardly surprising as ten thousand delegates had booked every available room in town. It seemed as if my plans had stalled. But the compulsion to travel would not be silenced and so I put a request on Facebook for accommodation somewhere-anywhere in Melbourne, not really expecting a reply. Imagine my surprise when I received a reply, within three minutes of my post appearing. Not only did I travel to Melbourne and go to the parliament, but I was welcomed with open arms into a family home, and this is how my friendship with Naza Cogo began. When she met me at the airport, it knew at once that we soul-sisters in Isis. When I left her almost three weeks later, I cried tears behind my big sunglasses. During our time together, it was as if Isis herself had joined us, she had most certainly brought us together. It is impossible to convey the intensity of the exchanges between Naza and myself, nor is this the place to do so. Naza will have her own story to tell but I will say that in Naza I recognized the breath of Isis in the first instant of our meeting. This extraordinary, beautiful and wonderful heart connection of course continues and it was

THE SORROW OF ISIS

during this time that Isis took up Her place in the Mystery School which She had knitted together with such patience over so many years. I suddenly knew that She had never been absent but only silent watching me stumble and fall so many times. How She must have wept at my stupidity and folly, my blindness to goodness and my deafness to counsel. What an arduous homecoming I have made of it.

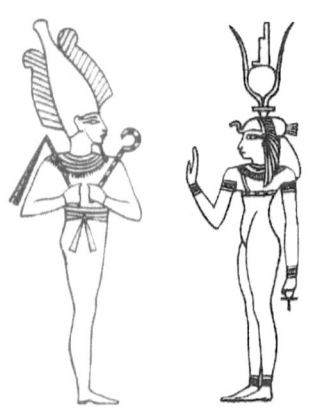

WORDS FROM THE ARCHIVE

BACKGROUND

When I began to write this book, this section was never planned but with the completion of my story, it appeared in my mind as a new idea. The following is a selection, chosen for their broad appeal. Since the archive represents the fruits of my labours in the field of mind, it might be timely to explain something of my own creative processes. I have prepared ritual scripts and meditations for over thirty years now. In the beginning my efforts were laboured and I was quite uncertain in these unfamiliar waters. But time brings experience, and I now recognize the landmarks which bring an idea to fruition.

The process invariably begins when a phrase, even a few words appear in my mind and will not leave. At this stage, I have no idea whatsoever where this idea will lead. I begin always to explore the idea intellectually with extensive related reading. I fill my mind with content and no matter what I am doing, I carry these ideas in my mind actively and continuously turning them over repeatedly as a gardener might turn the soil. Especially I review the ideas before sleeping and sometimes it happens that I will gain insight through a dream. Finally, I sit at the computer to review the texts I am working with. Now the intellectual work is done, and I must hand the task over to intuition and insight. As I sit at the keyboard, some phrases jump out at me screaming to be chosen, others just shy away into

THE BREATH OF ISIS

a quiet corner as soon as I see them. When I have collected enough ancient words like a great unsorted heap, I need to create a structure which is quite correctly Psyche's quest. Here I must draw upon a library of ritual experiences: beginnings, endings, openings closing, composition of place, invocations, meditations, solo speeches, group speeches, pauses, music, cues, spaces for oracles and all the directions associated with a theatrical play. But all the while this structure must serve a purpose, it must cleanly and precisely build a bridge between two levels of mind, it must create a stable container, a microcosm of the macrocosm, it must provide for engagement with archetypal powers and also for disengagement by mortal minds.

I see it all in my mind as it unfolds but it is impossible to explain what this will yield, until the container becomes filled as the ritual unfolds, it is just a sequence of words on a page. While I am writing I have no idea what the end result might be, in fact even as the performance draws closer, I have no idea what will come from it. Nevertheless, I know from experience that there will be results, both personal and transpersonal.

Immediately following a ritual, in the first few days, there are often a flurry of synchronicities. These are of some interest and are seen as, 'signs following,' they are not however the full outcome of the work but more like randomly generated stirrings, much like the dust thrown up as a heavy cart passes over a stony path. Nevertheless, 'signs following' are an indication that the applied correspondences have impacted upon the matrix of collective consciousness. The deeper and lasting effects are more difficult to discern. Sometimes, it has to be said, the results do not manifest for a generation. Now this may seem very odd to people who regard, 'magic' as spell-craft and seek immediate self-gratification in the form of a visible result. The life and work of Dion Fortune is a good example of this long- term view. Hindsight enables this present generation to look back and see her legacy which is encapsulated in the appearance of a new constellation of ideas and values. However, her legacy is not accidental or coincidental but fully in accord with the Magical Work of her life. In other words, the seeds that were planted in full consciousness and under the auspices of divine intent have flowered broadly along the lines so intended. This transpersonal character indeed an essential characteristic of what has been called, High Magic. Although the term has fallen out of favour, there is nonetheless a qualitative difference between magical work undertaken for personal result and magical work undertaken by the few for the benefit of the many; it is the difference between spell-craft and theurgy.

COMMENTARY
It should now be clear that ritual which often takes the form of sacred drama, is not theatre but a continuous, extended, three-dimensional meditation employing all the senses. It should be undertaken in this light and in the spirit of soul-service. The high sense of vocational calling should never be lost even though the preparations for such events are totally mundane and practical.

Ritual dynamics can produce bizarre effects, interference with electrical or technical equipment is not uncommon. It is however very annoying: a projector suddenly fails, a sound system won't start, computers become erratic. Once at the Runnings Park centre, all the lights in the block failed for no reason only to miraculously start again just in time for the ceremony. This has happened too many times in my experience to be merely coincidence, just remember the energy generated by the group may be invisible to the eye but not in effect.

It is common to devote one session to a rehearsal, especially if working with large numbers of people. This is entirely as matter of ritual logistics never of dynamics. The purpose is simply to ensure that everyone is familiar with entrances, exits, movements, sequence, where to stand, who to stand next to etc. The run-through gives

THE BREATH OF ISIS

everyone confidence in the physical form, it is a straightforward affair, always low key and good humoured. It should directly precede the ritual, so that the rehearsal period is followed by a brief interlude only. If the preparations have been thorough, all participants will be as racehorses at the starting gate, highly tense, keyed up and ready to run.

The experience of the ritual is quite unlike that of the rehearsal, the rehearsal is merely a movement in an empty container but as soon as the ritual opens, the dynamics begin. Circumnambulating, that is, processing the area three times is an effective opening as the focussed walking sets up a powerful momentum it begins to feel like, 'wading through treacle' – my best description. Once everyone has taken their pre-arranged positions, allow a few moments of quiet to settle the group mind. The script is essential, (unless everyone has time to learn a part by rote!) but it is not a place to hide. Look out from the script across the room and your inner eye will show you subtle changes of radiance and vitality in your companions. You are not obliged to follow every speech via the script, if you have prepared well enough, you will be primed for your cue so that you can absorb what is meant by the words you are hearing. If your part is short, keep your focus and be vigilant with your thoughts so that your attention is fully present at all times. Know that Members taking on the identities of the *neteru* are asked to engage in thoughtful and extended meditation.

When creating a scripted drama, a communion of some kind is always included. This is placed towards the end of the ceremony after the intention of the work has been effected and it provides a brief climbing-down plateau. Interludes for silent meditation are essential as places in which to gather one's thoughts for later reflection. And so, the divine act will come to its close and all participants will return to their chosen places in the world. But the divine act has not ceased, it has just begun its work, its effects will ripple in ever increasing circles and like a tiny enzyme, it will produce immense and beneficial change.

WORDS FROM THE ARCHIVE

I have attended rituals where even after the event, I cannot say what has been achieved. This feels most disconcerting, but experience tells me this happens when consciousness has not been extended sufficiently. In other words, my mind has not connected to the levels at which the bridge has been constructed. I have seen something similar when taking guided visual meditations. It is always my practice to ask for a brief report straightaway after meditation. The purpose of the instant debrief is to elicit a response before it has faded. Bear in mind that the report follows immediately upon the visualised journey, yet it is not uncommon for a report to be incomplete and fragmented, sometimes recall simply ceases and the memory is blank. Sometimes people say that they fell asleep. But when loss of memory replaces recall, awareness has merely shut down. It is not sleep but the sleep of forgetfulness. At other times participants cheerfully report that in preference to the images described on the journey, they 'saw' a variety of other scenes, usually 'more interesting' images and followed these with the mind's eye. This firstly excludes from the group mind-set being created and secondly reveals a jumbled consciousness akin only to a waking day-dream. When participants report seeing the image a mili-second before it is described, then the tradition is making itself known. Report writing, shared debriefing sessions and personal diary keeping, play an important role in training the mind, most especially in the early years.

It is important to state at the outset that the western esotericism provides a curriculum which trains the heart-mind through the presentation and assimilation of its Magical Images. This is a path of Restored and Revealed Imagination. The western way is to fill the mind with numerous symbolic memes to create a rich internal vocabulary of connections, multiple meanings and multi-layered associations. This fertile mind-set is primed for creativity, revelation and realisation. Moreover, the developing mind is by nature one of an expanded consciousness and increased receptivity. There is a regrettable tendency to associate the imagination with the play of children, with make-believe and with pretence. However, all works of art in all fields begin first in the imagination. All social reformers are able to, 'imagine' a better and different society.

Training the mind is a matter of training the imagination. The words, magic, magician, image, mage, magus and imago all share something with the word imagination and the path of magic inevitably and inexorably opens into the arena of mysticism and The Mysteries. The word, 'Mystery' in its religious context is derived from the Greek word, myein meaning, 'to close' referring to the lips or eyes. The gesture of silence, the finger raised to the lips, is familiar to students of the Mysteries. However, it does not carry the usual connotation of a secret that must not be told, its meaning is far more subtle. It refers to an experience so sublime that its essence cannot be conveyed by words. This is not so unusual even in ordinary life, for how might you convey the sound of a symphony to a deaf person or the sight of sunrise to a blind person. It is perhaps unusual to hear that an experience nominally described as 'religious' in form is impossible to convey in content. Modern religiosity mainly takes the form of worship as prayer, hymns, sermons and set services. It is an essentially passive process. There is no equivalence in the Kemetic tradition. There is no Egyptian word for worship in the modern sense, instead the word, iau implies the establishment of a relationship between the participant and the divinity. This describes an active and personal engagement rather than the uniformed and standardised response of the congregation. Though there is no word for worship, several terms converge in the word, mystery. The word, sheta means mystery. In daily use it means 'hidden', 'concealed' or 'unprecedented.' However, in a religious context the same word means, 'a truly religious secret.' The word djeser is usually translated as 'magnificent' or 'exalted,' but it also means, 'secluded,' 'inaccessible' or 'hidden.' The verb bes means, 'to usher in' or, 'to enter.' It is used to describe the investiture of

WORDS FROM THE ARCHIVE

the pharaoh or the installation of a priest and a cultic secret. These words take us beyond the gesture of silence into the Mysteries : hidden, magnificent, exalted, and unprecedented, experiences which usher in a relationship between the divinity and the devotee.

Welcome to the archive House of Life. If your group should decide to enact any of the scripts given to you, please observe the protocols developed by the group over the years. Although it is common enough to use the terms, god or goddess, this is an inadequate rendering of the ancient Egyptian understanding. The deities were called neter in the singular and neteru in the plural. These figures were regarded as the life-giving powers of renewal in cosmic and mundane existence. The scripts use the western divine names but this can easily be amended to the Kemetic if preferred.

PREPARATION

Allocate parts in good time. Ask all participants to meditate and reflect on the meaning and significance of the words in their care. Everyone should be familiar with any references to actual places in the script, easily achieved via the internet. All members should become familiar with ritual procedures and their significance; lighting candles or offering incense indicate that the space is being sanctified and made ready for the divinities. Members taking on the identities of the neter are asked to engage in thoughtful and extended meditation and to make an internal connection with the nature and characteristics of the divinity. The meaning of all emblems such as the Djed Pillar or the Tet amulet for instance should be fully understood by all participants. On occasion it will be necessary to physically create particular items, the making of beautiful artefacts is an integral part of this tradition, so let all objects be made with care and meditative thought. Once created, all ritual objects deserve to be stored with care.

THE BREATH OF ISIS

GROUP PREPARATION

Use individual meditation, shared discussion and active listening to firstly deconstruct the ritual according to its sequence, structure and meaning. Allow space for all participants to share their personal understanding of the words in their care. Sharing begins the process of reconstruction so that when the performance arrives, all participants will have absorbed and internalised the group's understanding.

PHYSICAL PREPARATION

In exactly the same way that a performance demands precision, pre-planning will ensure that all goes as a smoothly as possible. Make sure that all physical items are planned for, that matches are provided for lighting, that blocks of charcoal are not damp, that altar cloths are clean. Make sure that all musical cues are in the safe keeping of a competent technical person. Do not leave candles burning in unattended rooms.

PSYCHO-SPIRITUAL PREPARATION

This is much harder to describe and define as maturity comes only with experience. Though the performance may resemble theatre, it is not theatre. You are creating a container of living energies so that divine energies may also enter and share the same sacred space. I remember the first time that I stood a part of a contacted ritual group, I thought I would faint; the energetic atmosphere of the space changes so very distinctly. On other occasions, my body has started to shake uncontrollably, at other times I have wept and wept. Experience creates stability.

As the ritual unfolds, it is possible, though not common, to see movements of energy through the group, more often it is quite usual to sense and feel a changed atmosphere. This charged environment does not switch off at the close of the ceremony but will remain palpable for some time afterwards. It is best left to settle and

WORDS FROM THE ARCHIVE

dissolve in its own time, so once the company has left the sacred space, do not re-enter immediately. In fact, the room is best left until the following day. All participants, especially those mediating the neter, should also be mindful of the energetic shifts required to effect this mediation. Opening the aura to receive and connect with energies moving more rapidly is one thing, closing the aura and returning to a stable waking consciousness is quite another. I cut my teeth in ritual environments where it was assumed that everyone knew how to ground themselves satisfactorily, experience shows this is not the case especially in groups of mixed ability and exposure to ritual dynamics.

Debriefing is an essential part of the process too, like a jigsaw puzzle, each person holds a single piece according to their abilities and aptitudes. The initial debriefing session is the first opportunity to piece together the various moments and many perspectives. Writing a fuller report is also important and often curious synchronicities will appear in the few days just after a ritual. These should be noted but not necessarily accorded any great meaning as they are merely signs that the work has stirred the ether and the reflecting correspondences spill out.

The preceding comments should indicate that this form of initiating ritual is not to be treated lightly. Ritual enactment in the Mystery Tradition is theurgy not pageant. As such it is a part of a committed spiritual journey and should always be seen in this context.

CHAPTER I
THE ASCENSION OF OSIRIS

BACKGROUND

The Ascension of Osiris – A Mystery Drama based on The Pyramid Texts, was the first of our Isian Assemblies. As usual, the phrase just appeared in my mind and would not let go so I was pushed into exploring what it might signify. I turned to the Pyramid Texts which describe the stellar journey of the Osiris-king. So my intellectual preparation consisted of reading the Pyramid Texts and the various commentaries on it. When I consider that the group was not formed until the January and the performance took place in May, I am quite astounded at our bold endeavour but we were very fortunate in being able to draw upon a pool of very talented people. We hired a large hall at a local university which permitted us to make the most of the space and we were fortunate in being joined by Robert Bauval who gave a talk on the significance of the Giza Plateau. He was on the verge of what has become an illustrious adventure in Egyptian metaphysics and we were the first group he shared his new ideas with.

COMMENTARY

This text was used as the preamble to the ritual on the day it was read to the group just prior to the sacred drama.

THE ASCENSION OF OSIRIS

Our assembly meets to perform a dramatized presentation of the Pyramid Texts. We meet in the ancient tradition of sacred drama. The texts which form our script were inscribed in pyramids dating from the Fifth and Sixth Dynasties. The most notable pyramid of this group is the Pyramid of Unas, the last of the Fifth Dynasty kings. In all probability these texts represent an older tradition. The discovery of these inscriptions came as something of a surprise as it was generally believed that the pyramids were silent tombs.

The first translation was hurried and it sadly established certain misconceptions which lasted well into this century. In essence the stellar influence within the texts was completely missed. It was not until 1946 that the significance of the star cult was belatedly recognised. Though academic Egyptologists may be slow to recognise it, these texts are not merely sacred writings but a ceremonial script. These words were recited, intoned and enacted. This was the Egyptian way. It is our way.

I would like you to reflect on the fact that the words you will hear today come straight from the Pyramid of Unas. You will hear the Priest of the Pyramid speak in exactly the same words used by the Priest of the Pyramid. You will hear Horus speak as Horus spoke, you will hear Osiris declaim his divinity as Osiris declaimed his divinity thousands of years ago.

We hope to understand the meaning of these texts not through scholarly research but through their active use. We no do merely read the words, we read them from an interior state of deep meditation. This interior awareness opens us to continuous realisation while the ritualised energy is flowing. We contemplate while we speak, even while we dance. We hold these new realisations as our presentation progresses and share these new thoughts together when the presentation is over. Those of you

THE BREATH OF ISIS

not familiar with this approach are enjoined to participate in our state of meditation and share your own realisations with us as part of formal group debriefing.

Though we present our meditation through drama, do not expect anything resembling contemporary acting. Sacred drama is theurgy. We can be certain that the rite we enact today had no audience. Indeed, it may have been a rite reserved only for the few, namely those initiated into the Sacred Science who had responsibility for the soul of the pharaoh and the office of divine kingship.

Our drama follows a particular sequence. It opens with a brief excursus into the ceremony known as the Opening of the Mouth. This ritual endowed the departed king with his new form. It is Horus the son who applies the adze, curiously shaped in the form of the constellation Ursa Minor, known by the Egyptians as the foreleg. As a ritual implement of great power, the adze was made from meteoric iron, the metal from heaven. Its unique shape was repeated by one of the shafts within the pyramid; route, constellation and implement for waking the divine soul are all represented. The Egyptians loved to weave an elaborate puzzle overlaying one symbol with another in a complex overlay of correspondences. Such devices are deliberate dead ends to the intellect which seeks to analyse and dissect. But the same devices are doorways to the intuition which seeks to synthesis and unite. Through the ceremonial Opening of the Mouth, the king steps into his astral body and becomes an Osiris. But the process of transformation is not over for Osiris will become as Orion, the far strider. The king will undergo a stellar birth. He will be born to another realm. The Egyptian envisaged a complex relationship between the gods and king. Each pharaoh was Horus-in-life and Osiris in death. As ruler, the king was the incarnation of the Horus ntr. This divine-human identification extended beyond

THE ASCENSION OF OSIRIS

physical life, all was but an aspect of the process of becoming. The sepulchral home, the burial chamber was known as the House of Gold, a symbol of perfection. Curiously the quarry famed for the finest alabaster was also called the House of Gold. The dual nature of kingship effected a complex succession. If the departed king was no longer the living Horus, how was the Horus ntr to be transferred to the king-to-be, the new Horus, the Horus-to-come? These themes are to be found in the rituals of state and the transfer of authority both earthly and divine was effected seamlessly. During the exoteric Ceremony of Accession, in the presence of the royal mummy, the new king ritually donned a stomacher around the chest and back. This ritual garment symbolised the embrace between father and son, the Horus-who-was and the Horus-who-will-be. It represents a transfer of royal authority from the old king to the new. As the departed king underwent his own transition to an Osiris, the new king donned the Horus mantle. For the Egyptians these complex transfers and transitions were essential the smooth running of their world. But where did this identification begin, where was the Horus seed planted?

The mother of Horus was Isis, wife and sister to Osiris. Isis is called, 'She of the Throne.' She is the kingmaker to Horus in life and to Osiris in death. She empowers the dual kingship. She empowers Horus in her capacity as mother. She empowers Osiris in her capacity as wife. She empowers Orion in her capacity as Sothis-Sirius, the star queen. She is addressed in all these roles in the Pyramid Texts.

Exoteric state rites were invariably mirrored by esoteric cultic rites. It may well be that here in the Place of Ascension at the moment of the king's perceived translation to another form, Isis, sister, wife and mother ritually received the seed of the Horus ntr holding it within herself in trust for the king to be, the Horus

THE BREATH OF ISIS

to come. We do not have to think of this act as being a literal coupling of divine representatives. To say the words and mediate the divine presence was sufficient enough.

The ascension text has a curious resonance with Christianity as you will hear. Osiris is the good god, the shepherd king, Isis is Stellar Maris, The Queen of Heaven, Regina Coeli and Nuit, the sky goddess speaks the words, "This is my beloved son in whom I am well pleased." This phrase surely has a familiar ring.

The pyramid does indeed represent a great mystery. Architecturally it remains astounding, symbolically it is the enigma of enigmas, ritually it takes us to the heart of a royal stellar cult. It has always been regarded as a tomb, but its precise teaching is veiled, its spiritual purpose is a transcendent mystery. We may glimpse an answer for ourselves here today. As we like Osiris walk through the Gateway to the Stars.

PREPARATION

As always the stages of preparation are firstly intellectual and secondly intuitive. In this instance, there are many possibilities for intellectual preparation since the ritual is centred upon probably the most enigmatic constructions of the world, the Pyramid and the Sphinx, personal preparation might include background reading about these two most famous structures. Statistics and calculations will undoubtedly awe the mind with Kemetic building prowess. Reading the Pyramid Texts aloud is another powerful preparation for it will open the mind to Kemetic purpose. Together the ancient words and monuments will move the mind from an intellectual grasp towards an intuitive apprehension so that the vast sweep of Kemetic cosmic vision might sweep into view.

THE ASCENSION OF OSIRIS

Dramatis Personae
PRIEST
PRIESTESS
ORACLE OF THE SPHINX
PRIEST OF THE PYRAMID
THE FOUR SONS OF HORUS
THE VOICE OF NUIT
THE VOICE OSIRIS
THE VOICE OF HORUS
THE VOICE OF ISIS
THE VOICE OF NEPHTHYS

CHOREOGRAPH NOTES:
In the centre of the space, let there be an altar covered with gold cloth and statue of the pharaoh. This place represents the heart and meaning of the pyramid. The Priest of the Pyramid attends here. The Four Sons of Horus will also take up positions of guardianship here standing one to each of the four sides and facing outwards. This is the tememos where those representing the neteru will assemble. There is additionally a second altar attended by Nuit as the sky goddess and the Oracle as the Guardian of the Sphinx. This altar is set with candles, incense, a small pyramid, statues or pictures of Isis and Osiris, a statue of the Sphinx and a representation of a mummy case. Any other participants who are not assigned speaking roles may be formed into a circle either around the grouping at the 'pyramid' or around the outer circumference. This will depend on the space available and the number of participants. The person taking the role of Osiris stands in the role of an initiate on the threshold of a stellar initiation.

The musical segment *Opened are The Double Doors of Heaven* from *Akhenaten* by Philip Glass provides the perfect accompaniment. At the first music cue all participants break positions and move swiftly around the hall in a fast moving circuit, even a swift run if

THE BREATH OF ISIS

space permits. This represents the ascent of the king moving from one level of conscious existence to another. The group movement is also part of the meditative consciousness, and no focus should be lost during this time. A simple procession will also suffice if space is limited. When the music is over, all participants resume their places. The second music cue is more celebratory in nature. It too is part of the continuous meditation.

THE WORDS OF POWER

Priestess:

Companions we are met to explore a great mystery, established by our forefathers in the Light of the Ancient Wisdom. Let us begin our inner journey to the sacred site at Giza. In the mind's eye, let us see the three great monuments rising from the plain. Let us remember that in these three structures, we also see the three stars of the great constellation Orion. Let us become attuned to the stars in the old tradition,
As Above so Below.

We draw closer to the Horizon of Khufu, commonly called The Great Pyramid. Its white faces reflect a brilliant clear light. At the summit, gold glints like a beacon of fire. The sky is blue above us. We draw closer to see that a great procession is also winding its way across the plain. We hear the melancholy note of a horn sounding and we understand that we are close to the rites of death. The procession draws closer, and we see the royal mummy being carried upon its bier. We see the priesthood in formation and as they pass, in respectful silence we join their procession.

Procession enters.
The Four Sons of Horus take up positions around the central altar. Osiris, Horus, Isis, Nephthys and Priest of the Pyramid wait in the area between the central altar and the outer circumference.

THE ASCENSION OF OSIRIS

Priest:
A great mystery holds a great revelation. The rites of death are the rites of birth. Let us hear the words of the Guardian of this place.

Oracle of the Sphinx:
I am called the Sphinx but my true name is unknown. I represent a great mystery for you cannot fathom my nature or my purpose. You cannot say how I came to be for your mind sees only easy answers and explanations. I preside over the great cosmic mysteries. I tell of patterns and cycles, of stars and space, of time and mind. I sit and wait for you to look to the skies and wonder about origins and destinations. I wait upon your questions age after age. When you seek I will answer. I will answer you through silence which is wisdom. I will answer you through mystery which only self- revelation can fathom. I will answer you through challenge which will call upon all that you are and can be.
I will take you to the stars.

I am the Guardian of Guardians, the Keeper of this Place. I am The Watcher on High. I have watched the ages pass and now I watch you as you seek to understand what is written here. Remember, all knowledge brings change. What you seek will change you. This is my challenge for you. Behold now this pyramid, mer, the Place of Ascension, the Mystery of Mysteries. I leave you to contemplate its meaning in your lives. Seek in peace and honour in the true spirit of Holy Wisdom which denies nothing to the server of truth. All gates are opened to the wise, all gates are closed to the foolish. Go then in wisdom to the stars.

Priestess:
Offers incense

I offer incense to Isis-Sirius, Opener of the Year who rises with the Nile's flood, Great Provider provide for us. Divine Isis, wife of Osiris, Mother of Horus, carry us on your wings of inspiration to heights of being where we may understand these Mysteries. Isis, Mother of Horus, enfold us in your starry mantle as we reach out to your realms.

THE BREATH OF ISIS

Priest:

Offers incense.

I offer incense to Osiris-Orion, Divine Osiris, he of the staircase, the good god who welcomes the priest-king, welcome us as we travel the Path of Ascension. Divine Osiris, king and god, star-becoming, Great God, Lord of Abydos, Foremost of the Westerners, King of Eternity and of Everlasting. As we seek to understand these mysteries cast in star and stone, let us reflect upon our own becoming. As we hear the ancient words let us contemplate origins and destinations.

The Four Sons of Horus:

1. I am the North face of this House in Eternity.

2. I am the South face of this House in Eternity

3. I am the East face of this House in Eternity.

4. I am the West face of this House in Eternity.

1. Together we hold a Great Mystery.

2. Together we are The Horizon of Khufu.

3. Together we form the Place of Ascension.

4. Together we are the road of going up, the gateway to the stars.

Priest of the Pyramid:

Enters 'Pyramid' by stepping forwards towards the centre from the periphery.

I am the Priest of The Horizon of Khufu. O all you gods who shall cause this pyramid and this construction of the King to be fair and endure: you shall be effective, you shall be strong, you shall have your souls, you shall have power, you shall receive your god's offerings.

O Atum, set your protection over this King, over this pyramid of his, and over this construction of the king, prevent anything from happening evilly

THE ASCENSION OF OSIRIS

against it for ever, just as your protection was set over Shu and Tefnut. O you Great Ennead which is in On, make the King's name endure for ever.

The Voice of Osiris:
Enters 'Pyramid' by stepping forwards towards the centre from the periphery.

I am Osiris, departed King, Horus who was, Orion becoming. I travel the Path of Ascension here in this place, the Horizon of Khufu. See me here in mummy form.

Priest of the Pyramid:
Let us hear the words of Nuit, mother of Isis and Osiris, Lady of Heaven who spreads her wings over the departed.

The Voice of Nuit:
The king is my eldest son who split open my womb; he is my beloved, with whom I am well pleased. The king my son is my beloved. I have given to him the two horizons that he may have power in them as Harakhti. I enfold your beauty within this soul of mine for all life, permanence, dominion health, for the king - may he live forever. I have given to your sister Isis that she may lay hold of you and give heart for your body. I have given you your sister Nephthys that she may lay hold of you and give you your heart for your body.

Priest of the Pyramid:
Re in the sky is gracious to you and he conciliates the two lands for you, night is gracious to you. The Two Ladies are gracious to you, graciousness is what has been brought to you, graciousness is what you see, graciousness is what you hear, graciousness is in front of you, graciousness is behind you, graciousness is your portion.

O Osiris, the King I bring to you your son whom you love, who will split open your mouth. Let us hear the words of Horus.

THE BREATH OF ISIS

The Voice of Horus:
Enters 'Pyramid' by stepping forwards towards the centre from the periphery.

O King I have come in search of you. I am your son, I am Horus, child of my father, king who-shall-be. I have struck your mouth for you, for I am your beloved son; I have split open your mouth for you. I have split open your eye for you with the adze of iron. I bring you Horus' own eyes, seize them and join them to yourself.

O King, Horus has split open your mouth for you, he has split open your eyes with the Gods-Castle-Adze, with the Great-of-Magic Adze, the mouth is split open.

O Osiris, the King stand up, Horus has caused you to stand up. Horus has given you his eye that you may see with it, Horus has split open your eye for you that you may see with it in its name of Opener of Roads. O Osiris the King, Horus has placed you in the heart of the gods, he has caused you to take possession of all that is yours. Horus has found you and it goes well with you.

Priest of the Pyramid:
The messengers of your double come for you, the messengers of your father come for you, the messengers of Re come for you, so go after the sun and cleanse yourself for your bones are those of the divine falcons who are in the sky.

May you go beside the god, may you depart and ascend to your son, may you fetter anyone who shall speak evilly against your name.
Go up for Geb has committed him to a low estate in his town so that he may flee and sink down weary but you shall bathe in the starry firmament, the sun-folk shall call out to you for the imperishable stars have raised you aloft.

Ascend to the place where your father is, to the place where Geb is that he may give you that which is on the brow of Horus so that you may

THE ASCENSION OF OSIRIS

have a soul thereby and power thereby and that you shall be at the ahead of the Westerners thereby.

O King, your messengers go, your heralds run to your father, to Atum. O Atum raise him up to you enclose him within your arms.

O King, you have not departed dead, you have departed alive. Sit upon the throne of Osiris, your sceptre in your hand that you may give orders to the living, your lotus bud sceptre in your hand. Your arms are Atum your shoulders are Atum, your belly is Atum, your hinder-parts are Atum. Your legs are Atum, your face is Anubis.

Priest of the Pyramid:

O Re-Atum, this King comes to you as an imperishable spirit, lord of the affairs of the place of the four pillars. Your son comes you. O Atum this one here is your son Osiris whom have caused to be restored that he may live.

This King comes to you, may you traverse the sky being united in the darkness, may you rise in the horizon, in the place where is well with you. O Re-Atum, your son comes to you, the King comes to you, raise him up, enclose him in your embrace, for he is the son of your body for ever. The doors of the horizon are opened, its bolts are drawn back.

Music
Company break positions and run or swiftly walk in a circle surrounding the central altar returning to previous positions at the close of music.

The Voice of Osiris:

I have come to you my father, I have come to you O Re.

I have come to you my father, I have come to you O Great Wild Bull.

I have come to you O my father, I have come to you O Soped.

I have come to you, O Nut. I have come to you, O Nuit.

THE BREATH OF ISIS

I have cast my father to the earth, I have left Horus behind me, my wings have grown into those of a falcon my two plumes are those of a sacred falcon, my soul has brought me and its magic has equipped me.

The Voice of Nuit:
Open up your place among the stars of the sky, for you are the Lone Star, the companion of Hu; look down upon Osiris when he governs the spirits for you stand far off from him, you are not among them and you shall not be among them.

Priest of the Pyramid:
Your son Horus has acted on your behalf. Hail to you wise one, Geb has created you, the Ennead has borne you. Horus is pleased with his father.

The Voice of Osiris:
I have succeeded to Geb, I have succeeded to Geb, I have succeeded to Atum. I am on the throne of Horus the first borne and his eye is my strength. I have come to my throne.

Priest of the Pyramid:
Enters 'Pyramid' Isis and Nephthy together by stepping forwards from the periphery.

Behold she comes to meet you as does the Beautiful West, meeting you with her lovely tresses and she says, "Here comes he who I have born." The Mourning-Woman summons you as Isis, the Mooring Post calls to you as Nephthys.

The Voice of Osiris:
Here I am O Isis, here I am, O Nephthys. Come that you may see your son.

THE ASCENSION OF OSIRIS

The Voice of Horus:

Wake O my father Osiris for I am your son who loves you, I am your son Horus who loves you, behold I have come, wake up, wake up O King, wake up for me, I am your son, I am Horus who wakes you. The two sisters who love you are Isis and Nephthys and they will support you. The king has come to you. You great and mighty companions who are in the eastern side of the sky lift the King and set him at the eastern side of the sky. 'Greetings' says Isis. "In Peace," says Nephthys when they see their brother in the Festival of Atum.

The Mourning-Woman calls to you as Isis, the joyful one rejoices over you as Nephthys.

Isis cries out to you, Nephthys calls out to you.

The Great Mooring Post speaks to you as Isis.

The West calls to you as Nephthys.

The Mourning woman cries out to you, the Great Mooring Post calls to you.

Hands are clapped, feet are stamped for you. You ascend here as a star, as the Morning Star.

O my father the King take this milky fluid of yours which is in the breasts of your mother Isis.

O Nephthys give him your hand.

The Voice of Isis

How lovely to see you when you ascend to the sky, your power upon you, your terror about you, your magic at your feet, you are helped by Atum just as he used to do, the gods who are in the sky are brought to you, the gods who are on the earth assemble for you, they place their hands under you, they make a ladder for you that you may ascend on it to the sky. The doors of the sky are opened, the doors of the starry firmament are thrown open for you.

THE BREATH OF ISIS

O Osiris, the King, I am Isis, I have come into the middle of this earth, into the place where you are.

I have come and have laid hold over you. Rouse yourself, turn yourself over O king for I am Isis.

I have come that I may lay hold of you and give you your heart for your body.

The Voice of Nephthys:
Osiris the King, I have come rejoicing for love of you O King.
Rouse yourself O King turn yourself about O King.
I am Nephthys and I have come that I may lay hold of you and give to you your heart for you.

Priest of the Pyramid:
Your sister Isis comes rejoicing for love of you.
You have placed her on your phallus and your seed issues into her.

She is ready as Sothis, and Harspod has come forth from you as Horus who is in Sothis.

It is well with you.

A mystery takes place deep in the Place of Becoming.

A mystery takes place deep in the Place of Ascension.

The Voice of Osiris:
May Orion give me his hand for Sothis has taken my hand.
Priest of the Pyramid:

Osiris awakes the languid god awakes, the god stands up, the god has power in his body.

The King awakes. The King's road is opened for the King, a road is made ready for the King.

THE ASCENSION OF OSIRIS

The Voice of Horus:

O my father, the king, may you climb and mount the sunshine, for to you belongs the half-light which is on the pole of the sky.

O my father the King, I will make this shout of acclaim because you have no human fathers and you have no human mothers, your father is the Great Wild Bull, your mother is the Maiden.

Live the life, for you have not died the death.

The Voice of Osiris:

The sky is clear, Sothis lives, because I am a living one, the son of Sothis, and the Two Enneads have cleansed themselves for me in Ursa Major, the imperishable.

My house in the sky will not perish. My throne on earth will not be destroyed. For men hide, the gods fly away.

Sothis has caused me to fly up into the sky into the company of my brethren gods.

Nuit the great has uncovered her arms for me. My seat is with you O Re and I will not give it to anyone else, I will ascend to the sky to you.

Music to accompany personal meditation

Priest:

Let us rejoice. We have witnessed a great mystery in the Place of Becoming.

Let us rejoice. We have witnessed a great mystery in the Place of Ascension.

Let a communion be shared to commemorate this homecoming.
Communion of white wine and dates

Priest:

Our joy is complete. Let the company depart in peace. Em hotep

THE BREATH OF ISIS

Group at the central turn anticlockwise led by Osiris, next Isis and Nephthys, then The Four Sons of Horus.

After one circuit, this group moves towards the greater assembly who follow in procession to complete two further circuits. This closing movement is also a meditation and all participants should visualise a returning descent towards all things manifest and known.

MEDITATION REPORT
THE KINGDOM OF THE FIRST TIME
– 29TH MAY 1995

I have enclosed the following report. At the time, it was as bizarre to me as it must appear to you now. Nevertheless, it is a faithful and accurate account. You are free to make of what you will. At the time I wondered if I had quite lost my mind and sent the report to a friend who just advised me file it in the usual manner without passing any judgement on it – which is exactly what I did.

> *In meditation, I passed through what I called, the 'Star-gate.' It seemed very easy perhaps because I have journeyed here often without realising it. This seemed a little different however from my usual journeys as for the first time I felt quite unaided. As soon as I emerged, images from the film Stargate came flooding in and I consciously thought, if I see a pyramid I shall know that I am quite deluded. Of course I did see a pyramid, in fact I soon realised that I was standing in the archetypal Kingdom of The First Time. Here was the prototype Giza itself. Everything was pristine and brilliant. It was quite unchanged by time.*

THE ASCENSION OF OSIRIS

I stood for only a brief period of time before I saw a small procession approaching. I was greeted thus, "Welcome, we are your ancestors and your descendants. We are your future and your past. We are The Kingdom of The First Time and you have returned to us. You have remembered the way home. We greet you and welcome you. You are free to travel here as often as you are able. Each time will become easier and you will prepare a way for others. We await your every coming and look forward with deep joy to the time when our priesthood stands here. For us, you will come in no time at all, for time has no meaning here with us. We will welcome you in the Great House of Life. You will sit among us and receive teaching which is much needed on earth. We give you a gift for your return." I was handed a box and I asked if I might look inside. I opened it and two white birds flew up, each held the end of a banner, it began to unfurl and I saw letters strung upon a skein. "This is the gift of Common Understanding, it contains all the scripts of the world." The banner then seemed to condense itself and return to the box which was handed to me.

I addressed the small assembly something along the following lines ."Kingdom of The First Time, I thank you for your gift for the peoples of Earth. I have been away and travelled far but I have never forgotten you. Our stellar priesthood shall return and you shall look upon us face to face, brethren to brethren. We shall come at the appointed time. Until then I go to prepare our coming."

I think then with due salutations I turned and departed the way I had come. The visit was very clear in my mind and I don't think I realised how far I had travelled. On returning I found it very difficult to inhabit my body. I could hardly move myself and finally drifted back to dreamless sleep. I did not surface fully for about four hours. I rested and watched the TV fairly aimlessly

THE BREATH OF ISIS

only to see an advert appearing which showed me the words, 'One Language' in large letters. I think I am sane enough to still question my sanity. Writing this report and submitting it to you is a way of keeping a watch on my mind.

It dawned on me some time later than our Mystery Play *The Ascension of Osiris* had been performed on the weekend of the week celebrating Ascension Day. This curious quirk of fate created a perfect synchronicity yet for my part no preplanning had been involved, I am oblivious to the nuances of the Christian calendar, and we took the booking offered to us by the university!

NOTES

1. Robert Bauval: author, researcher, alternative historian. Robert Bauval has written numerous popular and controversial books focused on an alternative view of ancient Egyptian history and culture. He is perhaps best known for *The Orion Mystery* which began his meteoric rise to public attention.

CHAPTER II

THE ADORATION OF SEKHMET

BACKGROUND

I became interested in Sekhmet when the phrase, The Adoration of Sekhmet appeared in my mind and would not leave. Her presence resides in a triplicity of statues in the British Museum and I have stood in front of Her on several occasions. I have no earth shattering experiences to report, but She certainly seized my mind with such force that I planned a weekend in Her honour. As I began to find out more about Sekhmet, I came across the book by Robert Masters, *Goddess Sekhmet: Psycho-Spiritual Exercises of the Fifth Way* which became my essential reading.

The Litany of Sekhmet is the script used for the weekend The Adoration of Sekhmet. It is indebted to the inspiration provided by Robert Masters, and quite unlike any other ritual script I have used before or since. I hope it is not seen as a plagiarism, but as a sincere attempt to place his words in a ceremonial context. Despite its brevity and apparent simplicity, the Litany is deceptively powerful as the entire rite is a lengthy extended invocation.

The book is a key text to approaching Sekhmet. Robert Masters has pioneered a path towards especially in her role as the mistress of the five bodies, or vehicles of consciousness. Curiously the two members of the group who experienced a strong attraction towards Sekhmet, were both deeply immersed in energy work as Reiki practitioners. I do not believe that this connection is merely

THE BREATH OF ISIS

accidental. It is very clear to me that Kemetic metaphysics included a deep, profound and utterly practical understanding of living energetic dynamics. However too proscriptive a comparison with our present understanding of the chakra system is bound to mislead.

A single experience from the weekend stands out in my memory. Within a couple of days, one of the participants alerted me to the fact that since the ritual his arms and hands had not stopped itching. Now one of the lesser known titles of Sekhmet is, 'she who scratches.' This epithet could be interpreted in many ways but speaking personally, it aligns Sekhmet with the kundalini fire which often creates strange physical sensations as high voltage energy runs through the nervous system. My friend's itching arms, and extremely overheated hands did not subside but became quite troublesome. Quite soon his symptoms were getting in the way of his work as a teacher. The GP proscribed all sorts of treatment but nothing provided more than a temporary relief. To cut a long story short, after several months, my friend began the process of applying for early retirement on health grounds, eventually it was granted. Was he unhappy at the outcome – not in the least!

COMMENTARY

Sekhmet is a neter embodied in the form of a lioness. Contemplate for a moment the power and intelligence of the lioness, skilled at hunting and quick to kill when required. She has a physical power and ferocity not given to humans. Yet She also shares the form of a woman and as such She embodies the fierce protective instinct of a mother.

An Egyptian myth states that when Ra was made discontent by humans, in a moment of rage he despatched Sekhmet to destroy them. But soon Sekhmet was beyond his control. She destroyed almost all and ravaged with such efficient savagery that Ra soon regretted his intention and wished to call her back. But her blood lust was so great that she could not be stopped. Ra called upon

THE ADORATION OF SEKHMET

Thoth for help and he suggested that vats of red beer should be laid out. Some authorities suggest that it was a perhaps beer spiked with red ochre or even ground haematite to resemble human blood. In any event Sekhmet drank her fill mistaking beer for blood and fell into a long drunken sleep. The slaughter was done. In some ways the story is a representation of a real physical manifestation since the Nile ran blood red with silt from upstream at the yearly inundation and the resulting flood waters were a danger to human life.

The name of Sekhmet means Power and this same force of Sekhem is embodied in the baton held as a sign of authority. Power is a gift to the wise and for those unwise enough to call upon its name prematurely, it will become a poison. Like a beautiful woman, power is alluring, tempting and provocative. The dream of power awakens desire for it opens all horizons and possibilities. This tincture is as slippery as quicksilver, as toxic as lead and as compelling as gold, once tasted, it cannot be forgotten. So, Sekhmet is the neter of Power. She will bring temptation and destruction unless your capacity for greed, avarice and self-aggrandisement has been tamed. When these self-satisfying voices have been despatched, Power becomes a servant and the essential ally of those destined to rule. The divine rulership of kings is over and in the age of men, rulership has become a civil and secular matter. Nevertheless, the exercise of power remains part of civil society, all institutions and organisations function with the assistance of a power accrued through time. Power is quite impersonal and when diverted for personal gain or satisfaction, the lioness will roar and bite in rebellion. Yet power is abused daily by self-serving individuals hiding in compliant hierarchies.

When kingship was a divinely conceived, Sekhmet was among the royal protectors and Mut the divine-wife of Amun at Thebes took on some of Sekhmet's leonine qualities. Though often recognisable by her vulture cap, Mut also absorbed Sekhmet's

THE BREATH OF ISIS

fierce protective power as part of her identification with the cult of queenship whereby queens embodied powerful the female neter in different capacities as Hathor, Isis and Sekhmet too.

Sekhmet had a temple in the Nile delta at the capital of the 11th nome. It was called Leontopolis by the Greeks since lions were kept in a spacious enclosure. Her statues were placed at locations calling for protective powers. It has been suggested that more than seven hundred statues once stood in the funerary temple of Amenhotep on the west bank of the Nile. Public festivals for Sekhmet were held at Thebes where her pacification was remembered and re-enacted with dancing, jubilation and much red beer. Her priestesses performed daily rituals of pacification before a different statue on each day of the year. Just as a lion requires to be fed daily so the lioness neter required to be pacified daily. Despite her bloody nature, or perhaps as a result of it, Sekhmet becomes closely associated with healing especially surgery. In this capacity, She is called The Lady of Knives.

Sekhmet is the consort of Ptah at Memphis where is he is the great craftsman and metal worker. His High Priest in likeness was also a master craftsman and architect. This priestly lineage assumed an importance in the Ramesside period as participants at the state rituals of coronation. The High Priests of Ptah retained a close link with royalty often marrying women of royal descent and played an important part at the Ptolemaic court. In this way Sekhmet's original role as protector to the royal lineage was diffused and spread through these connecting priestly functions.

PREPARATION

There are several levels and stages of necessary preparation, intellectual, intuitive and imaginative. Unusually the Litany includes mantras or words of power and these should be taken as themes for reflection so that they are not merely sounds upon the air.

The mantra is vibrated, not merely spoken by the whole company. It expresses a threefold transformation. The hieroglyph,

THE ADORATION OF SEKHMET

'sa' includes meanings of safety and protection but it also means the will to bring things to pass, the ability to translate action into substance, the power to manifest a vision and turn an idea into physical reality. Sekhem is the power willingly received and applied to the process of transformation as a flame beneath a cooking pot. The sahu is the body of gold or the perfected vehicle of consciousness. So this seemingly simple mantra of just three words holds a powerful sequence: from will, through applied power the glorified consciousness will arise. The mantra should be applied forcefully, powerfully and backed by a focussed intent.

The beautiful statue of Sekhmet at the British Museum should be included as a meditation moment. If this is not possible, find an image of Her for your reflection. Generally speaking, unless Sekhmet calls you directly, you have little reason to call on Her.

SEKHMET AND THE HOUSE OF LIFE
Extracts from a talk delivered at the Isian Assembly, 15th September, 1996

I greet you in the name of the House of Life which has drawn us here together. For the House of Life magnetises the soul and imprints its image deep in memory and imagination. Egyptologists would of course not wax lyrical about a vague and poorly understood institution. While there can be no doubt about the existence of the Per Ankh, Egyptologists are unclear about its purpose. Was it a merely the place where scribes were trained? Was it a priestly training college? Was it a university for higher learning, a library where archives were maintained, a place where texts were copied generation to generation, or was it something outside a contemporary frame of reference?

Professor C.J. Bleeker "The only useful guiding principle in Egyptology is: one must learn to think Egyptian to be able to penetrate the religion of ancient Egypt." Here is the single key, to penetrate the nature of the House of Life, we must learn to think

THE BREATH OF ISIS

in an Egyptian manner. It is clear that the Egyptian mindset is not our own. The writer Arthur Versluis reminds us that, "The gulf between modernity and antiquity is not temporal but mental."2 the philosopher and alchemist R.A. Schwaller de Lubicz also recognizes this gulf of understanding. "Our own confusion is the consequence of a mistaken way of seeking, which is the path taken by rationalism." The ancient Egyptian mindset was entirely symbolic, the ancient Egyptian civilisation was constructed upon the symbolic relationships of myth thereupon ritualised into festival and institution.

Pythagoras who spent twenty-two years in Egypt and was initiated into the temple tradition adopted this mindset and made it the cornerstone of his teaching. Iamblicus records that, "The method of teaching he wished to introduce was the symbolical one, in a manner similar to that which he had been instructed in Egypt."3 Pythagoras encouraged students to train the memory and develop a state of inner serenity. He taught a philosophy which integrated psychology with political philosophy, astronomy with ethics, music with piety, geometry with divinity. He taught metaphysics and mathematics. We remember Pythagoras but forget who taught him.

The House of Life, the Per Ankh combines two powerful symbols, that of a dwelling and that of the ankh. The house represents residence, and habitation, it is a container. The ankh, the most familiar of all ancient Egyptian symbols is derived from the thoracis spine of the bull and represented its mighty virility and power. The ankh is seen to be held by the gods and extended often it towards the nose, the most subtle of the sensory organs with immediate access to the brain. The Per Ankh was the residence and container for the life-giving powers held in divinely inspired writings. The ancient Egyptians believed in the power of the word, an emanation or, 'soul of Re' and the scribes in the House of Life were described as followers or servants of Re. The Egyptologist C.J. Bleeker understood that *"The aim of all cultic rites is the renewal*

THE ADORATION OF SEKHMET

of the life of the world, of the community and of the individual." Ancient Egypt was vitalised by the theme of perpetual renewal both in myth and ritual through the numinous power of the word under the aegis of Djehuty- Thoth.

The evidence for the House of Life is sparse and the historical record is vague. Recorded references are few until the reign of Ramesses 1V who expressed a particular interest in all things literary, archaeological and magical. He is described as investigating, *"the annals of Thoth who is in the House of Life."* Elsewhere he is described as being, *'excellent of understanding like Thoth.'* It is said that he, *"penetrated into the annals like the maker thereof,"* having, *"examined the writings of the House of Life."* At El Amarna two small buildings were constructed with bricks individually stamped with the hieroglyph for the per ankh. The temples at Memphis, Abydos, Akhmim, Coptos, Esna and Edfu included a House of Life, it is most likely that this is true of every major city

Tombs of a number of scribes from the House of Life have been found. Amenwahsu from the Nineteenth Dynasty at Thebes is described as, *"scribe of the sacred books in the house of Amun, wab priest in the House of Amun, conducting the festivals of all the gods at their seasonal feasts, scribe who wrote the annals of the gods and goddesses in the House of Life."* His son Khaemope carried the same title and is described as, *"one who wrote the annals of all the gods in the House of Life."* Amenmose is called, *"scribe of the sacred books, scribe of the House of Life of the Lord of the Two lands."* The prince Mentjuhotep is called, *"Master of the Secrets of the House of Life."* The scribe Iha from El-Bershah, is described as, *"one who propitiates the gods, an overseer of writings in the House of Life, to whom all private matters are revealed."* Later In the Thirtieth Dynasty, a chief lector priest is described as, *"leader of the masters of magic in the House of Life."* A relief from Bubastis depicting the Hb Sd festival shows a priestly procession described as, *"friends and masters of magic,"* and two

THE BREATH OF ISIS

persons present are described as, *"magician-protectors of the King of Lower Egypt."* These inscriptions link the House of Life to the festivals of state, to magic, to the power of the written words, to the gods, and to the pharaoh. An inscription in the name of the chief physician, Udjehorressnet, clearly describes one purpose of the Per Ankh.

> *His Majesty king Darius commanded me to return to Egypt in order to restore the department(s) of the House(s) of Life .. after they had fallen into decay. I did as His Majesty commanded me; I furnished them with all their staffs consisting of persons of rank, not a poor man's son among them. I placed them in charge of every learned man (in order to teach them) all their crafts. His Majesty commanded them to be given all (manner of) good things that they might exercise all their crafts. I equipped them with all their ability and their apparatus which was on record in accordance with their former condition. This His Majesty did because he knew the virtue of this art to revive all that are sick and to commemorate for ever the name(s) of all the gods, their temples, their offerings and the conduct of their festivals.*

This text affirms the view that The House of Life was connected with the practice of medicine. However, another inscription is more enigmatic and magical.

> *As for the House of Life, it shall be in Abydos. Build it in four bodies, the inner body being of covered reeds. As for the four 'houses' and the four presences of Life, as for the living one, He is Osiris, and as for the four they are Isis, Nephthys, Horus, Thoth, Isis being on one side and Nephthys on the other; Horus on one side and Thoth on the other. These are the four sides. Gebb is its ground and Nut its heaven. The hidden one who rests within it is the Great God. The four outer bodies consist of a stone that contains two wings, and its lower part, its floor is*

THE ADORATION OF SEKHMET

sand, and its outside has severally four doors, one south, one north, one west and one east. It shall be hidden and very large. It shall not be known nor shall it be seen; but the sun shall look upon its mystery. The people who enter into it are the staff of Re and the scribes of the House of Life. The people who are in it, the fkty-priest is Shu, the slaughterer is Horus who slays the rebels for his father Osiris, and the scribe of the sacred books is Thoth, and it is he who will recite the ritual glorifications in the course of every day unseen, unheard. Hale of mouths and secret of body and mouths. They are far removed from sudden cutting of. No Asiatic shall enter into it, he shall not see it thou art very far removed. The books that are in it are the emanations of Re wherewith to keep alive this god and to overthrow his enemies. As for the staff of the House of Life who are in it, they are the followers of Re protecting his son Osiris every day.

This mysterious model takes us straight to the numinous, in it we recognise an archetypal construction much like a mandala or magic circle with Osiris the god of resurrection at its centre. Like all mandalas and magic circles, this particular model can be internalised as a map for the psyche. Yet the mundane is never far away for these gods bring practical gifts to Egypt. Thoth, the self-created, is the inventor of astronomy, astrology, the science of numbers and mathematics, geometry, land surveying, medicine and botany. He established the worship of the gods and laid down the rules concerning the times and nature of offerings. He composed hymns and prayers by which the gods should be addressed and drew up liturgical works. He invented the letters of the alphabet, the arts of reading and the skill of oratory. He was the author behind every branch of knowledge whether human or divine The Books of Thoth numbered 42. As scribe of the gods, Thoth was the god of scribes and the great unseen mind behind the House of Life itself. Isis and Osiris as the rulers of Egypt bestowed the civilising forces of law and established the mysteries.

THE BREATH OF ISIS

Other less well-known among the neteru had special connections with the Per Ankh. Seshat was called The Lady of Plans and the Lady of Writings in the House of Life. Khnum the builder god par excellence was a protector to the House of Life and was called Lord of the House of Life. But the divinity we should never forget in relation to the House of Life is Sekhmet, the Mistress of Transformation. The word sekhem simply means, 'the power.' This is the force behind all magic, the raison d'etre of The House of Life. Thus is Sekhmet rightly called, The Great Lady of the House of Life.

The nature and qualities of Sekhmet perhaps above any other single deity provide insight into the nature of the House of Life. Her leonine nature, wild and fierce made her the ideal figurehead for the activity of the slaughterhouse and the work of butchers. But this same power also made her the aegis for surgical and medical practice. Yet if we describe Sekhmet only as the patron goddess of medical practice, we miss the essential unifying function of her presence and we have failed to touch the Egyptian mind. Sekhmet unifies the arts and science, the mundane and the metaphysical, the medical and the magical. All of these are extensions and expressions of the one life constantly transformed. She is called the Lady of Transformation. The application of medicine brings transformation. The application of magic brings transformation. The application of metaphysical knowledge brings transformation. The application of knowledge itself brings transformation. Transformation is the key to initiation, the renewing function of festival and myth, and all esoteric practices.

Sekhmet embodies the active power of transformation, for she is as Shakti. To engage with Sekhmet is to actively court transformation. She is Kundalini, the raised serpent on the brow of her father. As Shakti is to Shiva, so Sekhmet is to Ptah. As Shiva lies beneath Shakti as a corpse, so Ptah is the bound mummiform awaiting the fertilising power of the feminine. Ptah is conceived of

THE ADORATION OF SEKHMET

as the creator of the physical world but he does not act without the life giving fire of Sekhmet. Like Shakti, Sekhmet is the awakener. As the rising Kundalini, she is fire, the gleaming one. As the risen Kundalini, she is the bringer of enlightenment. Hear the path of transformation through her titles.

> Sekhmet, Great One of magic
> Lady of Transformations
> The Source
> Awakener
> Opener of Ways
> Flaming One
> Sparkling One
> Gleaming One
> Destroyer by Fire
> Giver of Ecstasies
> Ruler of Serpents
> Sublime One
> Enlightened
> Great Serpent on the Head of her Father
> Lady of all Powers
> Beloved Sekhmet

According to Robert Masters, it was at Memphis where the system of Sekhmet, Ptah and Nefer-tum was taught. In this triad we find the same enduring themes of Egyptian sacred life. Through the fertilising power of Sekhmet, Ptah brings forth mathematics, philosophy, the sciences, literature, painting, sculpture and music. Nefer-tum brings medicine. Sekhmet herself brings a systemized knowledge of higher states of consciousness and the interrelationship between the subtle bodies and the physical form. Robert Masters has restored a system which unites and integrates the five bodies into a composite centre of active consciousness. As he openly admits, there is much more to bring through, for more has been lost than found.

The Egyptians understood the relationship between the creative powers and the world itself. Like a stone dropped into water, the impact of the causal ntr created ripple upon ripple in the world of effects. Medicine, the veterinary sciences, astronomy, the arts, the sciences, music, dance and more besides all flow from a single source and centre. They are not separated but the gifts of single blessing. In our fragmented world, knowledge and wisdom have been split asunder, knowledge itself has become fragmented. Mathematics, architecture, astronomy, music, philosophy, art, medicine are seen to be separate and quite distinct. Mathematicians do not mix with medical men, architects do not mix with astronomers. They have little to give each other. Above all, the spiritual and the material have been prised apart. Arthur Versluis understands this well. He writes that, '*In a very real sense our modern age represents an anomaly, a discontinuity, and a time of dissolution, in which by making contact with the ancient past, we also contact the future, serving very much thereby as a means of continuity for the perennial truth, the realisation of the transcendent. Whether we know it or not, this is the single most important function one could perform in this, or any other age. For indeed contact with the primordial is that for which one exists, and initiation is the 'turning about in the consciousness' which signifies this very change in the direction of one's life, turning from the dispersed to the concentrated, from the irreal to the Primordial.*'

The House of Life is rightly named. It is no simple training school for the scribal arts but the House of the Mysteries of Life. At its heart we find Osiris, lord of all cycles of renewal. In the typically labyrinthine complexities of Egyptian theology, Ptah and

THE ADORATION OF SEKHMET

Osiris merged as Ptah-Seker-Asar, the triune god of resurrection, the architect and builder of the world, self-begotten, self-born, the giver of everlasting life, perhaps a fitting mystery in the House of the Greatest Mysteries.

In our current struggle for holism, The House of Life presents a powerful model. The House of Life does not belong to the past but to the eternal present. The House of Life lives, its magic lives, its vivifying centre lives, the deities live. Let me close by addressing you with the words of one Petearpokrates, king's scribe and prophet of Mehyt in Abydos.

> *O all you priests who penetrate into the words of god and are skilled in writings, you who are enlightened in the House of Life and have discovered the ways of the gods, who have penetrated into the archives of the library and can interpret the mysteries of the emanations of Re, who are skilled in the work of the ancestors and who open up the heart of what is upon the wall, you who carve the tombs and interpret the mysteries, who shall come to Rostau and if you all shall, approach the sacred land.*

THE LITANY OF SEKHMET

Dramatis Personae:
PRIEST
PRIESTESS
THE COMPANY OF SEKHMET, THE SHEMSU

On the altar:
Many pictures and statues of Sekhmet placed on a red cloth
2 Candles
Incense

THE BREATH OF ISIS

CHOREOGRAPH NOTES:

This is mainly a static rite with an opportunity for free dance, the altar may be placed in one quarter with the company completing a circle. The mantras are to be spoken by the whole company. The remaining script can be divided in many equally valid ways, either for choral or solo voices. For instances the Voices can be allocated a line to each person simply moving around the circle and the name of Sekhmet can be spoken by the assembly. If this is the case, the lines should follow swiftly as a continuous and seamless.

THE WORDS OF POWER

Priestess:

Lights candle and incense.

We meet to offer Adoration to Sekhmet.

Priest:

Lights candle and incense.

We meet to offer Adoration to Sekhmet.

Shemsu omnes:

We meet to offer Adoration to Sekhmet.

Sekhmet, Lady of the Place of The Beginning of Time,

Sekhmet, Whose Essence is Fire,

Tempestuous, Forever,

Great One of Magic, Grant us

Success in our endeavour.

Blessed be the Name of Sekhmet

Beloved Her Image

THE ADORATION OF SEKHMET

As it was at Memphis
So be it here now.

•

Hear us, we beseech Thee
O Powerful One

•

Lady of Rekht,
Lady of Pekhet,
Lady of Set,
Lady of Rehesaui,
Lady of Tchar and of Sehert
Mother in the Horizon of Heaven,
In the Boat of Millions of Years,
Thou art the Great Defender,
Thou art Overthrower of Qetu,
Preserve us from the evil chamber
of the souls of Hes-hra
Deliver us from the Abode of Fiends . . .

•

O Thou Who Art
Sekhmet,
Life-Giver to the Gods,
Sekhmet,
Lady of Flame,

THE BREATH OF ISIS

Sekhmet,

Great One of Magic,

Sekhmet,

Ennead is thy Name,

O, Hear Us Now

Sekhmet,

With Lioness head

Sekhmet,

Whose colour is Red

Sekhmet,

Daughter of Ra

Sekhmet,

Consort of Ptah

Sekhmet,

Mighty is thy name,

O, Hear Us Now

Sekhmet,

Goddess of Pestilence

Sekhmet,

Goddess of Wars

Sekhmet,

Queen of the Wastelands

Sekhmet,

Terrible Is Thy Name

THE ADORATION OF SEKHMET

O, Come to us.

Sekhmet,

Destoyer of Rebellions

Sekhmet,

Scorching Eye of Ra

Sekhmet,

Protector, Ruler

Sekhmet,

Holy is Thy Name

O, Reveal Thyself to Us.

Sekhmet,

Mother of the Gods,

Sekhmet,

Mistress of the Crowns

Sekhmet,

Thou art the Only One

Sekhmet,

Beloved is Thy Name.

Possess us now, O Great One.

Sekhmet,

Greater than Isis

Sekhmet,

Greater than Hathor

Sekhmet,

Greater than Bast

THE BREATH OF ISIS

Sekhmet,

Greater than Maat

Sekhmet,

Mysterious is Thy Name,

We are Lost in Mystery

Sekhmet,

Pre-eminent One

Sekhmet,

Light beyond darkness

Sekhmet,

Sovereign of Her Father

Sekhmet,

Hidden is thy name

Rapturous is our dying

Lady of Amt,

Lady of Manu,

Lady of Sa,

Lady of Tep-Nef,

Lady of Heaven,

•

Thou art Ammi-seshet,

Destroyer, Upholder,

Thou art the Terror,

Before Which Fiends tremble,

THE ADORATION OF SEKHMET

Thou art Lust,

Thou art Life,

Ever-burning ONE.

Tekaharaesa - Pusaremkakaremet

Sefi-per-em-hes-hra-hapi-tchet-f

Mistress of Enchantments,

Source and Word of Power,

Forbidden Is Thy Name.

•

I am the sealed One.

Do not consume us

With thy Fire.

Give us Light.

O Lady, Mightier than the Gods,

Adoration rises unto Thee,

All beings hail Thee,

O Lady, Mightier than the Gods

Preserved beyond Death

That Secret Name

O Being

Called Sekhmet

At the Throne of Silence

even, shall no more be spoken than

EncircIng One

I lose myself in you.

THE BREATH OF ISIS

Sustained Silence to be broken by the ringing of a chime by the priest

Priest:
Lady of the Words of Power
We speak the Words of Power.

Voices of the Shemsu Omnes:

SA

SEKHEM

SAHU

•

SA

SEKHEM

SAHU

•

SA

SEKHEM

SAHU

Priestess:
Let music and dance be offered in celebration.

Music and Dance

Voices of the Shemsu:
Lady of Images
We contemplate your image and say your name.

•

Sekhmet, Great One of Magic
Mother of the Gods.

THE ADORATION OF SEKHMET

One Who Was Before the Gods Were

Lady of the Place of the Beginning of Time,

Beloved of Ra, her Father

Beloved of Bast, her Sister

Beloved of Ptah, her Husband.

At whose wish the Arts were Born.

Beautiful Eye which giveth Life to the Two Lands.

Beautiful Face, Image most beloved by Art.

Flaming One

Sovereign of Ra, her Father.

Protectress of the Gods.

Lady of the Scarlet-Coloured Garment.

Pure One.

Destroyer of Rebellions.

Eye of Ra.

Eye of Horus.

Pre-eminent One in the Boat of the Millions of Years.

Roamer of Deserts

Wanderer in the Wastes.

Self-Contained.

Only One.

Awakener.

Lady of Enchantments.

Opener of the Ways.

Lady of Transformations.

THE BREATH OF ISIS

Lady of the Many Faces.

Enrapturing One.

Giver of Ecstasies.

Satisfier of Desires.

Inspirer of Males.

Victorious in Battles.

Overcomer of all Enemies.

Ruler of the Desert

Ruler of Serpents and of Dragons

Ruler of Lions.

Complete One

Sublime One

Enlightener

Empowerer

Sparkling One.

Great one of Hekau.

Lady of the Magic Lamp.

Mother of the Dead.

Lady of the Bloodbath.

Destroyer by Plagues.

Great one of Healing.

Lady of the Waters of Life.

Mistress and Lady of the Tomb.

Great One in the Places of Judgement and Execution.

Guide and Protectress from the Perils of the Underworld.

THE ADORATION OF SEKHMET

Great One of the Place of Appearance in Silence.

Lady of the Way of the Five Bodies.

Unrivalled and Invincible One.

Ruler of the Chamber of Flames.

She Whose Opportunity escapeth her Not.

Winged One.

Powerful of Heart.

The Aware

The Gleaming One.

Sekhmet, who reduceth to silence

Sekhmet who Rouseth the People.

Lady of Jubilation.

Adorable One.

Shining of Countenance.

Mother of Images.

Incomparable One.

Lady of Intoxication.

Mightier than the Gods.

Most Beautiful.

Most Strong.

Great One of Laws.

Protectress of the Divine Order

The One who Holds Back Darkness.

The Beautiful Light.

Warrior Goddess.

THE BREATH OF ISIS

Goddess of Love.

Great One in Heaven.

Great Serpent on the Head of her Father.

Great One the Incenses of the Ennead.

Great Lady of the House of Life.

Queen of the Venerable Ones.

Lady of the House of Books.

Devouring One

Sekhmet of the Knives.

Burner of Evildoers.

One Before Whom Evil Trembles.

Terrible One.

Lady of all Powers.

Eternal as her Father.

Lady of the Manifold Adornments.

Most Beautiful Among the Gods.

Bountiful One.

Sekhmet who Gives Joys.

Unwavering Loyal One.

Beloved Teacher.

Beloved Sekhmet.

Priest:
Lady of the Words of Power
We hear the Words of Power.

THE ADORATION OF SEKHMET

Shemsu Omnes

SA

SEKHEM

SAHU

•

SA

SEKHEM

SAHU

•

SA

SEKHEM

SAHU

Voices of the Shemsu:
Lady of Enchantments
Enrapturing One
Giver of Ecstasies
We bring life to your sanctuary.

Priestess:
Lady of the Words of Power, we embrace the Words of Power.

Shemsu Omnes

SA

SEKHEM

SAHU

•

SA

THE BREATH OF ISIS

SEKHEM

SAHU

•

SA

SEKHEM

SAHU

Sustained silence to be broken by the ringing of a chime by the priest

Priest:
Lady of Silence. We contemplate your image in the Hall of Silence.

Sustained silence to be broken by the ringing of a chime by the priestess

Priestess:
From the silence of Her contemplation, let inspired words arise.

Inspired speech from the Shemsu

Priest:
Let a communion be shared.

Communion of red wine and dates distributed.

Priest:
Sekhmet is satisfied. Let the company depart in peace. Em hotep.

Priestess:
Sekhmet is satisfied. Let the company depart in peace. Em hotep.

Company departs

THE ADORATION OF SEKHMET

NOTES

1. C. J. Bleeker: pastor, academic. Dr Claas Jouco Bleeker studied in Leiden and was a pastor in Apeldoorn, Culemborg and Enschede. After the war he was appointed professor of religious history and phenomenology of religion at the University of Amsterdam. He received an honorary doctorate from the University of Strasbourg and wrote a large number of studies, including several books on ancient Egyptian religion intended to interest a wider audience.

2. Arthur Versluis: academic, writer, scholar. Arthur Versluis holds the Chair of the Department of Religious Studies and Professor in the College of Arts & Letters at Michigan State University. He has published numerous books and articles on the fields of magic and mysticism with a special interest in Christian Theosophy. He has also written on the Egyptian Mysteries. He was awarded a Fulbright scholarship to Germany, and is the founding editor of Esoterica, and co-editor of the Journal for the Study of Radicalism. He is the founding president of the Association for the Study of Esotericism.

3. Iamblichus: classical writer, Neoplatonist philosopher, priest. He is among the most important of the Neoplatonic philosophers. He studied with Porphyry, a pupil of Plotinus, the founder of Neoplatonism. He established his own school and designed a curriculum for studying Plato and Aristotle. He was an influential figure in his own time, although many of his works are lost to history, Theurgia, or On the Mysteries of Egypt and his biography of Pythagoras exerted a considerable influence on later generations.

4. Pythagoras: Initiate, mathematician, mystic, philosopher. He and studied In Egypt for 22 years and based his own school on these teachings.

CHAPTER III

THE BLESSINGS OF HATHOR

BACKGROUND

The Isian Assemblies were going well. I was inspired to create an event based upon the Mysteries of Hathor and I offered the idea to the FOI. It was agreed that *The Blessings of Hathor* would be included in the next conference. But nearer the time I was informed that there was no space left on the programme, so I had to decide whether to abandon the idea or make other arrangements. I decided to make other arrangements and continued with the planning. We hired a beautiful hall in north London and sent out invitations.

Creating a public ceremony presents a special set of challenges. The group was expected to be quite large but without the cohesion of a stable group mind and I could not set preparatory tasks for a group unknown to me. Nevertheless, we had a small core group who could be relied upon to undertake any of the necessary tasks. A meaningful event needed to arise from these disparate strands, so our engagement followed the simplest of structures.

I had asked six women to take on the role of priestesses. They were each experienced in differing degrees and each person made a beautiful contribution. Everyone made a beautiful dress in golden fabric since Hathor is called The Golden Goddess and as part of their personal preparation everyone had made a menat necklace too. It was arranged so that the core group would arrive in the

THE BLESSINGS OF HATHOR

morning to help set up the hall for the afternoon, so I had some quiet time with the priestesses. In my own preparations, I had become increasingly aware of the significance of the menat as an epiphany of Hathor, and it seemed to me that the menat expressed a special relationship between the priestess and the ntr Het-Her. Seated with these contemporary priestesses, the veil of time seemed to momentarily part and once again each priestess ritually received the menat through The Presentation of The Emblems, a spontaneously generated ceremony of investiture.

The Blessings of Hathor opened with a guided meditation which I had spontaneously received immediately some years earlier upon hearing the piece of music that Debe (Nix- Merwin) had kindly sent me called *Golden Hathor*. The meditation is an extended composition of place and in this respect the journey worked very well to attune us to the Hathoric presence. A model of Hathor in her bovine form had been constructed, it was mounted on a large base painted gold and set into long carrying handles, so that her Epiphany might be processed around the hall.

Quite simply our template was to be the map of the Hathor's temple at Denderah and through dance, song, drumming, spontaneous invocations and oracular speeches we intended to travel through its various levels culminating in a meditation in the heart of the temple. To set the scene and provide the most fleeting of group-minds, I delivered the talk, *The Blessings of Hathor*. There was no script other than the few simple statements of intent which punctuated the different sequences. Between the offerings of dance and song, brief meditations served as short minor compositions of place which took us from hall to hall. Unusually no communion was provided as the numbers mitigated against this.

THE BREATH OF ISIS

SEQUENCES

Meditation
The Beauteous Ones – priesthood processes

Free Dance to the temple, led by Debe Nix-Merwin

Visualised meditation
Entering the temple

"Let incense be offered to Hathor. Let dance be offered to Hathor."

Solo dance offered

"Let joyous dance and sound be offered to Hathor."

Group drumming

"Let song be offered to Hathor."

Solo song offered by Debe Nix-Merwin

Meditation
The Hall of Appearance

Spontaneous invocations offered

"Let the Mantle of Hathor descend."

Oracles given

"Let the Blessings of Hathor be received."

Priesthood bestow blessings

"Let the joy of Hathor be radiated."

THE BLESSINGS OF HATHOR

All turn outwards – radiate loving energies

Closing

"Let the priesthood withdraw."

Image of Hathor is processed out

"Let the company withdraw."

COMMENTARY

The priestesses of Hathor were called The Beauteous Ones. Now beauty and the sacred have become irrevocably separated, beauty is connected with womanly ways: allure, sexuality, desire, seduction even danger. This is a male perspective for men are aroused to desire or recklessness through the presence of beauty and this real sense of losing self-control demands a corrective. Helen of Troy was famously so beautiful that a war was fought to win her. But the ancient Egyptians perceived the beautiful to be sacred. The same impetus that created beautiful artefacts, images and ornament also embraced embodied beauty as a divine blessing. However, beauty in the name of divine service is stripped of its self-serving personal function and produces neither vanity nor self-absorption. Instead, it becomes the face of the goddess manifest and the priestess truly becomes the garment of the neter. This transpersonal beauty is radiant, graceful, innocent and mesmerising. If a man might lose his heart at the sight of a beautiful woman, a man might lose his heart to a beautiful goddess, the Nfr, Ntr, at the sight of The Beauteous Ones.

It remains curious to me that the priestesses from The House of Life were on one occasion criticised for being, 'too beautiful to be role models for ordinary women.' This protest was voiced by women clearly not aligned to the sacred-beautiful axis but moved by a restricted and modern view of a sacred role were blinded to an exalted and magnificent quality of engagement.

THE BREATH OF ISIS

Dance too has been desacralized by men in positions of religious authority, conditioned to see only licence and debauch in swaying hips and stamping feet, preferring instead the silent, covered and obedient version of womanhood. This loss is not only measured in the lives of women but in the entire cultural milieu that follows upon such restrictions. Where dance becomes forbidden, it becomes forgotten as a vehicle for generating and distributing life force. Just as th paced and graceful movements of Tai Chi are visible expressions of an invisible life force described as Chi, so it is possible for certain forms of danced movements to also effect the same. So, the sacred dance of Hathor's House of the Sistrum was not the mundane dance of movements set to music but a formalised and taught tradition of movement charged with life force, variously described as chi or prana. Priestess danced at public festivals, at funerals and even to nourish the ka of the king. This was no ordinary dance but the distribution of life force disseminated through danced movements and conferred as blessings. This is the essence of sacred dance, long may it live.

PREPARATION
As The Blessings of Hathor was built upon the idea of travelling through the temple, it is helpful to become familiar with its layout and structure. This is easily done with some internet research and the pictures so readily available soon build a visual vocabulary. It is important to gain an understanding of the sistrum and the menat which are Hathor's special emblems. The sistrum is not merely a musical instrument and the menat is not merely a decorative necklace.

Apart from the event described here, I have facilitated other events which also bring the Blessings of Hathor. These invariably included elements of discussion, meditation and ceremony which call upon intellectual, intuitive and imaginative responses from all participants. I have found the litany created by Rosemary Clark in

THE BLESSINGS OF HATHOR

THE MANSION OF THE SISTRUM

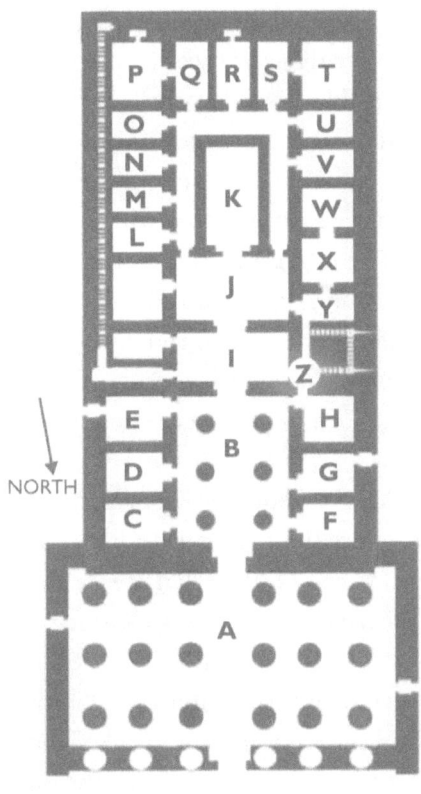

A. First Hypostyle Hall
B. Second Hypostyle – The Hall of Appearance
C. Incense Chamber
D. Storage Room
E. Entry into the Hall of Offerings
F. Treasury
G. Exit to Well
H. Access to Stairwell
I. Offering Hall
J. Hall of the Ennead
K. Great Seat (central Shrine) /Main Sanctuary
L. Shrine of the Nome of Dendera
M. Shrine of Isis
N. Shrine of Sokar
O. Shrine of Harsomtus
P. Shrine of Hathor's Sistrum
Q. Shrine of Gods of Lower Egypt
R. Shrine of Hathor
S. Shrine of the Throne of Re
T: Shrine of Re
U. Shrine of the Menat Collar
V. Shrine of Ihy
W. The Pure Place
X. Court of the First Feast
Y. Passage
Z. Staircase to Roof

her book *The Sacred Wisdom Ancient Egypt* to be an invaluable source of inspiration. There is a regrettable tendency to reduce Hathor to a love-goddess, but Het-Her held a vast significance for Kemetic philosophy.

THE BREATH OF ISIS

The following text provides an intellectual overview, this primary scaffolding will serve to create intuitive and imaginative responses.

THE BLESSINGS OF HATHOR
The name Hathor, Ht Hr is usually translated to mean the House of Horus or the Womb of Horus. It has been suggested that her early rise to eminence coincided with the political rise of the falcon nome, the falcon-folk who worshipped Horus. Hathor takes the form of a cow, sometimes as a cow headed woman and sometimes simply as a cow, often carrying the sun disk between her horns. Now this image needs to be understood in its ancient agricultural setting where wild herds once roamed the delta lands. The domestication of the cow brought a supply of life sustaining milk and created an entirely new relationship as human beings became intimately involved in the life cycle of cows, bulls and herding. In many parts of the world, wealth is still counted in cattle. So, her bovine form represents a life-giving power, stability and human settlement.

Hathor is not the only cow headed Kemetic deity, but in time she absorbed the characteristics and qualities of earlier cults. A cow faced deity appears on the top of the Narmer Palette as the patron deity of the seventh nome (district) of Upper Egypt during the pre-dynastic and Old Kingdom. This is more likely to be an earlier divinity, Ba't whose name derives from ba meaning soul with the addition of the letter 't' indicating a feminine ending. So, the cow headed icon also intrinsically implies soul, even though the ba is more often represented as a bird.

Mehet-Weret was another cow headed deity. Her name means, 'Great Flood.' She was connected with the creative powers of the waters both as the Nile and as the first primeval waters of creation from which the sun emerged. She is called the one who gives birth to Ra and she wears the sun disc between her horns. She is connected with the celestial Nile which is the Milky Way and with the waters of birth itself as a means of rebirth in the underworld.

THE BLESSINGS OF HATHOR

In this capacity as a midwife to the deceased, she is depicted as a cow standing in papyrus plants at the foot of the mountains of the West with her head poking out. Hathor is also depicted in the same manner. Curiously in the Bible, the story of the great flood is one of destruction but for the Egyptians, the great flood is an image of primeval creation. Mehet-Weret is depicted as a recumbent cow often lying on a reed mat, as a woman with the head of a cow, or as a beautiful woman. She also sometimes is shown wearing a menat. However, this ancient cow goddess had no independent cult of her own, and all her attributes and qualities were subsumed by Hathor.

THE HATHOR-HEAD
The façade of her temple at Denderah is uniquely faced with Hathor headed columns. These show the Hathor-head made up from a gently smiling woman's face, the ears of the cow both set within a very particular curled hairstyle. Even though the effect is aesthetically pleasing, this is to miss the intended purpose. Hathor, Het-Her is called The Womb of Horus and the Hathor-Head is indeed The Womb of Horus.

The internal organs of cow and woman are remarkably similar with the container of the cervix topped by the two fallopian tubes on each side. Now the whole image is remarkably similar to the long and broad face of the cow with its ears one to each side. So, the Hathor-head is both the womb of the woman and the womb of the cow simultaneously. The happy smiling face is the contented womb, the ears represent the fallopian tubes and the uterine horns of the cow have become the stylised curling wig. Here is The Womb of Horus carved as the Hathor-head in the pillars which uphold the façade of the temple which is Hathor's house, The Mansion of the Sistrum where she resides.

HATHOR'S HOUSE
Her temple at Denderah was known as the Mansion of the

THE BREATH OF ISIS

Sistrum and the House of Hathor and She was called, The Lady of Denderah. In its present form the temple is Ptolemaic though earlier temples were constructed and rebuilt here in the 4th and 6th dynasties. According to a crypt inscription, the temple was founded in the ancient almost mythical period dated to the Followers of Horus, a common device for attributing great age and therefore great importance to a temple. The site included a sacred lake and wild cows were kept here.

The architectural style typically opens with a courtyard which leads into the first hypostyle hall and then a series of increasingly smaller chambers eventually leads to the sanctuary, where a shrine held her statue. This shrine area stands at the farthest depths of the temple, and was attended only by the pharaoh or his deputed representative. On the exterior wall there is a huge Hathor head where the people were free to congregate and take a blessing from her face so close to the sacred shrine in the sanctuary area. In the same area but built into the walls and foundations of the rear and side wall there are twelve small underground chambers, 'whose content no stranger knows, whose doors are concealed.' Hidden with great care and by concealed entrances, the walls here are covered by images of resurrection.

The central halls which lead one into another finally culminate in the Sanctuary, known as the Great Seat. It is, 'the dwelling place of the Golden One' where Hathor is present in Her cult image. Here only the pharaoh or a direct representative is permitted to gaze upon Her face in adoration. The Great Seat is surrounded on three sides by a processional corridor which opens onto a number of further chapels. Here is the Resurrection Room, the place of renewal. Ptah-Ta-Tenen, one of the ancient creator gods is here. Here is the Birth Room, depicting the birth of Isis. In the next chapel of Sokar, a neter of the realm of light, resurrection scenes link Sokar with Un-neffer, that is Osiris. The next chapel is dedicated to a constant theme, the Union of the Two Lands. Here we see the birth of Hor-

THE BLESSINGS OF HATHOR

Sma-Towy, Harsomtus, son of Hathor and Horus, the Uniter of the Two Lands. A further shrine was dedicated to Upper Egypt, and another known as The Flame room was dedicated to Lower Egypt. In this Pr-Nu, the chamber of Wadjet, Hathor's travelling shrine was stored and taken out for the annual voyage to Edfu. This room also had connections with the protective nature of Sekhmet-Hathor. As Hathor's special emblem, the sistrum was recognised for its vitalising and protective powers in the Room of the Sistrum which significantly had connections with the rooftop shrine. The Throne Room of Re revealed Hathor's fearsome solar aspects and the nearby Purification Room include rites of purification. Finally, the New Year's Room or chapel of Nut housed statues connected with the annual festival and included references to Ihy, the divine dancer and son of Hathor.

At the culmination of the New Year's celebration, her image was carried to the Chapel of the Disc so that, 'Hathor might meet her father.' The chapel on the roof has twelve Hathoric columns and no permanent roof. Instead, a wooden covering could be drawn back at the appropriate time so that the statues could receive the rays of the sun. During this ritual Hathor received various gifts including eight crowns from the gods of Hermopolis, pectorals, necklaces, ointments, perfumes, coloured cloths and offerings of food. Led by the king, the priesthood carried her image up the staircase into the sunlight for the union of Hathor and Re. As they walked in procession, they sang:

> *How beautiful is your passage.*
> *Living one of the horizon when you glide through the air in joy.*
> *Hathor, Lady of Denderah, Eye of Re, Lady of the sky, sovereign of the gods.*

Sunlight shone upon the image, 'She unites her rays with those of her father in the horizon.' This meeting of lights was believed to establish harmony throughout the temple and imbue Her with vital life and light. This festival of Re was celebrated to coincide with the rising of the Nile at the New Year's Festival when Hathor was called, 'the ruler over Sirius, the great one who makes Hapi come.' The encounters with Horus and Re highlight Hathor's solar identity. She is the sun-eye, and The Golden One. The hieroglyph for gold symbolises the perfected state of being and accordingly the pharaoh as the living Horus takes the name, Horus of Gold. Hathor's cult developed powerful solar connections especially during Dynasty V when the cults of Re and Hathor co-existed in the Heliopolitan sun temples. In this solar guise as the sun-eye she is sent forth from Re to chastise mankind which she almost destroyed. In this capacity, she is identified with both Sekhmet and Tefnut.

Worship Hathor, the lady of Denderah, in all lands,
For she is the mistress of fear.
Worship Hathor, the lady of Denderah in all lands,
For she despatches the gods of vengeance against the foe.

The temple is a microcosm of the macrocosm, from the hidden crypts concealed in the depths to the zodiac ceiling in an upstairs chamber, it is an image of the Kosmos rendered in stone, and image, relief and word, all presided over by Hathor, the womb of heaven.

HATHOR AND ROYALTY
The pharaoh called himself the oldest son of Hathor and on ritual occasions he wore a ceremonial apron ornamented with Hathor heads. Hathor was present at vital cultic performances, she was represented at the Heb-Sed, the important festival of renewed kingship. At the preliminary festivals for the Heb-Sed of Amenhotep 111, Hathoric influence abound: Princesses wore the menat and shook sistrums while Hathor was enthroned behind the pharaoh a place normally reserved for the queen.

The great female Horus, Hatshepsut was a lifelong devotee of Hathor. Hathoric imagery abounds at her funerary temple and a

THE BLESSINGS OF HATHOR

text reads: 'I am thy mother who formed thy limbs and created thy beauty.' Hathor assisted at the birth of a royal child and suckled the future divine king. In the city of Apis, the high priestess carried the title, 'She who gives suck.' At the temple of Denderah, in the mammesi which depicts the tale of divine parentage, it is Hathor who is shown suckling the royal infant; only through divine milk might the young prince become a true king. This divine ichor holds a mundane and earthly meanings of nourishment, but it is also the white splash of the stars and it connects the king-to-be with the heavenly celestial realms. Hathor was invoked at the royal birth to give oracle and protect the fate of the king, a function shared with Seshat and Hathor was believed to guard the king throughout his life.

Het-Her, as the womb of Horus, not only empowered kingship but through the sacred marriage with Horus, continued to legitimate it by annually affirming victory over the adversary Set. In the Festival of The Joyous Reunion, Hathor's flotilla left Denderah to reach Edfu stopping along the way. On the first day Hathor visited Mut at Thebes. On the second day she reached the sanctuary of Anukis. On the third day she arrived at Nekhen where she was met by the local Horus who now accompanied her on the last part of the voyage to Edfu. In the meantime, Horus of Edfu had set out to meet her. The two companies met north of Edfu and finally after further ceremony, the two flotillas arrived at Edfu to the joy of cheering crowds. The divine effigies of Horus and Hathor were placed in the temple and rituals were celebrated by the joint priesthoods. The divine pair remained together for 14 days to consummate The Festival of the Beautiful Embrace. It is also stated that on the fourth day the young Horus was conceived by the goddess. The sacred marriage was a complex ritual of state, Hathor was simultaneously consort to the Horus neter yet also mother to the future Horus. This cyclic pattern confounds d linear mental processes; Kemetic thought is always multi-dimensional, holistic and relational. The Horus neter empowers the living pharaoh while Horus is empowered by the Divine Feminine through Hathor and also through Isis.

HATHOR AND OTHER DEITIES
Hathor was intertwined with other key divinities including Isis, Osiris, Neith and Min. In this capacity certain priestesses of Hathor were also priestesses of Neith as revealed in the titles, 'Possessor of reverence with Hathor, Mistress of the Sycamore, Mistress of Denderah, Priestess of Neith, Opener of Ways' and, 'Priestess of Hathor, Possessor of Reverence with the great god, Priestess of Neith, Priestess of Hathor, Mistress of Denderah.' Hathor was also connected to Min, in the form of the white bull as a sign of earthly fertility. Min in ipthyphallic form represented manifest power of the celestial Horus. This continuity between the above and the below was symbolised by a ceremonial pole as the axis mundi. A sky pole was set up at Kusae and probably at another temple of Hathor's in the tenth nome which had special connections to the celestial Min. Hathor was also related to Ptah of Memphis. It appears that these two divinities were jointly worshipped at Memphis, Medinet Habu and in the Sinai. Hathor also assimilated and shared the functions of other deities. She is sometimes addressed as Maat and shares the title, 'Queen of writing' with Seshat as The Lady of Books. Like Nuit she is a cosmic receiver of the dead and She is intimately connected with both Isis and Nephthys. Hathor was worshipped at five main centres and at another nine lesser centres. She was frequently given a place of recognition in the temples of other key divinities including a chapel on the island of Philae, a place in the temple of Ptah at Karnak and a shrine within Hatshepsut's funerary temple. Her worship extended beyond Egypt into Syria, the Sinai peninsula and Nubia. Hathor's remaining temple stands at Denderah, the capital of the sixth nome.

THE BLESSINGS OF HATHOR

HATHOR AND WOMEN

Hathor was served almost entirely by women, though men held some administrative posts. She answered their needs in matters such as love, childbirth and fertility. As a mother goddess of the sky and earth, fertility is central to Her nature. She appeared as a fertility figurine in human guise and as a funerary charm in tombs and Her functions as nursing mother were stylised into ritual jars with spouting breasts. Hathor is the mother sky goddess, her son is the sun. She is called, mistress of the sky, queen of the stars, mistress of the stars. As goddess of the nocturnal sky, she is also the receiver of the dead for the night sky was thought of as the netherworld. I am Hathor, mistress of the northern sky. The wings of the sky-doors will be opened for thy beauty. As a mother goddess she presides over birth. She is called, 'the one who is giving birth.'

As Hathor was called Mistress of the Sycamore, so her daughters likewise took this title. In a hierarchical structure, titles reflected the exercise of power and authority. Accordingly, The Mistress of the Sycamore served in one sanctuary, The Mistress of the Sycamore in all Her Places held authority in two temples and finally the office of Hathor in All Her Places, had a broad jurisdiction and was only answerable to The Chief Priestess of Hathor in All Her Places. It was common for priestesses of Hathor to hold subsidiary titles indicating a royal connection: King's Acquaintance, King's Jewel, King's Only Jewel, and King's Noblewoman.

HATHOR'S INSIGNIA

The priestesses of Hathor were clearly identifiable through their cult regalia, the menat and the sistrum. The menat necklace was a heavy beaded neckpiece formed from many strands of small beads with a weighted counterpoise at the back. It is unlike the familiar broad jewelled collar. Originating in the Old Kingdom, its precise derivation is obscure. It has been suggested that the counterpoise weights were originally two in number and may indeed have denoted the testicles. Such physical symbolism is in keeping with the Kemetic mind, but this seemingly sexualised imagery is merely a representation of human fertility. The strings of small beads are certainly reminiscent of seeds.

As Hathor was immanent within her statue, so she was also present within the sistrum and menat. Though the sistrum has been described as a musical instrument, it is more properly understood as an epiphany immediately signifying Her presence. Hathor is sometimes depicted as the menat, itself. She is called the, 'the possessor of the Menat', 'the great menat necklace' and, 'the divine menat necklace.' At Denderah, she is called, 'the great menat in the house of the menat.' The menat necklace might be shaken to make a soft percussive sound but more often it was held by the priestess so that the beaded part could be extended at arm's length and offered strongly to the recipient. It is difficult to fully convey the significance of the gesture, since this tradition is now without a social or cultural context. However, if the menat is derived from the papyrus seeds and the custom of offering papyrus flowers to the beloved, then the gesture of offering the many seeded necklace, is one of offering a gift of love. In other words, she is the divine prototype for the one who chooses the beloved with the gift of papyrus. Iconography shows Hathor offering the menat to the king. In this way the king becomes the beloved of the goddess, the chosen one of Hathor.

The sistrum takes two forms, the loop sistrum and box sistrum. The first is like a more elaborate ankh, similar in shape to the ankh, it has a number of cross bars, most often four in which small metals discs are threaded. Based on the ankh, the key of life and the Key to the Mysteries, the sistrum conveys the same life-giving powers. Its ratting sound was most probably derived from the papyrus head which rattles when dried. The papyrus itself has connections with Hathor since the emergence of the new brilliant green show of plants signified the return of life. The papyrus plant is the

THE BLESSINGS OF HATHOR

pharaonic emblem of Upper Egypt under its more common name of the sedge plant; the royal connection is implicit. Not only did the papyrus plant provide the raw material for paper but its strong fibre was used for shoes and plaited baskets. Its rhizome could even be eaten. Nesut, the sedge or papyrus plant was clearly of immense importance as a royal symbol, a food, and a valuable raw material. No wonder then that one popular feast day was celebrated among the papyrus groves. The Festival of Plucking the Papyrus took place among the ripe papyrus and flowers were picked to give in the hope of winning the favour of a chosen beloved, what better symbol of enduring life, nourishment and sustenance.

The sistrum carries the same symbolic meanings and additionally, the looped sistrum replicate the shape of the ankh, and in doing so it forms the shape of the hieroglyph for, 'sa' meaning, to protect. Coincidentally this same shape is reminiscent of the uterus both human and bovine. Once again even the simple sistrum, reveals the Egyptian love for compressing multiple meanings into form so that many meanings coincide in a single moment. Here ideas of life, protection, fertility, and divinity reside in the sistrum. The box sistrum resembles a shrine and it too signified the presence of Hathor. It may have first taken shape as a sacred box, a simple rattle containing loose objects bearing comparison to the pregnant womb. When held by one of Hathor's daughters, the sistrum immediately signified her presence and power. Hathor is called, the "Mistress of the sss and the shm sistra." The tinkling percussive sound created by shaking the sistrum signifies that the divine was present, its sounding conveyed protection and it was used to clear sacred space against profane incursions. So, the sistrum is symbolically complex, a world away from the simple musical rattle it is usually taken for. It was carried by the Hathor's, the priestesses who accompanied processions both in the temple and beyond its walls for the populace. At Denderah, when the pharaoh and his queen walked in procession to the temple roof for the ritual on New

THE BREATH OF ISIS

Year's morning, the queen rattled two sistra. The accompanying text reads, "I have taken the sss sistrum, I grasp the shm-sistrum and drive away him who is hostile to the mistress of heaven," and it was commonly said, "*I dispel what is hostile by means of the sistrum in my hand*." Priestesses were presented with the regalia of their authority at the Ritual Presentation of the Emblems. In this ceremony, it was believed that Hathor transmitted the essence of her divinity to these sacred emblems, so that through the cult regalia, Hathor's divine essence might enter and merge with the priestess as her living embodiment. These emblems united the *netert* with the priestess. The emblems were recognized as the manifestations of Hathor herself. When the priestess was dressed as Hathor complete with these emblems, the state of identification was complete, the emblems united ntr and priestess. When wearing this divinely empowered regalia Hathor herself was seen to be incarnate and present. Her daughters, her musician-priestesses were thereby empowered to confer divine favour and blessings on her devotees in a moment of sacrament. But this sacrament is not merely about the promise of an after-life, it is a covenant forged in life, through dance, joy, beauty and the celebration of physical love. This merging of the divine and the human is outside contemporary experience, it belongs to the mystical tradition of the temple and its wisdom teachings. Though we cannot fully understand or experience this blended consciousness, we can recognized its validity and by a leap of faith we can imagine feelings generated through such an encounter. In the Kemetic temple tradition, this identification between the priestess and the Goddess was complete; the priestess embodied the ntr Hathor as an epiphany. Moreover, her daughters were quite simply called Hathor.

HATHOR'S FESTIVALS

Hathor was renowned for her beauty. She was called, 'the beautiful, the lovely one who stands at the head of the House

THE BLESSINGS OF HATHOR

of the Beautiful; the gods turn their heads away in order to see her better.' Priestesses walked in public processions offering the blessings of life, stability and happiness upon eager and devoted crowds by extending the menat and the sistrum. During public festivals they processed through the streets, stopping at houses to bestow life-giving blessing to the populace through Hathor's unique cult emblems. At festivals the musician-priestesses processed through the streets offering the extended menat to confer the blessing of life, stability and happiness upon eager and devoted crowds. Secular society has lost touch with the spiritual essence of movement, sound and dance. These are personal pleasure zones not transcendental experiences. Imagine if you can women schooled into the strength of Yoga, the grace of Tai Chi and the power of breathwork combined with the discipline of the ballet and the beauty of the beloved, this is sacred dance in the Kemetic tradition.

Hathor was called mistress of the dance, the queen of happiness, mistress of inebriety, of jubilation and of music. Her son Ihy was the divine dancer. Dance was a sacred act, performed in situations outside our present norms, we dance primarily for social pleasure and entertainment. Sacred dance was not designed to entertain or amuse but to evoke particular cosmic principles. The current religious mind-set cannot permit a procession of women, adorned in evocation of beauty, to step and dance in honour of the divine. But in Ancient Egypt dances were performed to honour the deities, to celebrate festivals but also at funerals to increase the vitality of the deceased. Acrobatic dance is depicted in tombs and dances were performed at state ceremonials. There were dances for fertility. At Denderah certain dances were performed at night by priestesses entranced by wine. Images of the divinities were welcomed with dance. Hathor's festivals were always joyous. At the Festival of Inebriety, wine was plentiful, drunkenness a joyous duty. Hathor brought joy and beauty to life. Her presence

THE BREATH OF ISIS

was celebrated with song, dance and delight. A poem on the sarcophagus lid of Wennofer describes the atmosphere at a feast of Hathor.

> *Singers and maidens gathered together,*
> *Made acclaim like that of Meret*
> *Braided, beauteous, tressed, high bosomed,*
> *Priestesses richly adorned,*
> *Anointed with myrrh, perfumed with lotus,*
> *Their heads garlanded with wreaths,*
> *All drunk together with wine,*
> *Fragrant with the plants of Punt,*
> *They danced together in beauty, doing my hearts wish,*
> *Their rewards were on their limbs.*

THE BEAUTEOUS ONES
> *Using the creative imagination, build the following scene in the mind's eye. Find yourself standing among an excited crowd waiting on the banks of the beautiful Nile. Today is a festival day. It is Hathor's festival and her daughters will be arriving very soon. All eyes are upon the river now. In the distance you hear the sound of drums. Everyone falls silent with a hushed expectancy and all eyes turn towards the river. In the distance, the shape of sails emerges on the horizon. You know that flotilla is drawing closer with every minute. Four small boats lead the procession, each one pulls the great ship by ropes like an umbilicus. The flotilla is drawing closer; now the pungent scent of incense drifts upon the air like a heady intoxicant, you know that Hathor and her daughters will be here soon. The anticipation among the crowd overflows and people begin to shout with joy. Now the flotilla is pulling up alongside its allotted moorings. Men step off and swiftly secure the leading boats, but you hardly notice, your attention is already elsewhere.*

THE BLESSINGS OF HATHOR

All eyes are on Hathor's sailing ship. Her face is carved upon the prow and from the decks clouds of incense fill the air. In the centre of the decks Hathor's sacred barque rests on its sledge. At its centre Hathor's most sacred shrine sits in perfect peace and harmony. The Golden One is here.

Now the sound of a chanted song is rising on the air and you can hear the faint tinkling of sistrums. The Beauteous Ones are here. Momentarily the crowd falls silent hearing the sweet sound of women's voices in light song. Then with a roar of approval and delight, the assembled crowd breaks out into wild jubilation.
Your eyes are filled by delight at what you now see. This living symphony steps forward as one, dark long wigs, plain pleated dresses, collars of shining colours and the emblems of Hathor, the beaded menat necklaces slung low. The Beauteous Ones bring Hathor to you.

Now the procession falls into a gentle rhythm and begins to move as one, with upstretched arms, hands open to the heavens drawing down its invisible divinity. Bodies stoop with graceful momentary bend to bless the earth; heaven and earth are united. Sistrums rattle and the dance takes on its shape. Here is a vision of utter loveliness.

The daughters of Hathor dance and your heart lifts in response. Their gestures are delicate, perfectly poised and exquisite, extended hands reach out towards the river, drawing in the invisible life force of the living waters beloved by Hathor. Arms are extended like living wings floating upon an invisible breeze. The procession glides as one, moved by feet in perfect time, by movements in perfect harmony, by minds in one accord. Sweet perfume fills the air as they pass. Sistrums shake with a silvered note and just for a moment, your body begins to shake too picking up the pattern of awakening. Blessed is the name of

THE BREATH OF ISIS

Hathor. Now perceptibly the line of Hathor's is beginning to move away from you. Little by little the procession is moving on. The Beauteous Ones are slowly moving on to bestow blessings on other devotees. Now gather up all your impressions, savour all the sensations, hold on tightly to the feelings, plant all your memories deeply in your heart-mind like a shining seed a divine blessings to you from Hathor, The Golden Goddess.

CHAPTER IV

THE ROSES OF ISIS

BACKGROUND

Our group met in the beautiful surroundings of The Runnings Park Conference Centre cradled in the Malvern Hills to create a weekend experience centred upon The Mysteries of Isis. In this case, I am now unable to remember the exact moment of inspiration or even the sequence of events which led to the decision to take this as a theme. But I expect that as usual my mind became mesmerised by a particular idea. I returned to *The Golden Ass*, the unforgettable text of Apluleius which had so miraculously provided the epiphany moment during the weekend, Isis of Ten Thousand Names in 1990. I returned to the description of the procession and allocated the various characters to members of the group.

"The woman attired in white vestments, and rejoicing, in that they bare garlands and flowers upon their heads, bedspread the wares with herbs, which they bare in their aprons, where this regal and devout procession should pass: other carried mirrors on the backs of their heads to testify obeisance to the goddess which came after. Other bare combs of Ivory, and declared by their gesture and motions of their arms, that they were ordained and ready to dress the goddess : Others dropped in the ways as they went Balm and other precious ointments: Then came a great number, as well of men as women, with candles torches, and other lights, doing honour to the celestial goddess: After that sounded the musical harmony

THE BREATH OF ISIS

of instruments: then came a faire company of youth, apparelled in white vestments, singing both meter and verse, with a comely grade which some studious Poet had made in honour of the Muses: In the mean season, arrived the blowers of trumpets, which were dedicated unto Serapis, and to the temple before them were officers and beadles, preparing room for the goddess to pass."

The site enjoyed an extensive garden, this enabled us to process around the entire grounds bearing a statue of Isis on a palanquin. Much effort had gone into the making of all the artefacts for the weekend but in exchange there had been much pleasure and enjoyment. Our procession came to its finish at the terrace where we lit a brazier and drawing upon the flames as a symbol of purification and each person made a dedication. The meditation *The Roses of Isis* arose in my mind when we sat as a group immediately after our session on the terrace. I have given the same meditation in varying contexts including a seminar given at The World Parliament of Religions.

COMMENTARY
The classical novel, *The Golden Ass* appears to be a bawdy picaresque novel in which the main character is turned into a donkey through his continued folly, a juxtaposition which sets the misuse of low magic beside the sublime magic of the soul. The salutory tale bears some similarity with the Italian folk tale of Pinocchio, the wooden puppet who journeys to become human. He too falls into bad company and becomes a donkey, a symbol of folly and low estate. His eventual salvation appears through the good auspices of the blue fairy and of course he achieves his wish to become a human boy. In *The Golden Ass* restoration and salvation comes at the behest of Goddess Isis. In heartfelt gratitude, the central character Lucius becomes a devotee and then one of her priests. The author, Lucius Apuleius was a student of Plato and also an initiate of several mystery cults. He called the work, *The Metamorphoses*,

THE ROSES OF ISIS

though it is more often called *The Golden Ass*; metamorphosis is nothing other than a series of transformations, this is the path of the initiate. Apuleius visited Egypt in his lifetime and rather like the hapless fool of his tale, he was accused of using magic to gain the attentions and fortunes of a wealthy widow. His account of his initiations into the Mysteries of Isis and subsequently into the Mysteries of Osiris are autobiographical.

Egypt may have faded but curiously its divinities remain. Isis has become a favourite goddess once more. Her appeal is timeless and of all the ntr Isis remains easily approachable. Her story is fully human, yet she is also divine. Some commentators suggest that she actually lived and if this is so, then she completely understands the human condition. In any case, her mythos tells the story of a human life and this of itself creates a bridge between Isis and her devotees. Not only is Isis a woman, wife, mother, but in her capacity as ruler she brings the arts of civilization to humanity. In Her divine aspect She is the embodiment of Wisdom and Compassion. These abstracted universal qualities cannot be gained as intellectual accoutrements but only through a total engagement with life. Such a deep commitment with the life of the world must bring both suffering and sorrow, where there is ignorance, great injustice and terror will flourish in the hands of the strong. Isis bears the name, the Lady of Sorrows just like another grieving mother, Mary the mother of another human-divine figure. The comparisons between Isis and the Virgin Mary have been made often. The two figures mourn the death of the beloved. Isis is the mourning queen demented by grief, the bereft widow, the woman reduced to rags wandering the desert disguised by despair. This mythic image is also recounted in the later Greek Eleusinian Mysteries where the story of loss and return is told through the story of The Two Goddesses Demeter and Kore. These traditions initiate through the story of loss and death, triumph, renewal and return to life. This is the Path of Wisdom and Compassion.

THE BREATH OF ISIS

PREPARATION

Lucius Apuleius wrote not merely to entertain but to educate and initiate. Reading The Golden Ass with a meditative mind is the best preparation for becoming attuned to the Mysteries of Isis.

THE ROSES OF ISIS

Use the creative imagination to build the following scene:

Find yourself transported in time. You stand among an excited crowd in holiday mood. The atmosphere of expectation and anticipation is palpable. This is the day when the servants of Isis shall process through the city. You wait expectantly, hoping beyond hope that the promise given by Isis herself shall be fulfilled. It is early in the morning. Crowds have already lined the streets. But looking down at yourself, you see that you are quite unlike any other gathered here, for you have become a donkey, traditionally a beast of burden. Now you recall the incidents and episodes, the follies and foolish choices that have robbed you of your humanity. Look upon yourself and recall the misadventures that created this dehumanised form. But while remembering your folly, also recall the words spoken in the depths your misery. 'I beseech you by whatever name and whatever aspect, with whatever ceremonies you deign to be invoked, have mercy on me in my extreme distress, restore my shattered fortune, grant me repose and peace after this long sequence of miseries.' You know only that you wish to regain your humanity, by losing it, you have come to value it above all else.

This day is very special, it holds a hidden promise. For the goddess Isis through her visionary presence has promised you a great transformation. You do not know what will happen. You do not know what to expect. You have joined the festivities in total trust. You have received very particular instructions. You nuzzle your way into a group; no-one takes any notice of an ass.

Now you hear the approaching sound of the procession. Here come the merrymakers, men and women in fancy dress who

THE ROSES OF ISIS

entertain and engage the crowd. The crowd cheer and laugh as the entertainers pass by. Next come devotees of Isis, women in white dresses pulling flowers out of the folds of their skirts. Next come women with mirrors tied to the backs of their heads, an illusion to be contemplated. Some women bear ivory combs, others sprinkle precious perfumes upon the road. Next, we see women bearing lamps, torches and candles. Their flames burn brightly. You recall that in your animal form you can do none of these things.

Now you see musicians and a choir of singers followed by a great crowd of initiates men and women of all classes and ages dressed in pure white linen. The women wear gauzy headdresses, the men are shaven headed. They all carry rattles and timbrels which tinkle on the breeze. Now you see the priesthood and your heart lifts. You see the oracular emblems of the deity, a boat shaped lamp spouting a flame, a golden pot, a miniature palm tree, a wand of Mercury, a rounded vessel shaped like a woman's breast, a winnowing fan and a wine jar.

You gaze upon them knowing that in this present form you have become separated from all good things. Now here come the representations of the deities. Here is dark faced Anubis, the messenger of the gods and a representation of the goddess in her nurturing aspect as a cow. And now the High Priest comes into view carrying the rattle and garland as promised. This is the signal you have waiting for. Pushing gently forwards, as an ass emerging from the crowd you make your way towards him. At once you know that you are expected, he gazes at your form and smiles knowingly. He too has been instructed by some private word of the goddess. He unmistakeably extends the garland of roses to you. As you nuzzle your face deeply into the garland, so the perfume from the roses fills your nostrils. You inhale deeply, it is as if Isis herself has breathed into your very soul. You eat a rose from the garland and savouring its taste relish, instantly a great change takes place. A miracle unfolds, the animal form is gone, you are quite transformed. In a rush you

THE BREATH OF ISIS

remember what it means to be truly human and you rejoice at your restoration. Those nearby stagger backwards in amazement but then a great cheer rises up for the goddess has bestowed a miracle on this her chosen day.

The High Priest speaks to you and finishes with the words, *"Rejoice now become a wearer of white linen. Follow triumphantly in the train of the goddess who has delivered you. Her service is perfect freedom."* In a state of gratitude and wonder, your mind slips into a deep state of awareness. Suddenly the crowds have faded, dissolving away at the instant like gentle phantoms and now you become aware of another procession drawing closer. As if from nowhere a procession approaches. Here are the Eternal Servants of Isis. Here are the linen clad priests, the Fathers of Wisdom bearing sacred objects. Here are the bearers of sweet incenses. Here are the white robed priestesses shaking the sacred rattles. You are surrounded by voices raised in adoration and joy.

Your communion deepens and it seems that the air begins to stir and shimmer. From the Eternal realm, the Eternal Servants from the House of Isis simply become visible. You are greeted as a returning soul and in return you greet those close by. You sense a rising wave of palpable expectation. The company are waiting. Now the air seems to shimmer and shine. The veil which separates the past and present, the physical and spiritual becomes transparent. Open the inner eye which is the eye of eternity, look with the eyes of the soul. A vision of transcendent beauty and glory begins to form. Emerging from worlds unseen and places unknown, She stands before us and about us, over and among us. She is crowned with twin plumes and set with a disc. Light radiates from her crown, her face is veiled within a shimmering iridescent light.

Beloved Family, You who shelter beneath my wings, we are together once again. You have heard my call deep in your being. We are united in service. We are joined in the heart's

THE ROSES OF ISIS

desire. Beloved Priesthood, You who are marked by my light, we are together once again. You have heard my call to awaken and remember. We are united in our mystery. We are united in eternity. All are welcome in my house. All are known by me. Some I know by many names for we are old friends. It is my delight to renew a friendship, yet I will always wait upon your remembering and asking. As I invite you into my house so you must invite me into your heart. I await your asking and if you invite me in, we shall be joined in eternity. If you would know me, open the heart and I shall reside there.

With these words she stretches out her arms as if to embrace the company. The Wings of Isis descend upon you. From her wings rose petals begin to fall like a shower of scented rain. Receive this blessing. The sweet perfume of roses fills the air. Each petal bestows its gift. The petals continue to fall. Isis speaks again. 'My house is open to you.' In the mind's eye, see the small temple of Isis at Pompeii. You stand together before the flight of steps. The Eternal Servants of Isis have gone on ahead. They flank the staircase on either side. You begin to climb the steps. The ancient brethren rattle sistrums in welcome and blessing. The doors to the small temple are already open and you pass over the threshold.

You know that the ancient priesthood has joined the procession and follows into the sacred place. We enter. Immediately you are surprised at the size of the interior which stretches before you. You stand in a great hall flanked with columns. Above you is a starry ceiling and everywhere the scent of incense pervades the air. Candlelight flickers from distant corners. This is the House of Isis. As you move forwards, see her statue raised on a plinth. This is the House of Isis and She inhabits it. Stone benches fill the hall and everyone takes a seat.

THE BREATH OF ISIS

A voice asks you to deepen your state and prepare to journey once again. Open to your deepest senses. The starry ceiling is now a starry sky. The walls of the temple have fallen away. Instead you are surrounded by columns of crystal. The walls and floor also seem to be made of crystal. Everywhere light reflects as if through prisms. Coloured lights dance and play. You hear light ethereal notes as if glass rods were being lightly struck one upon another. Look now upon your form and see that you have emerged as a body of light. Colours play through you and every thought produces a counterpart in coloured light. You hear a long sustained note, and in response the company rise from their seats and walk forwards. Ahead of you, you see two thrones side by side. These too seem to be cut from crystal or perhaps cut from something quite unknown. Shafts of light from an unseen dome bathe these twin thrones. One throne is quite empty. Hieroglyphs set into the back of the seat reveal the name of the owner.

However, the second throne is fully occupied. This is the seat of Isis, She of the Throne is upon her throne. She is crowned and arrayed in splendour. She stands to greet us. She speaks to us each individually yet simultaneously. The air is filled with the colours of our exchanged thoughts; blues and purples, rosy pinks, gold and silver fills the air.

A profound silence falls. Isis stands before us. She reaches up and in a single gesture takes off her crown. She holds it before us. It seems to be made of pure light. She speaks, "I alone may bestow my crown at the time of my choosing." She replaces her crown and is seated again. Muted colours fill the air as our thoughts arise yet again. She accepts our questions and our concerns. She understands our fears and worries. For each there is an answer. We now sit in silent meditation in the House of Isis.

THE ROSES OF ISIS

I ask you all to assemble your thoughts. Hold on to all that has been given to your heart-mind. Now it is time to begin the journey of return. A veil begins to form before your eyes. The Throne of Isis is now veiled from you. Now you must become focused on the return to the physical plane. The shining glory of the temple has now dimmed, you see only walls of stone and columns of marble. You are seated upon the stone benches in the little Pompeian temple.

Turn your minds towards the outer world and the life that you know is yours. Prepare to leave this temple when you are ready. Make your way towards its door and cross the threshold back into our physical reality. You take as much time as you need to readjust and become fully integrated into the physical levels of your existence.

These words which spontaneously arose in my mind settled upon the site of the little Iseum at Pompeii. This has always remained something of a curiosity, since at the time I had no special interest of my own in it, though it figured in my own far memory recall, (assuming of course that this has some substance and it not mere mental fabrication). At Pompeii the Iseum was especially rich in frescoes and these reveal how the essential Egyptian iconography had been translated into a new form. Perseus, Andromeda, Mars and Venus now appear along with Eros, Priapus, Heracles and the white heifer Io. These frescoes tell a story, one depicts a ceremony: on a flight of steps a young woman, probably taking on the role of Isis, extends her hands towards a figure who is most probably Heracles. She is crowned and adorned with necklaces and bracelets. Two processions are taking place simultaneously, winding into and out from the temple. Scholars have suggested that this scene represents the marriage of Heracles.

Ancient Kemetic and Isian themes are now dressed in a new

THE BREATH OF ISIS

guise, though the essential themes remain unchanged the modus operandi of the Egyptian tradition is becoming dilute. Now allegorical references must point towards esoteric truths. The heroic figure of Perseus, the conqueror of the sea symbolises a victory over the Sethian powers of chaos as he liberates Andromeda from her bonds and her fate at the hands of a monster. Eros and Priapus represent the twin aspects of love both physical and divine. Venus is here too and curiously she is also to be found in The Golden Ass in a tale about Cupid (Eros) and Psyche whose name means soul. These interconnected allegorical characters are somewhat lesser in stature than the great timeless divinities of ancient Egypt but here in Pompeii, so far from home, symbol and code must again serve to reveal a hidden truth again. Andromeda awaits her liberation and personal salvation, the sacred marriage is perhaps a reference to the Hieros Gamos, a vestigial feature of ancient religious thought and in the story of Io we find familiar themes. Io, a priestess of Hera, or a beautiful nymph, depending on the version, was seduced by Zeus. To hide her from the enraged Hera, Io was turned into a white heifer. But Hera still managed to set a constant watch on her. However, Hermes slew the guard and released Io to wander the world whereupon she wandered to Egypt. Here Hera agreed to restore her to human shape, so far away now, that she was beyond the reach of Zeus. Io became a queen in Egypt and her descendants included King Belus and his sons Cadmus and Danaus who were destined to return to Greece. So a single fresco tells a magical tale of journeys, transformations, restored queenship and interaction with the gods. These are familiar the Isian themes. But now there is a new message, not only is Io a go-between moving between Egypt and Italy, where both Greek and Roman cultural influences mingle, she is also the mother of a royal lineage destined to return to Greece and Io herself is freed by Hermes, (a later form of Thoth) to wander through the whole world. It is no wonder then that the fresco shows Isis receiving Io for Io is also Isis, The Goddess of Ten Thousand Names.

THE ROSES OF ISIS

Far away from the mother country, the Iseum had incorporated its own unique and familiar motifs including a megaron, a small crypt building set slightly away from the temple itself. Plain and undecorated, its several purposes included providing a catchment for rainwater. The symbolism of the annual flood was too deeply imbedded in the Egyptian psyche for it to be easily forgotten, so the megaron became the new Nilometer. Renewing water became a significant feature of the newly emerging cult of Isis and Serapis (a Graeco-Roman merging of Osiris and the Apis bull). More than half of the newly constructed sanctuaries in Italy included a permanent water facility derived either from collecting rainwater or by drawing upon a local source such as a river.

In Egypt the significance of the Nile was immediate and clear cut. To any native Egyptian Nile water was life itself. Nile water flowing from the neter Hapi was also considered to be the body of Osiris itself. For those born outside Egypt however, the connection was to become more symbolic than real. Nevertheless, the water which flowed into the crypt took on a sacramental power as Osiris. These new fresh waters symbolised the triumph of life over the inhospitable saline sea waters of the ocean.

Water representing both the Nile and Osiris was carried in utmost reverence with veiled hands. The blessing, 'May Osiris give you cool water,' was derived from the simple observations of daily life but at the same time it referred to the gift of eternal life bestowed by the glorified Osiris. Sacramental water was distributed from two different vessels, the urnula and the Osiris hydreois. The urnula is described in The Golden Ass as a gilded and decorated vessel with a rounded lower portion, a spout like the beak of a bird with a handle in the shape of a uraeus serpent. The Osiris hydreois was the subject of adoration as the container of the body of Osiris. Its base was garlanded with flowers and on the top was the head of the god, the hair arranged in a distinctive crown style. Sacramental water was reverently carried in procession in the veiled hands of the Osiris hydreois.

THE BREATH OF ISIS

In this way Egyptian symbolism was continued and modified where necessary while key elements retained their recognisable form in this new landscape. Here Anubis or perhaps an Anubis priest is depicted bearing a caduceus, this is a new Hermetic symbol not found in Egypt though it may have evolved from the serpent entwined staff carried by Thoth. Isis as the mistress of the temple is seen extending the ankh on a panel over the central doorway. The sistrum is much in evidence and frescoes show a choir probably drawn from a supporting laity association. Music making is depicted including a woman playing a tambourine. Offerings of fruits and flowers are given. Here priestesses wear a costume much like that described by Lucius in his vision of Isis, a white linen undergarment, covered by a fringed mantle knotted between the breasts with a wide adorned band, hung over the shoulder. The lotus flower as the symbol of immortality is also much in evidence, it was worn at the top of the head for ceremonial purposes much as it had been in Egypt. Rings of spiritual significance were worn and inscribed with images of the deities on the inner side these doubtless belonged to the priesthood. Two engraved silver goblets indicate that both priests and priestesses carried out sacred duties together. One shows a priestess crowned with a serpent, the ancient symbol of initiation, she carries a tray set with a cake, probably in celebration. This new Graeco-Roman Isis is no longer the winged Isis of Kem, She has drawn closer to the human condition and is friend to women and men alike.

It is interesting to speculate on the fall of the Isian Mysteries and the rise of Christianity. History cannot be re-run and history is always written by its winners. The words spoken by Cyril of Alexandria are symptomatic of a mind-set consumed by male self-righteousness in the name of the one God. He stated, 'It is the custom of the Egyptians especially for the women to visit temples wearing linen garments, reverently supplying their left hands with a mirror and the right with a sistrum; these women, when they have

THE ROSES OF ISIS

been chosen among others and have been made initiates of such a religion with difficulty, are deemed worthy of honour - therefore of wantoness.' In the space between his time and ours it is very sad to report that nothing much has changed.

The pompous Cyril would have been stunned to learn that even in its ruined state the Iseum could still communicate a hidden truth. In 1769, the young Mozart aged only 13 visited here and in maturity he was inspired to write *The Magic Flute*. Performed around the world to this day, its message is that of the most ancient mysteries in surprising disguise. In the closing scene the Mozart's characters are victorious and the people hail Isis and Osiris as the embodiments of Wisdom. Isis would be pleased.

CHAPTER V
THE RE-MEMBERING OF OSIRIS

CHOREOGRAPH NOTES:

Place the altar centrally. The priesthood attend the altar. The company stand in a circle this providers space for the several processional circuits to be undertaken. The members of the company taking the part of the oracle and the divinities stand in the circle formed by the company and move to the altar as necessary.

Dramatis Personae:
FIRST PRIESTESS
SECOND PRIESTESS
FIRST PRIEST
ORACLE OF OSIRIS
THE VOICE OF ISIS
THE VOICE OF NEPHTHYS
THE VOICE OF HORUS
THE VOICE OF THOTH
THE VOICE OF GEB
THE VOICE OF NUIT

On the altar:
Three candles; Djed Pillar; Bed of Osiris
6 amulets Tet, Wings, Eye, Palette, Star, Phoenix
Scented sand or sand filled with barley seeds.

THE RE-MEMBERING OF OSIRIS

THE WORDS OF POWER

First Priestess:

Lights candle.

We stand in the presence of the Lux Occulta.
We meet seeking the Illumination of the Lux Occulta.

Priest:

Lights candle.

We stand in the presence of the Lux Occulta.
We meet seeking the Illumination of the Lux Occulta.

Second Priestess

Lights candle.

We stand in the presence of the Lux Occulta.
We meet seeking the Illumination of the Lux Occulta.

First Priestess:

Our assembly is gathered. Our temple is opened.

Priest:

Companions, we are met in the Spirit of Truth which is named Ma'at.
Let us quest in the Name of Truth.
Let us stand in the Cause of Truth.
Let us be blessed by the power of Truth.

Second Priestess:

Let it be known that we travel under the auspices of a Threefold Mystery
which we hold to be sacred.

Priest:

Processes the Bed of Osiris.

THE BREATH OF ISIS

We travel together on this the Great Quest. Like Isis who searched without ceasing for the body of her best beloved, we too will quest until Osiris is re-membered.
We are met to re-member Osiris and celebrate his Mysteries which hold the secrets of death and rebirth.
Behold the bed of Osiris lies vacant.

First Priestess:

Processes the Djed Pillar carrying it horizontally.

Companions and Shemsu of The House of Life,
we are met to re-member.
We are met to celebrate the Mysteries of Isis which hold the secret of triumphant love and eternal truth.
Behold the Djed of Osiris is fallen.

Second Priestess:

Priestess processes alone.

Priesthood, Initiates, Bearers of the Ancient Wisdom, Shemsu under the direction of Lord Thoth, we are met uphold the Ancient Rites which are things both sacred and glorious.
Behold the House of Osiris is empty.

First Priestess:

In preparation for our journey, let us hear the Oracle of Osiris.

Oracle of Osiris

Behold that which is in separation. Behold that which is fragmented. Behold that which is divided. Behold that which is forgotten. How may I be restored except that you remember me. You have given me your pledge that you will quest without ceasing; only thus may I be restored. Only when the human heart remembers what has been lost, will it be found, only when the human heart remembers what has been taken

THE RE-MEMBERING OF OSIRIS

may it be returned. I ask you to quest in the spirit of the human heart. I who was broken shall be whole. I who was lost shall be found. I who was scattered shall be united. I who was forgotten shall be remembered. Quest on behalf of the human heart which has forgotten and I shall be remembered.

First Priestess:
Offers incense.

*In the name of Glorious, I offer incense to Isis, the great Goddess who quested without ceasing, who never forgot the beloved.
Let us remember too.*

Priest:
Offers incense

*In the name of Magnificence, I offer incense to Osiris, the great Goddess who was never forgotten by the beloved.
Let us remember too.*

Second Priestess:
Offers incense.

In the name of Exalted, I offer incense to Lord Thoth, great tongue of Re, Lord of Hieroglyphs, Prophet of Truth seated upon his throne. We acknowledge spiritual realms unknown and divine powers unseen. We acknowledge the vast divine pattern and its holders.

Priest:
Let us hear of the Body of Osiris.

First Priestess:
What has been lost to us?

THE BREATH OF ISIS

Second Priestess:
What has been lost to us?

Shemsu 1-14

1. *The head of Osiris is lost to us.*
We have lost the higher mind which knows eternity.

2. *The face of Osiris is lost to us.*
We have lost our mirrored likeness.

3. *The eye of Osiris is lost to us.*
We have lost the sight that pierces darkness.

4. *The tongue of Osiris is lost to us.*
We have lost the tongue that speaks of truth.

5. *The ears of Osiris are lost to us.*
We have lost the gift of inner hearing.

6. *The heart of Osiris is lost to us.*
We have lost the love which flows without ceasing.

7. *The interior of Osiris is lost to us.*
We have lost the place of all inner knowing.

8. *The backbone of Osiris is lost to us.*
We have lost the axis which brings stability.

9. *The body of Osiris is lost to us.*
We have lost the outer sign of presence.

10. *The fist of Osiris is lost to us.*
We have lost all sense of crook and flail.

11. *The bones of Osiris are lost to us.*
We have lost the strength that upholds the body.

12. *The arms of Osiris are lost to us.*
We have lost the link of shared endeavour.

THE RE-MEMBERING OF OSIRIS

13. *The fingers of Osiris are lost to us.*
We have lost the way of sacred counting.

14. *The feet of Osiris are lost to us.*
We have lost the step which walks the path.

Priest:
Osiris is lost to us.

First Priestess:
What do we seek?

Second Priestess:
We seek the Body of Osiris

Shemsu 1-14

1. *We seek conscious alignment to the divine order.*

2. *We seek the full identity of our own nature.*

3. *We seek the eye of wisdom which strips away illusion.*

4. *We seek the words of truth which uphold natural order.*

5. *We seek the inner hearing which speaks in the silence.*

6. *We seek the great heart which knows no boundaries.*

7. *We seek the interior life which shows us meaning.*

8. *We seek true stability which gives us definition.*

9. *We seek sacred form which enshrines a mystery.*

10. *We seek the firm grasp which holds all together.*

11. *We seek divine structure which gives us a blueprint.*

12. *We seek the joint commitment which brings us together.*

THE BREATH OF ISIS

13. We seek sacred measure which shows us the immanent presence.

14. We seek firm footing which paces our journey.

Priest:
We will journey to Abydos the home of Osiris.

First Priestess:
We come as the Shemsu of Re.

Priest:
We come as the Scribes of Thoth.

Second Priestess:
We come as the Protectors of Osiris.

First Priestess:
Let us remember Abydos. This is the House of Osiris. This is the place of the Osirion where king and god were made as one.

Priest:
Let us hear of the House of life at Abydos.

Second Priestess:
As for the House of Life, it shall be in Abydos. Build it in four bodies, the inner body being of covered reeds. The living one he is Osiris. The hidden one who rests within it is the Great God. The four bodies consist of a stone that contains two wings, and its lower part is sand and its outside severally has four doors, one south, one north, one west and one east. It shall be hidden and very large. It shall not be seen but the sun shall look upon its mystery. The people who enter into it are the staff of Re and the scribes of the House of Life. The people who are in it, the fkty priest is Shu. The slaughterer is Horus who slays the rebels for his father Osiris,

THE RE-MEMBERING OF OSIRIS

and the scribe of the sacred books is Thoth, and it is he who will recite the ritual glorifications in the course of every day unseen, unheard. The books that are in it are the emanations of Re wherewith to keep alive this god and to overthrow his enemies. As for the staff of the House of Life who are in it, they are the followers of Re protecting his son Osiris every day.

Priest:
Let Osiris be assembled.

First Priestess:
Let Osiris dwell in his house.

Second Priestess:
Let Osiris be re-membered.

Shemsu 1-14
Each holder brings scented sand as the Body of Osiris and pours it into the Bed of Osiris.

1. I bring the head of Osiris.
Let conscious understanding be restored.

2. I bring the face of Osiris.
Let ancient recognition be restored.

3. I bring the eye of Osiris.
Let inner vision be restored.

4. I bring the tongue of Osiris.
Let truthful speaking be restored.

5. I bring the ears of Osiris.
Let inner hearing be restored.

THE BREATH OF ISIS

6. I bring the heart of Osiris.
Let divine love be restored.

7. I ring the interior of Osiris.
Let inner knowing be restored.

8. I bring the backbone of Osiris.
Let stable life be restored.

9. I bring the body of Osiris.
Let sanctified space be restored.

10. I bring the fist of Osiris.
Let personal rulership be restored.

11. I bring the bones of Osiris.
Let wise structure be restored.

12. I bring the arms of Osiris.
Let deep communion be restored.

13. I bring the fingers of Osiris.
Let sacred measure be restored.

14. I bring the feet of Osiris.
Let the union of spirit and matter be restored.

First Priestess:
Let the house in which he dwells be re-established.

Priest:
Let the divinities who uphold this house come forwards.

Second Priestess:
Let Heaven and Earth meet.

THE RE-MEMBERING OF OSIRIS

The Voice of Isis:
I am Isis, I am the East Face of The House of Life.
My name is Love.

The Voice of Nephthys:
I am Nephthys, I am the West Face of The House of Life.
My name is Protection.

The Voice of Horus:
I am Horus, I am the North Face of The House of Life.
My name is Perfection.

The Voice of Thoth:
I am Thoth. I am the South Face of The House of Life.
My name is Wisdom.

The Voice of Geb:
I am Geb, I am the Lower Face of The House of Life.
My name is Foundation.

The Voice of Nuit:
I am Nuit, I am the Upper Face of The House of Life.
My name is Eternity.

First Priestess:
Let the House of Life receive its blessing.

Priest:
Let the divinities who shall bless this house be present.

Second Priestess:
Let heaven and earth be united.

THE BREATH OF ISIS

The Voice of Isis:
I am the daughter of Nuit. It is I who breathe life into this Per-Ankh that it shall be restored.

The Voice of Horus:
I am the daughter of Geb. It is I who protect this Per-Ankh that it may be restored.

The Voice of Horus:
I am the son of Isis and Osiris. It is I who empower this Per-Ankh that it may be restored.

The Voice of Thoth:
I am the tongue of Ra. It is I who give name to this Per-Ankh that it shall be restored.

The Voice of Geb:
I am the father of Isis, Osiris and Nephthys. It is I who support this Per-Ankh that it may be restored.

The Voice of Nuit:
I am the mother of Isis, Osiris and Nephthys. It is I who endow this Per-Ankh that it may be restored.

First Priestess:
Let the House of Life be reconstructed.

Priest:
Let the divinities who shall establish this House of Life be present.

Second Priestess:
Let the House of Life receive its divine portion.

THE RE-MEMBERING OF OSIRIS

The Voice of Isis:
Each divinity places an amulet around the Bed of Osiris

My name is Divine Love. My sign is the Tet.
I bless this place with my presence.

My name is Undying Support. My sign is the outspread wing.
I bless this place with my presence.

The Voice of Horus:
My name is Spiritual Rebirth. My sign is the eye.
I bless this place with my presence.

The Voice of Thoth:
My name is Eternal Wisdom. My sign is the palette.
I bless this place with my presence.

The Voice of Geb:
My name is Earthly Existence. My sign is the phoenix.
I bless this place with my presence.

The Voice of Nuit:
My name is Cosmic Truth. My sign is the star.
I bless this place with my presence.

Priest:
Is it your wish that Osiris should dwell in his house?

Shemsu Omnes:
It is.

First Priestess
Is it your wish that the House of Life should live again?

THE BREATH OF ISIS

Shemsu Omnes:
It is.

Second Priestess
Then let Osiris come to his house.

First Priestess:
Let us meditate on this mystery.

Priest:
Let us now hear the words of Sefkhet-Abu, Mistress of Writing, Lady of Builders, She of the sacred foundation.

Second Priestess:
Thy house is completed, thy monument is embellished, those who are in it are in joy, mayest thou rest in thy august temple, every god being thy protection, who is in thy mansion of triumph in the west of Abydos. I have founded it together with Sokar; it is Ptah who performs my work on it. I have stretched out the cord in the interior of its walls, my utterance is for it, containing the great spells of glorification. Thoth is therein with his scrolls; Khnum has established its works; Ta-Tanen, he levels its foundation soil; Atum is upon it forever.

The head of the baton of gold is in my hand; I struck the rod therewith, thou being together with me in thy forms of Sokar, thy hands holding the hoe. He has set in place its four walls which are fixed to perfection like the four supports of the sky. Nut utters her magical spells; its protection is effected by Neith, Selkis being satisfied with the eternal work. Its walls are in their proper places. Mayest thou come anew. The columns are firmly fixed, all its doors being of copper. Hu is in it, bearing provisions. Sia proclaims its beauty, every, good god resting within it, under supervision together with Osiris. Mayest thou cause him to rest on his seat in its Great Mansion, his sacred image being distinguished.

THE RE-MEMBERING OF OSIRIS

Amun is in, as the head of them all. How divine is thy temple; his face and his dignity being a protection round about it.

First Priestess
Behold the House of Osiris is complete.

Priest:
Behold the Bed of Osiris is complete.

Second Priestess:
Raises pillar and accompanying music.

Behold the Djed of Osiris is raised.

First Priestess:
Let each come before the House of Life to make a dedication.

Each person walks to the altar and makes a silent dedication

Priest:
Let joyful communion be shared.

Communion of bread and wine

Second Priestess:
*Our joy is complete. Let the company depart in peace.
Em hotep.*

Company departs

CHAPTER VI
THE MARRIAGE OF HEAVEN AND EARTH

BACKGROUND

It is not possible to express a deep interest in Ancient Egypt without encountering Isis and Osiris. These two divinities were seminal to the beliefs and hopes of ordinary people. Their shared story is utterly human and readily understood. The re-telling of it is an affirmation of triumph over despair and loss. Yet simultaneously both Isis and Osiris have a larger part to play in Kemetic culture as initiating models of rulership. The Isis-Osiris-Horus trinity is the template upon which the kingship is built both in life, as the Horus-king and beyond life as an Osiris. Moreover, both Isis and Osiris take a stellar identification as Sirius and Orion. Few divinities fully bridge the human, divine and stellar realms like this. I have included one ritual at each of these three levels.

When I began to explore the meaning and significance of Isis and Osiris, I had no idea where it would lead. I have used the Osirian template of seeking-finding-rejoicing on several occasions and at different levels of experience. This triple sequence in its phases of destruction and reconstruction, clearly states the processes necessary for personal re-orientation, it is the blueprint for all initiations. I have used the Osirian pattern for personal initiatory processes and also for rituals intended to embrace the transcendent.

I have presented three rituals. *The Ascension of Osiris* is undeniably stellar in scope. *The Marriage of Heaven and*

THE MARRIAGE OF HEAVEN AND EARTH

Earth is a beautiful and mystical evocation of renewal using the initiatory template based on the twelve hours of the night. This rite undoubtedly brings about personal regeneration and renewal, it gifts the greening of the psyche. *The Re-membering of Osiris* is another rite of reconstruction, it embraces both the personal and the non-personal.

COMMENTARY

The Mysteries of Isis and Osiris are central to understanding the metaphysics of ancient Egypt. This story might be compared to the centrality of the Christmas story in Christianity. The nativity is enacted as a children's story in December and the passion is told at Easter but in ancient Egypt, the entire cycle of life, both the death and rebirth of the divine king was enacted with great fervour and intensity throughout the length and breadth of the land. We might compare these intense public pageants with the street processions of Catholic Europe or the massive religious events of India. However, the temple enactments are quite another matter altogether. Within the body of the temple, the house of the neter where the divinity abides in perpetuity, daily rituals affirm the divine presence. The annual commemorative celebrations re-state and renew the primal root connection to the patron divinity of the sacred house. The act of retelling and re-enacting the mythos, perpetuates the bond between the divine and earthly worlds. To be present at such an enactment is to stand in a sanctified space face to face with the living presence of the divinity. No wonder then that these enactments are the things glorious, magnificent and exalted.

Although both Isis and Osiris dwelled in temples dedicated in their name, there can never be a sense in which the divinity is present as a solitary figure. The indwelling divinity may be seen as the sole proprietor but by the same token, the connective and essential relationships with other relevant neter are also recognized and substantiated. At the Osirion, there are chapels to Horus and

THE BREATH OF ISIS

Ptah. At the island temple of Philae ostensibly the home of Isis, there is a sanctuary to Hathor and of course Osiris figures largely here too. So, the annual enactments are major events in the life of the temple and the kingdom, these conjunctions between the human and the divine serve to revivify the sacred network through which the culture of Kem exists. Accordingly, these divine acts which create the living heart of the temple tradition, follow established protocols and procedures. Theurgy applies patterns and procedures so that the divine life is disseminated and assimilated via the temple tradition to the life of the land and its people.

PREPARATION
The figures of Isis and Osiris are so well known that many approaches of understanding are all possible. There are hymns, images, statues and numerous representations to draw upon. So your preparation can be driven by your own interests. I would like to recommend the classical works by Plutarch's and Apuleius and the modern work Awakening Osiris and Dreams of Isis by Normandi Ellis. These key texts will provide a full range of intellectual, intuitive and imaginative keys. It might also be appropriate to create a shrine honouring both divinities as a key part of your personal preparation. Your private meditations and invocations will begin to build the bridge in consciousness necessary for effective ritual encounter. Theurgic ritual is never theatre or even a sacred drama, this means of identification is merely the appropriate modus operandi not the intended outcome.

CHOREOGRAPH NOTES
Place the altar in the centre attended by the priest. Ensure there is sufficient space to receive the 14 offerings. The company form a circle. The rite uses a repeating structure of question and answer. This refrain provides a stable pattern upon which the ritual dynamics are built. The question is followed by an answer in two

THE MARRIAGE OF HEAVEN AND EARTH

forms, firstly by the Shemsu who brings offerings to the altar and secondly by the answering voice of Osiris. These parts may be allocated in various ways. Ideally the rite requires 14 voices plus the voice of the priest. Each participant speaks both as a Follower and as the Voice of Osiris. In this case, allocate the voices in pairs across the circle space so that question and answer move dynamically across the space. The voices of the cardinal points may also be shared among the company. These anchor points should obviously be placed in the cardinal directions. Since the Four Sons of Horus do not match the western correspondences for the four quarters, some prior preparation might be helpful.

Dramatis Personae:
PRIEST
VOICE OF THE EAST
VOICE OF THE SOUTH
VOICE OF THE NORTH
VOICE OF THE WEST
THE VOICE OF OSIRIS 1-12
THE VOICE OF THE SHEMSU 1-12

On the altar:
Representations of Isis and Osiris, either statues or images.
Cloths of green and gold; Incense; 3 candles

THE WORDS OF POWER

Priest:
Beloved Shemsu,
We are met to enjoin The Mysteries of Isis and Osiris.
Let the company make way.
Awake in peace,
Those whose faces are beautiful

THE BREATH OF ISIS

Welcome is your coming.
To those whose hearts are open,
You are welcome in this your divine sanctuary.

Lights first candle.

Let this flame shine in the name of, Glorious.

Lights second candle.

Let this flame shine in the name, Magnificence.

Lights third candle.

Let this flame shine in the name of Exaltation.

The fire is laid.
The incense is laid.
Your perfume comes to me, O incense
May my perfume come to you.
O Incense, your perfume comes from me to you gods.
Let all here be pure.

Lights incense – circumnambulates area with incense.

Voice of the East:
We are met in the Light of the Ancient tradition to celebrate the Mysteries of Isis and Osiris. Let us glorify his name, establish his body and praise his spirit.
The fallen one will rise, the broken one will be restored, t he forgotten one will be remembered.
This is the sacred marriage of heaven and earth through which all things are renewed.
Open your heart to the Mystery of the restoration of life through the resurrection of the good green god and the birth of the golden child.
We gather in the shade of the Tamarisk Tree which binds the Above and Below.

THE MARRIAGE OF HEAVEN AND EARTH

Voice of the South:
In your mind's eye see now the four directions, the pathways of the infinite. At the axis of the four directions stands the holy tree, the divine pillar of fire which draws together the lower, middle and upper worlds of the full life. Its roots reach down into the inner earth, its canopy stretches up to heaven. It is the route upon which men and gods may journey.

Voice of the West:
Send the eye of the mind upwards to the far heavens into the unseen realm of the sacred bride who brings forth all life continuously. She is invoked in her name of Great One, Mother of the God, Starry One, Unknowable, Beyond Measure, Infinite, Majestic, Seed Bearer, Divine Mother, Nuit-Isis. All Hail to the goddesses who blesses the world with the power of becoming.

Voice of the North:
Send the eye of the mind downwards to the inner earth, to the unseen realms of the sacred bridegroom who brings forth all life continuously. He is invoked in his name of The Green God, The Good God, The Shepherd of his People, The Mysterious One, Divine Earth, The Ever Becoming, Seed Bearer, Divine Father Geb-Osiris. All hail to the green god who blesses the world with the power of becoming.

Priest:
Behold now the beloved whose form rests before you held in the pillar of the Tamarisk tree. Let us speak the words of lament.

Shemsu Omnes:
He who illumines the Duat with the rays from his eyes has gone far from us. He has gone far from us. Come now let us weep for Osiris. O you divine beings of the Northern and southern sky. The vigil of the god has begun. We shall justify the Foremost of the Westerners.

THE BREATH OF ISIS

Priest:
The Resurrection of Osiris commence at the first hour.

Shemsu Omnes:
Who will restore the Body of Osiris at the first hour?

Voice of the Shemsu 1:
Places offering of water on the altar.

Hail to you Osiris. Let him be established among the resplendent ones. May the Duat be opened to him. I will restore the Body of Osiris. I bring water to Osiris.

The Voice of Osiris 1:
That which is remembered lives. As I am, I was and I shall be a thing of matter and of heaven. That which is written shall be remembered. Osiris lives in the land of his birth. This day I am within you. Stabbed by the light of the great mind I awake. I am called from my house. My heart leaps. I stir from my place of rest. A voice reaches me on the still air. It drops into my mind like a pale feather from heaven. It rests with a secret word, it is the name of my becoming. From my names rises the story of Egypt. Give me my name, say it over red jasper dipped in unguent. Give me my name that gods may call me to soar like the hawk. Flood me with purpose and memory. Refresh me with water. Submerge me in living water. Osiris awakes.

Shemsu Omnes:
Who will restore the Body of Osiris at the second hour?

Shemsu 2:
Places offering of flowers on the altar.

Hail to you Osiris. Let him be established among the resplendent ones. May the Duat be opened to him. I will restore the body of Osiris. I offer flowers to Osiris.

THE MARRIAGE OF HEAVEN AND EARTH

The Voice of Osiris 2:
Beside the well, the sycamore rises. Beside the well bright cornflowers grow - the smell of growing things. Blessed are the cattle and the sheep. The lotus rises struggling towards the sun. The perfume of the lotus fills the air. There are channels to fill with quick water life to pour through the desserts to make the garden bloom. Lord of the winds deliver me like a seed blown to fertile ground. I smell a change coming, a shape turning leaves in the wind. What is your secret name? I am the sweet smelling flower of the olive tree. Let me lie with the heat of the sun. Eating figs and smelling hay. Osiris awakes.

Shemsu Omnes:
Who will restore the Body of Osiris at the third hour?

Shemsu 3:
Places offering of grain on the altar.

Hail to you Osiris. Let him be established among the resplendent ones. May the Duat be opened to him. I will restore the body of Osiris. I offer grain to Osiris.

The Voice of Osiris 3:
I am the plant of life, which comes forth from Osiris, which grows upon the ribs of Osiris which allows the people to live, which makes the gods divine, which enlivens the living. I live as corn the life of the living. I live upon the rib of Geb. I can show you the world in a kernel of wheat. I am the life appearing from Osiris. I am greeted by voices on the road. Look what corn and grapes we share. Bake me into bread, smelt me into gold. I eat the bread I baked. I offer what I have made, my bread, my peace. I gather and build my life. The fields, flowers and rocks, are mine, even the serpent and the bee. All existence is the measure between light and dark. Darkness gives way to light. There is no rest. The act is now. In your lives you will make children make peace, make errors, you will make

THE BREATH OF ISIS

trouble, you will dance under sun and moon. As long as you live you will create life, you will rise and fall many times. It is like the making of a good loaf of bread, you will be nourished. Osiris lives in the land of his birth. Osiris awakes.

Shemsu Omnes:

Who will restore the Body of Osiris at the fourth hour?

Shemsu 4:

Places offering of light on the altar.

Hail to you Osiris. Let him be established among the resplendent ones. May the Duat be opened to him. I offer light to Osiris.

Voice of Osiris 4:

I wake in the dark to the stirrings of birds, a murmur in the trees, a flutter of wings. It is the morning of my birth, the first of many. The past lies before me knotted in its sheets asleep. Out of darkness the earth spins towards light. I feel a change coming. My thoughts flicker, glow a moment and catch fire. Come and a welcome awaits the wanderer here. I speak of the creator and the creation, the ordinary life extraordinarily. I am the pieces of myself a man longing for unity. I am a creature striving for light. Mine is the double soul of the universe, heaven mingled with earth. I am a creature of light striving for light battling in oppression and darkness. I am a creature of history, human and divine, I am the scroll of numerous myths, one teller of a single story. I see myself by the light of my own becoming. Osiris awakes.

Shemsu Omnes :

Who will restore the Body of Osiris at the fifth hour?

Shemsu 5:

Places offering of herbs on the altar.

THE MARRIAGE OF HEAVEN AND EARTH

Hail to you Osiris. Let him be established among the resplendent ones.
May the Duat be opened to him. I will restore the body of Osiris.
I offer herbs to Osiris.

The Voice of Osiris 5:

I have offered up saffron and myrrh to the goddess. Long tables are set with cakes. The scent of sandalwood arises. Green herbs heal the sorrows of men. My hearts bursts into light like a seeds, such things are made everyday: grapes, pomegranates, melon, cypress palm, Osiris. No greater joy exists than a walk among gardens smelling herbs and flowers. I am lifted from the fretful earth as the green plant lifts clods of dirt. The sun pours its grace upon my head. It is good to be here, a husband of earth. Osiris wakes.

Shemsu Omnes:

Who will restore the Body of Osiris at the sixth hour?

Shemsu 6:

Places incense on the altar.

Hail to you Osiris. Let him be established among the resplendent ones.
May the Duat be opened to him. I will restore the body of Osiris.
I offer incense to Osiris.

The Voice of Osiris 6:

The ka of Osiris walks where he pleases. I am thought, shadow and bone. The ka of Osiris grows bright wings. My face grows white with heat. Within you are myself, my ka. The ka of Osiris grows bright wings his face glows with white heat. This is the going forth of the god into the land of triumph. Osiris lives in the land of his birth as the fire of god. May I create words of beauty. May I draw down heaven's blessings. I come in the power of light. I come in the power of wisdom. I Osiris rise and hurry into the two lands of the living. I speak the word from which I

THE BREATH OF ISIS

was made. I speak of truth and splendour and of the honour of death and the power of return. Osiris awakes.

Shemsu Omnes:
Who will restore the Body of Osiris at the seventh hour?

Shemsu 7:
Places offering of beer on the altar.

Hail to you Osiris. Let him be established among the resplendent ones. May the Duat be opened to him. I will restore the body of Osiris? I offer beer to Osiris.

The Voice of Osiris 7:
I drink the beer I brewed with my own hands. Making, making, making, your life is craft, your supple body moulded by word, sculpted by deed. I am myself perceiving myself making, making, making. Oh offers of cakes and bearers of beer, let me not starve for love or thirst for wisdom. My beer is made of red barley. Hungrily I eat the god's food and join a feast of mystery. Let my spirit be stronger today than it was yesterday, my heart more peaceful, my mind more fertile, my hands more gentle. Osiris awakes.

Shemsu Omnes:
Who will restore the Body of Osiris at the eighth hour?

Shemsu 8:
Places offering of wine on the altar.

Hail to you Osiris. Let him be established among the resplendent ones. May the Duat be opened to him. I will restore the body of Osiris. I offer wine to Osiris.

THE MARRIAGE OF HEAVEN AND EARTH

The Voice of Osiris 8:

My heart weeps for what it remembers. May my heart increase, may it open as wide as the sky. May his arms and legs be strong and his strength used for dancing, sowing fields and holding his wife and uplifting his children. My heart is a field above which the sun rolls. I am Osiris, man and god, black obsidian reflecting light. My heart is a casket of jewels. Mine is a heart of carnelian blood red as the crest of a phoenix. My heart, my mother, my heart of becoming; the heart leaps and answers to its name, its words are the deeds of my body. Its deeds have been my own thoughts, its blood the fluid of gods, river of joy and sadness. In my heart are the names of the things I have loved. The power of myself is moving. My heart, my birth, my coming into existence; on earth I walk daily but in the house of heaven my feet are still. That which was ravaged is made whole. Osiris awakes.

Shemsu Omnes:

Who will restore the Body of Osiris at the ninth hour?

Shemsu 9:

Places offering of linen on the altar.

Hail to you Osiris. Let him be established among the resplendent ones. May the Duat be opened to him. I will restore the body of Osiris.
I offer linen to Osiris.

The Voice of Osiris 9:

The god is walking, walking, a million years – the beat of his left foot, his right – the flux of the universe. Is my backbone straight? a column of fire thrown up from the mountain peak. In the dark marrow of my bones. I have made myself light. Do I rise like a flame dispelling light? My flesh glows. The god of light springs up all around. My bones and intestines fill with light. This day I make myself anew. I create life, my flesh coils about me foot to head, my breath rushes through my blood. This body is the book of all I've remembered. Osiris awakes.

THE BREATH OF ISIS

Shemsu Omnes:
Who will restore the Body of Osiris at the tenth hour?

Shemsu 10:
Places offering of unguent on the altar

Hail to you Osiris. Let him be established among the resplendent ones. May the Duat be opened to him. I will restore the body of Osiris. I offer unguent to Osiris.

The Voice of Osiris 10:
The plug has been lifted from the unguent jar. The past has been written rolled and sealed in a scroll I'll not see again. Body rise up singing. Bones, I rise my spine is of bone, sinew and flesh. In the dark marrow of my bones I have made myself light. Bind up the bones in my neck and back, wind the sheets tight around me. Gather my bones and place them in my body. Bind my vertebra with thick grapevines dipped in saffron water, cover me with the blanket of sky. It is as if I had seen my bones for the first time and knew how they fitted together. It is as is I fell in love with by bones and was born in their form. My bones and intestines fill with light. These are the bones of a living god, these bones know where I have been. I am a living god with the earth millions of years.
Osiris awakes.

Shemsu Omnes:
Who will restore the Body of Osiris at the eleventh hour?

Shemsu 11:
Places offering of milk on the altar.

Hail to you Osiris. Let him be established among the resplendent ones. May the Duat be opened to him. I will restore the body of Osiris. I offer milk to Osiris.

THE MARRIAGE OF HEAVEN AND EARTH

The Voice of Osiris 11:

I wake as from a dream. My heart opens, fills with light. My hair drips as if I rose new from the sea. Beads of crystal light surround me. I live a million years. Is my face radiant? Does it glow like a sun on the horizon? The god within shows himself, the soul walks out, the mind of fire burns. I am a changeling, a man become God. Touch me, I burn with fever. With my hands I make visible thoughts. I weave the cloth of life. I wear its shining robe and live a million years. I have come home I have entered humanhood bound to rocks and plants, men and women, rivers and sky. I shall be with you in this and other worlds. It is myself I see and a thousand colours swirling in liquid light. I am this body. I am that star rising above clouds hung by a thread from the ocean moon. Neither death nor spite nor ignorance stops my love for you. I am Osiris shining. A creature of light am I. Bless this body where the world is gathered. Osiris awakes.

Shemsu Omnes:

Who will restore the Body of Osiris at the twelfth hour?

Shemsu 12:

Places offering of oil on the altar.

Hail to you Osiris. Let him be established among the resplendent ones. May the Duat be opened to him. I will restore the body of Osiris. I offer oil to Osiris.

The Voice of Osiris 12:

I am anointed in oil. The power shivers from my heart down to my arms. I have made a reckoning of myself, the things I have said and done and of my intentions. The doors of perception open; what was hidden has been revealed. It is myself I see and a thousand colours swirling in liquid light. I have come home. May we come in and go out of heaven through the gates of starlight. As the houses of earth fill with dancing and song,

THE BREATH OF ISIS

so filled are the houses of heaven. I come, in truth. I sail a long river and row back again. It is joy to breathe under the stars. I am the sojourner destined to walk a thousand years until I arrive at myself. I see you as stars in the utmost distance. O listeners who hear my voice, come to me that I may know my name and purpose. I have been many things, lived and died many times and loved as often as possible. In this moment, I regret nothing for the paths that I chose led me here. I offer you my life. In this moment as the veil opens and before it closes, I see that we are gods and that all that exists and can be named is god coming from the body of god. Blessed are we in eternal change. I am a man blessed by becoming millions and millions of times. I am in this body, I am that star rising above the clouds. Hail myself traversing eternity walking among gods, a shuttle flying through the threads of time. This is all one place, one cloth, a man's life endures. I have come home, though apart I am a part of you. One of the million things in the universe, I am the universe too. You and I together are a single creation, neither death nor spite nor fear nor ignorance stops my love for you. May we come and go out in and out of heaven through the gates of starlight. I come in truth, I am the sojourner destined to walk a thousand years and arrive at myself.
Osiris awakes.

Priest:

Behold Osiris lives in eternity. The god is aroused. Osiris awakes. Osiris inhabits the body of gold. The body of Osiris shines. The Tamarisk Tree shines. A bird descends from its highest branches. Isis comes to her beloved. The kite descends. She beats her wings upon the air. She beats her wings upon the air. She beats her wings upon the air. She revives that which was dead. She restores that which was lost. She breathes life.

Company visualises the Ascent of Osiris and the Descent of Isis for their nuptiual meeting.

THE MARRIAGE OF HEAVEN AND EARTH

Company turn outward in silence — a crystal bowl
or singing bowl is struck

Priest:
Places hand over heart.

We witness the birth of Mystery for the Golden One is conceived in light. The spirit of light flies into every heart, seeding its divine image. The breath of Isis comes like a fragrance on the breeze. As the child draws its first breath upon life, so breathe now with the breath of new life at the hour of the second birth.

Silent Group Meditation

*Drink deeply from the cup of grace extended to you now. Let all rejoice for we have attended at the birth of a great mystery.
Osiris wakes, Isis is blessed, the Golden Child is conceived.*

Priest:
Let us hear inspired words.

Oracular Voices from the Shemsu.

Priest:
Let a communion be shared.

Communion of Wine and Bread

The Voice of the East:
Our Mysteries are completed.
You have made your transformations.
May we repose in this glorified frame.
Go in peace.
Khep em hotep.
Let the Shemsu depart in peace.
Khep em hotep.

THE BREATH OF ISIS

The Voice of the South:
Our Mysteries are completed.
You have made your transformations.
May we repose in this glorified frame.
Go in peace.
Khep em hotep
Let the Shemsu depart in peace
Khep em hotep.

The Voice of the West:
Our Mysteries are completed.
You have made your transformations.
May we repose in this glorified frame.
Go in peace.
Khep em hotep.
Let the Shemsu depart in peace.
Khep em hotep.

The Voice of the North:
Our Mysteries are completed.
You have made your transformations.
May we repose in this glorified frame.
Go in peace.
Khep em hotep
Let the Shemsu depart in peace.
Khep em hotep .

Shemsu Omnes:
Let the Shemsu depart in peace
Khep em hotep.

Company departs

Addendum I
AN AQUARIAN MYSTERY SCHOOL OF DIVINE PARTNERSHIP FOUNDATIONS

The new wine age of a New Age cannot be poured into the old bottles of outworn codes. There must be fundamental changes in the way of national life because a fundamental change has taken place in Life itself as the sun moves from Pisces to Aquarius in the Precession of the Equinoxes.
Dion Fortune, *The Magical Battle of Britain*

A BUILDING requires a strong foundation, building a Mystery School, a School for the soul, likewise requires a firm foundation not of bricks and mortar but of mind. This emergent school is based on the House of Life in ancient Egypt and the Hermetic tradition guided by the teachings of Dion Fortune. In the new spirit of the incoming Aquarian age, this school is built upon principles of inclusiveness and a non-hierarchical foundation of sacred geometry, specifically the Flower of Life. This template offers a foundation of organic growth and independent formation within the shared cooperation of community.

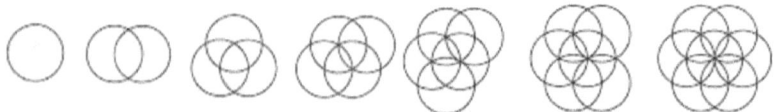

ADDENDUM I

The starting point is YOU, your experiences, interests, and aspiration with the tradition of western spirituality. This first stage is represented by the circle, a primal image of birth and potentiality, you are most likely to already have one or more likeminded friendships and in this small way, the process of formation begins and develops through sharing ideas and information. It is also likely that in some way, you have already been drawn to the tradition perhaps through the images of the Tarot or through the mythology and teachings of one of the Great Wisdom Teachers: Isis, Athena, Demeter, Hermes, Thoth, Hathor for example. This magnetic spiritual attraction is the voice of the heart-deity emerging in your life expressing the star-seed at the centre of the sacred circle.

The Flower of Life offers a sevenfold progression, however the group comes into existence from inception even before the seven faces of the flower have opened. The House of the Heart comes into being with the sounded power of the name in accordance with the ancient Egyptian idea. This template encompasses multiplicity within unity and diversity within community. Each new foundation is based upon the Kemetic understanding that the sacred house is as a dwelling place wherein the divinity and its living presence comes to reside. Accordingly, in keeping with the tradition, the newly founded house takes the Kemetic name beginning Per and is completed by naming the indwelling presence.

The House of Life takes its name from the Per Ankh of the ancient Egyptian temple tradition. It might be described as a storehouse of written protocol, the holder of sacred litany and the divine letters. It was a place dedicated to the power of the word at the behest of the speaker of the word, the Master of Wisdom, Djehuty-Thoth. Although as an institution, it is without a western equivalent, it might be compared to the work of monks in the creation of parchment manuscripts for divine purpose. In a similar way scribes were held in high esteem as servants in the retinue of Lord Thoth, the oversoul of the temple tradition. The House of

THE BREATH OF ISIS

Life was a nodal centre dedicated to the transmission of knowledge both mathematical and medical; without knowledge there can be no gnosis; knowledge is a divine unction always present for the parched soul in need of life-giving water.

The House of Life offers the gifts of life. This House of Life offers a pathway into the Wisdom of the West based on the contemporary symbols already charged with numinous power by previous generations: the Tarot, The Tree of Life and the Barque of Millions of Years creating a Path of three complexities.

Spiral One: Tarot – The Lesser Mysteries of preparation and purification of being through the Elemental Initiation of Synthesis.

Spiral Two: The Tree of Life – The Greater Mysteries of dedication and soul-service through the Mystical Initiation of Universal Being.

Spiral Three: The Barque of Millions of Years – The Supreme Mysteries of devotion and identification through the Cosmic Initiation of Eternal Becoming.

The Core Curriculum is to be found in the following texts:
The Element Tarot Handbook:
An Initiation into the Key Elements of the Tarot, Element, 1994

The Watkins Tarot Handbook, Watkins 2005

The Aquarian Qabalah – reissued as *The Kabbalah Experience*, Watkins 2003, 2006

Becoming a Garment of Isis – A Nine stage Initiatory Path of Egyptian Spirituality, Inner Traditions, 2022

The Elements of the Egyptian Wisdom, reissued as *The Way of Egyptian Wisdom*, Element Books, 1994, 2003

ADDENDUM I

In the Footsteps of Dion Fortune – Initiation for the Aquarian Spirit, Thoth Publications 2025

Daughter of the Goddess, The Sacred Priestess, Thorsens, 1994,

Becoming Hathor, A Rite of Passage into the Mysteries of Het-Her, E Book 2024

All titles within the core curriculum offer practical engagement for individuals and groups. I will be also be providing ritual scripts for key ceremonies and other support papers as the need arises. There are no fees for this school. My role is that of consultant and soul-friend for your journey.

Addendum II
THE HOUSE OF LIFE OVERVIEW

The reason that the occultist seeks his inspiration in the remote past is because the nearer the source, the purer the stream. The wisdom of the initiates is not so much a body of doctrine that has been built up by experimental research, each worker handing on the fruits of his studies to his successors, as in large part a revelation received from sources other than those to which humanity normally has access.
Dion Fortune, *The Headwaters of Occultism*

IT IS VERY clear that DF anticipated dynamic change in the structure of society and in the structure of Mystery school; these changes might best be described as Aquarian by nature: inclusive, holistic, person centred, and emergent from the grass roots upwards rather than superimposed from the top downwards. The emergence of the nineteenth century mystery schools was necessarily for the few and this selective environment matched the limited interest in all things esoteric. Since then, there has been a revolution, a much-needed spiritual renaissance aided in large part by the internet. However, this dissemination should not bring a dissolution of principles lost in the broader thrust of New Age spirituality. DF made her views clear. She established the principles required of an occult student, laid out the pathway and its stages, and defined the container of the school as an interface with the Inner Planes. Her words of wisdom

ADDENDUM II

have lost none of their power to inspire and initiate. This work is dedicated not merely to her memory but also to her legacy which lives on. She extended an invitation to enter into the tradition of western esotericism and this is the invitation offered here. In keeping with the spirit of our times, an Aquarian Mystery School must reflect the Aquarian values that she saw emerging in her lifetime. Accordingly, a new template, non-hierarchical, inclusive and organic is hereby offered. Here is a school fully in the tradition of the Mysteries yet aligned to a new template whereby the participants co-create the development of the school. This is a radical movement away from the hierarchical forms necessary in the past and this new template is in keeping with the incoming Aquarian ethos. There is no 'teacher' within this school but rather a presentation of 'teachings' which are expressed in the curriculum of the school in alignment with both the Hermetic and Kemetic traditions.

The foundational template for this new model is the aptly named the Flower of Life – a symbol of organic growth. This image can be seen carved in the Osirion at Abydos – a sacred space based on the cosmic processes of growth through renewal and rebirth under the aegis of the green faced divinity Asar. The sequence of growth can be applied to the founding and organization of a group dedicated to the same purpose.

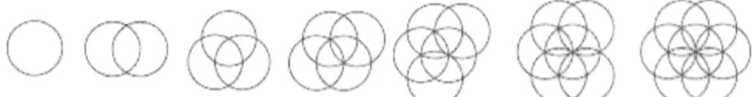

The starting point is the circle. This is a profound image that Pythagoras called the Monad, it represents the divine seed of inspiration. The second image is that of the Vesica Piscis (meaning a fish bladder) or mandorla (meaning an almond). This shape is also called, the Mother of Form since key geometric figures are generated through the intersection of the two circles. This stage represents the transition of an idea into manifestation. In actuality, this represents the stage wherein the divine is emerging in the life of an individual complemented by the desire to share with others. The sequential images finally unfolds into the Flower of Life, formed by seven circles intersecting equally with the first and from this a six petalled star-flower emerges. The sequence may represent seven persons equally engaging with the central point of emergence which represents the Divine Seed within the group. The completed Flower represents the harmonious relationship between the group to give birth to the star-secret, the mystical connection with all existence. The completed flower is always open to continuous growth, it might be seen as a single cell in a vast organism. This symbol therefore provides a foundational template for a small group of persons to share and partake of the Divine Seed always present at the centre, a point of potentiality within the pleroma, a word meaning fullness. The notion of cellular growth provides for an unlimited number of small groups focused on one aspect of a multilevel experience. Each person is free to establish a House according to their own light and the organic nature of the model brings growth and relationship through both simplicity and complexity in unity.

The Flower of Life is found on the wall of the Osirion thereby embracing the Kemetic tradition. Additionally, the same symbol embraces the Tree of Life and the Hermetic tradition. This symbol perfectly represents your invitation into the ever-open door of the mystery tradition. The growth implicit in the model fulfils the promise of the Monad which is the Divine Seed.

The symbol for the ancient Egyptian House of Life, the Per Ankh depicts an enclosure surrounding an ankh. The ankh has become a familiar symbol though its original meaning has been blurred by modern and spurious ideas of sexual symbolism. It's origins have been clarified by the work of Andrew H. Gordon and Calvin W. Schwabe, an Egyptologist and a vet in the groundbreaking study *The Quick and the Dead – Biomedical Theory in Ancient Egypt*. The ankh is clearly derived from the thoracic spine of the bull,

ADDENDUM II

the Key of Life bestows power in life. It is frequently shown being offered to the nose. As a person might savour the perfume of a rose, so the Key of Life is inhaled on an in-breath as pneuma the divine breath of the gods.

It is clear that ancient cultures created forms of living which preserved harmony with the natural world. Modern life offers many wonders but it seems altogether to have lost any sense of wisdom. By contrast many cultures envisaged wisdom in a divine form. It was an attribute held by the divine intermediaries and bestowed upon humanity through a reciprocal interchange. In ancient Egypt the ibis headed form of Djehuty-Thoth embodied the unseen source of wisdom and its many fields of knowledge, feminine divinities such as Aset-Isis and Ma'at likewise embodied wisdom in its many forms from the Intelligence of the Heart to the social and cultural value of Truthfulness. Without truth there can be no wisdom and without wisdom there can be no truth. There is much to gain from re-establishing relationships to the Avatars of Wisdom in our age so much in need of wisdom. The School welcomes you as a Co-creator in an ancient tradition now serving Aquarius.

Addendum III

THE HOUSE OF LIFE

MYSTERY SCHOOL OF DIVINE PARTNERSHIP APPLICATION

WRITE a letter introducing yourself to Naomi ozaniec@gmail.com using the following guidelines:

Your Journey – kindly share some significant markers on your journey to date

Your interests – intellectual and devotional – kindly share which writers have inspired your thinking and which deities have inspired your life.

Your Aspirations – kindly share the ideas you have to establish an independent House within the House of Life

I look forward to hearing from you.

Postscript

MY TALE of being and becoming does not end with the many stages and faces of sorrow but in resurrection and rebirth. I write about this new chapter of my life from a beautiful home in a secluded valley in central Portugal where I moved in 2015; the renewing of my life happened thus. I was living with my brother in Portsmouth and one afternoon even while I was chatting with my sister-in-law, I became aware that my focus of attention was shifting away from the cup of tea in front of me to a different vista. I took myself outside into the garden and sitting quietly and closing my eyes began to observe the unexpected flow of images arising in my mind. This might be compared with watching an internal cinema screen, quite where such images originate is an answered question. In my mind's eye, I found myself standing at one side of a large and long wooden table opposite a figure who I knew carried the title of Ur Hekau, the Great One of Magic and that is all I knew. Neither of us spoke but reaching down he picked up a papyrus scroll and with a flourish unfurled it across the table, I saw it was a map. Then with a gesture filled with tremendous force, he jabbed a finger down upon the map, accompanied by a single word, *"There."* I knew instantly that I would move home and leave the UK. He spoke to me at some length, that is to say ideas were placed in my mind, none of which I could recall even later that day and certainly not now.

It took me time to discover where I would be moving and it happened in the following way. In that summer I had treated myself

POSTSCRIPT

to a week of dancing with Suraya Hilal in Dusseldorf. During the week I made friends with a woman from Australia, who like so many Australians had just completed a year of travel around Europe. Prior to the dance week I had already spent hours researching far-flung possibilities such as Turkey, Croatia and even Bulgaria. She asked if I had ever thought about moving to Portugal – "No, never." She then pointed out a woman from the group, "Go and ask her about Portugal." It turned out that here was woman who worked for the Portuguese government. It would be simple to say that the 'rest is history' which is true but there is still a little more to tell.

When I returned home, my first task was to look at property prices, my budget was limited but miracle of miracles I would have enough to buy a property in a rural area in Portugal. My attention was focussed on one property and when I spoke with the owner, she told me that a prospective buyer was already on the horizon, so I asked her how much was needed for the deposit and it is at that point that I may finally say 'and the rest is history.' I found out only recently that she thought it was quite mad to buy a house unseen and the story of the mad English woman went around the village. Incidentally my sister-in-law and brother moved over in 2020 and later that same year my sister also relocated. A good friend and his new partner moved three months after me, another very old friend moved over in 2022 and a good friend from Peru will be moving into her house here after retirement in 2025. So, my story does have a happy ending. I now live in a beautiful valley in a forest in sight of the Mondego River. I grow vegetables and write words; my life has begun anew. I live surrounded by green on all sides, here is the colour of Osiris-Asar, the green faced neter of renewal. Now in 2024 I am opening a School of the Mysteries, Isis has given me a new task.

Naomi 2024 © Rob MacWhirter

CONTACT DETAILS

I warmly invite your comments and questions after reading my story. I look forward to hearing from you and making new friends around the world.

I can be contacted at naomi.ozaniec@gmail.com
Website is www.thehouseoflife.co.uk

OTHER TITLES BY THOTH PUBLICATIONS

AN INTRODUCTION TO RITUAL MAGIC
By Dion Fortune & Gareth Knight

At the time this was something of a unique event in esoteric publishing – a new book by the legendary Dion Fortune. Especially with its teachings on the theory and practice of ritual or ceremonial magic, by one who, like the heroine of two of her other novels, was undoubtedly "a mistress of that art".

In this work Dion Fortune deals in successive chapters with Types of Mind Working; Mind Training; The Use of Ritual; Psychic Perception; Ritual Initiation; The Reality of the Subtle Planes; Focusing the Magic Mirror; Channelling the Forces; The Form of the Ceremony; and The Purpose of Magic – with appendices on Talisman Magic and Astral Forms.

Each chapter is supplemented and expanded by a companion chapter on the same subject by Gareth Knight. In Dion Fortune's day the conventions of occult secrecy prevented her from being too explicit on the practical details of magic, except in works of fiction. These veils of secrecy having now been drawn back, Gareth Knight has taken the opportunity to fill in much practical information that Dion Fortune might well have included had she been writing today.

In short, in this unique collaboration of two magical practitioners and teachers, we are presented with a valuable and up-to-date text on the practice of ritual or ceremonial magic "as it is". That is to say, as a practical, spiritual, and psychic discipline, far removed from the lurid superstition and speculation that are the hall mark of its treatment in sensational journalism and channels of popular entertainment.

ISBN 978-1-870450-31-7 Deluxe Hardback limited edition
ISBN 978-1-870450-26-3 Soft cover edition

PRINCIPLES OF HERMETIC PHILOSOPHY
Dion Fortune & Gareth Knight

Principles of Hermetic Philosophy was the last known work written by Dion Fortune. It appeared in her Monthly letters to members and associates of the Society of the Inner Light between November 1942 and March 1944.

Her intention in this work is summed up in her own words: "The observations in these pages are an attempt to gather together the fragments of a forgotten wisdom and explain and expand them in the light of personal observation."

She was uniquely equipped to make highly significant personal observations in these matters as one of the leading practical occultists of her time. What is more, in these later works she feels less constrained by traditions of occult secrecy and takes an altogether more practical approach than in her earlier, well known textbooks.

Gareth Knight takes the opportunity to amplify her explanations and practical exercises with a series of full page illustrations, and provides a commentary on her work

ISBN 978-1-870450-34-8

THE WESTERN MYSTERY TRADITION
Christine Hartley

A reissue of a classic work, by a pupil of Dion Fortune, on the mythical and historical roots of Western occultism. Christine Hartley's aim was to demonstrate that we in the West, far from being dependent upon Eastern esoteric teachings, possess a rich and potent mystery tradition of our own, evoked and defined in myth, legend, folklore and song, and embodied in the legacy of Druidic culture.

More importantly, she provides practical guidelines for modern students of the ancient mysteries, 'The Western Mystery Tradition,' in Christine Hartley's view, 'is the basis of the Western religious feeling, the foundation of our spiritual life, the matrix of our religious formulae, whether we are aware of it or not. To it we owe the life and force of our spiritual life.'

ISBN 978 1 870450 24 9

THE CIRCUIT OF FORCE
by Dion Fortune.
With commentaries by Gareth Knight.

In "The Circuit of Force", Dion Fortune describes techniques for raising the personal magnetic forces within the human aura and their control and direction in magic and in life, which she regards as 'the Lost Secrets of the Western Esoteric Tradition'.

To recover these secrets she turns to three sources.
a) the Eastern Tradition of Hatha Yoga and Tantra and their teaching on raising the "sleeping serpent power" or kundalini;

b) the circle working by means of which spiritualist seances concentrate power for the manifestation of some of their results;

c) the linking up of cosmic and earth energies by means of the structured symbol patterns of the Qabalistic Tree of Life.

Originally produced for the instruction of members of her group, this is the first time that this material has been published for the general public in volume form. Gareth Knight provides subject commentaries on various aspects of the etheric vehicle, filling in some of the practical details and implications that she left unsaid in the more secretive esoteric climate of the times in which she wrote.

Some quotes from Dion Fortune's text:

"When, in order to concentrate exclusively on God, we cut ourselves off from nature, we destroy our own roots. There must be in us a circuit between heaven and earth, not a one-way flow, draining us of all vitality. It is not enough that we draw up the Kundalini from the base of the spine; we must also draw down the divine light through the Thousand-Petalled Lotus. Equally, it is not enough for our mental health and spiritual development that we draw down the Divine Light, we must also draw up the earth forces. Only too often mental health is sacrificed to spiritual development through ignorance of, or denial of, this fact."

"....the clue to all these Mysteries is to be sought in the Tree of Life. Understand the significance of the Tree; arrange the symbols you are working with in the correct manner upon it, and all is clear and you can work out your sum. Equate the Danda with the Central Pillar, and the Lotuses with the Sephiroth and the bi-sections of the Paths thereon, and you have the necessary bilingual dictionary at your disposal – if you known how to use it."

ISBN 978-1-870450-28-7

SECRETS OF A GOLDEN DAWN TEMPLE
by Chic Cicero and Sandra Tabatha Cicero

A Hands on Manual for Building a Complete Golden Dawn Temple and Understanding its Symbolism.

The act of constructing a wand or other ritual object is an act of magic. The magician spends an extraordinary amount of time creating ritual objects, not because it is only through these objects that magic can rightly be performed, but because the act of creating is a magical process of growth, one which initiates the development of the will in accordance with the divine intent or purpose. This in turn contributes to the success of the ritual.

The construction of a ritual object should be treated like any othermagical operation. It should focus all parts of the magician's mind (intellect, creativity, imagination, spiritual self) into one purpose – to manifest an object which will be a receptacle for higher forces, in order that the magician too can become a worthy receptacle of that which is divine.

It is not necessary to create a perfect work of art. A person who works long and hard on a wand that looks crude will ultimately have more success than a person who purchases a ready-made wand that is flawless. With this book, clear instructions are finally available on how to fabricate the wands and implements of the Golden Dawn, some of the most significant, profound and beautiful of all the ritual tools that have ever been produced in the Western Magical Tradition.

The various tools presented here each have a very specific symbology attached to them. With the materials and tools available to the modern magician, these instruments can be recreated with stunning accuracy and magnificence.

Chic Cicero and S.Tabatha Cicero have been instrumental in preserving the mystical wisdom of the Hermetic Order of the Golden Dawn. Their *Secrets of a Golden Dawn Temple: The Alchemy and Crafting of Magickal Implements* was the first book to bring you detailed instructions on crafting and using the ritual implements of the Golden Dawn system of magic. Now their classic text has been updated.

This is the most complete book to date on the construction of the many tools used in the Golden Dawn system of magic. Here is a unique compilation of the various tools of the Golden Dawn, all described in full: wands, swords, elemental tools, Enochian Tablets, altars, temple furniture, banners, pillars, thrones, lamens, mantles and robes, ritual headdresses and ceremonial clothing, admission badges, and much more. This book provides complete step-by-step instructions for the construction of nearly 80 different implements, all displayed in photographs or drawings, along with the exact symbolism behind each and every item.

ISBN 978-1-870450-64-5 400 pages

www.ingramcontent.com/pod-product-compliance
Lightning Source LLC
Chambersburg PA
CBHW020350170426
43200CB00005B/119